Student Study Guide

to accompany

Abnormal Psychology

Second Edition

Susan Nolen-Hoeksema
University of Michigan

Prepared by
Robert N. Davis
University of Houston

Boston Burr Ridge, IL Dubuque, IA Madison, WI New York San Francisco St. Louis
Bangkok Bogotá Caracas Lisbon London Madrid
Mexico City Milan New Delhi Seoul Singapore Sydney Taipei Toronto

McGraw-Hill Higher Education

A Division of The McGraw-Hill Companies

Student Study Guide to accompany
ABNORMAL PSYCHOLOGY, SECOND EDITION
SUSAN NOLEN-HOEKSEMA

Published by McGraw-Hill Higher Education, an imprint of The McGraw-Hill Companies, Inc.,
1221 Avenue of the Americas, New York, NY 10020. Copyright © The McGraw-Hill Companies,
Inc., 2001, 1998. All rights reserved.

This book is printed on acid-free paper.

2 3 4 5 6 7 8 9 0 BKM/BKM 0 3 2 1 0

ISBN 0-07-241286-0

www.mhhe.com

Table of Contents

Why and How to Use this Study Guide

WHY: The Motivation

Why would you want or need a study guide such as this one? What benefits should you expect from it? These are easy questions to answer. Now that you've bought the textbook and are enrolled in your abnormal psychology class, the results that follow depend entirely on **you.** It is your responsibility to accumulate and retain knowledge in the most efficient manner possible, and show that you have mastered the material on your exams. Needless to say, the process of reaching this stage first requires a substantial amount of time spent studying.

Clearly, some people are better at studying than others. Unfortunately, many of your educators from your precollege years may never have bothered to teach you how to study most efficiently in order to comprehend and retain information. However, you would not be where you are today (that is, in college looking at this study guide) if you had not adopted some type of strategy or set of techniques for understanding and remembering information. The purpose of this study guide is to provide you with the best tools and methods available so that you can master the material in the textbook and earn an excellent grade in your abnormal psychology course.

If you look around the bookstore, you may find that this study guide differs from others. **The purpose, and *only purpose*, of this study guide is to help you learn the most essential material in the shortest amount of time.** For this reason, you will not find any games, puzzles, or pictures to entertain you, as you might find in other study guides. By contrast, this guide assumes that your time is valuable, and that you are buying it as an aid to learn better, **not** as a source of entertainment! This guide will ask that you work hard. The payoff will be that if you use the tools and follow the principles of this guide, you **will** master the material in the textbook and earn an excellent grade in your class. Achieving a high grade is intrinsically rewarding, and the benefits that follow will make your hard work well worth the effort.

In writing this guide, your situation has been anticipated. If you are like most students, abnormal psychology is not the only class you're taking this term. Moreover, the textbook may not be the only reading that you've been assigned: you may have journal articles, book chapters, or other books about abnormal psychology to read and study, as well as class lectures that do not always overlap with the textbook. Such demands upon your time and energy suggest a basic set of principles for you as a student: spend time effectively, distinguish the important ideas from unimportant details, learn a lot of information, and learn it well enough to retain over time.

This study guide has been designed to provide you with a set of study principles and the conceptual tools necessary to comprehend, assimilate, retain, and integrate the information in the textbook. Taking these actions will give you a solid grasp of abnormal psychology that you can take into your exams with confidence and use for the rest of your life to advance your personal goals, whatever they might be. Interested? Then turn to the next page to learn more.

HOW: The Method

THIS MATERIAL IS IMPORTANT! READ IT TO SUCCEED!

Here is the method recommended to master the material in your course.

General Tips

- Attend **all** of your scheduled lectures and discussion/recitation sessions.

- Keep a personal calendar and write your examination dates and assignment due dates in it. Write these important dates and times in your calendar first, and then schedule any other extracurricular or social activities that might interest you.

- Keep up with the scheduled readings for the class. Make every attempt to read the pages assigned to you before the lecture. This will enable you to ask any questions you might have about the chapter during the lecture, as well as dazzle your instructor with your conscientiousness and knowledge of the material. This is particularly important should you desire to pursue graduate school or a career in psychology. Identifying yourself as a competent student (vs. a face in the crowd) will help your instructor know who you are, which can be a useful step toward getting involved in research or other projects with that instructor.

- While in class, sit in the front and not by your friends, unless they are also your study partners. If you do not define what you want and why, then you're waiting for someone else to do this for you. What you want is the knowledge that your instructor presents during lecture. Don't let your friends con you into talking to them during the lecture or criticize you for studying too much. Stand up for your right to perform as well as you possibly can.

- Look explicitly for connections among the information sources in your course. Keep an eye out for overlap between the textbook and the lecture, the lecture and the discussion, the articles, chapters, or other books and the lecture, and so forth. It is this material that is the siren screaming for you to learn it, and learn it well.

- Read each textbook chapter section by section, but definitely read the whole chapter in its entirety once. Take notes in the margins, outline key points, rephrase ideas in your own words, invent abbreviations and enumerate points that you want to remember. Underline or highlight as little as possible. Your goal should not be to have a page that is yellow with highlighter marks or dark with underlined passages, but a mind that knows and can summarize the information on the page without looking. Work hard at both understanding and memorizing the material in your own way. Stop every few paragraphs or every page, cover up the page, and ask yourself, "What have I been reading?" Review the main points by writing them down, or rehearsing them in your mind or out loud to yourself. (Talking to yourself in this context is fine, and no one will think that you are abnormal.) Actively speaking to yourself and asking yourself questions will help you remember the material better.

- While you read, establish a deliberate intent to remember the information. Do not save any concepts or ideas for the "second time around." Get it over with instead! Read the chapter completely only one time, but absorb it deeply the first time. The second time around, you'll only need to re-read underlined or highlighted passages, your notes in the margins, and review your work in the study guide.

- Pick a place to study where you will not be disturbed, whether it is the library, a coffee shop, or your own room. People differ in how much background noise they prefer when studying, but don't choose a spot where a TV is blaring or where people are blowing cigarette smoke in your face. Choose a spot where you can relax and think hard for hours at a time. Make this space **your** space.

- Studying with friends or classmates can be beneficial only if they take the task as seriously as you do. Partners are best used during exam review time, but only after you've already studied and reviewed the material on your own. Take turns quizzing one another, testing your individual comprehension and retention of key concepts. Even if you end up playing teacher to everyone in the group, you'll still be forced to articulate the information you studied clearly, and that helps you, too. If you're worried that your friends may not take the task as seriously as you do, then set the terms. Say, "I only want to study with you (all) if we're actually going to get something done. I want to ace this exam."

- Take breaks every 45-60 minutes while studying. Even if you're feeling good, it helps memory and recall to break up the time during which you're trying to learn and retain information. Walk around, stand up and stretch, get a drink of water, etc. But do not go somewhere where you're likely to become distracted and not finish studying. In other words, throw that remote control in the trash!

- Take care of yourself. The flip side of not trying hard enough is trying too hard and obsessing over the material even when you know it well. Reward yourself when you get excellent grades on papers, assignments, or exams throughout the term, and keep a positive attitude. Occasionally, you might encounter some difficulties. Always remember that they are temporary, but you and your abilities are not!

Using the Study Guide to Master Course Material

Assuming that you attend **all** of the scheduled lectures and discussions, here's how to best use the study guide to achieve your goals:

- First, skim over the chapter to get a sense of what you're about to learn. Read the section headings and the short summary of each heading at the start of the chapter. Look over the pictures briefly and read the chapter summary. This is called surveying, and it has been shown to cut down the need for study time by 40% when done correctly and in conjunction with the methods that follow. You should think of learning as a process like building a spider web: surveying is the process of building the web and getting the conceptual net in your head to catch the factual and conceptual bugs that your mind will now trap tightly in its clenches.

- Second, read the **learning objectives** and **essential ideas** for the chapter in the study guide. Read these closely. Again, you're setting the trap for what is to follow. If you don't survey or read these sections, you'll be like a zookeeper bringing home a flock of animals with no cages to put them in. They'll run in all different directions, and you'll lose important points and key integrations.

- Third, look over the **guided review** questions for the section of the chapter that you're about to read. Make your mental net so sticky that no information will break free from it. Now, you're ready to start reading the chapter.

- Fourth, begin to read the chapter section by section. Read actively, and search for the answers to the questions that you read over before you began. If ideas come to you, write them in the margins. As new facts and concepts are introduced, write them in your own words in the margin. Generate abbreviations for lists of things that you want to remember. Enumerate points that lead to a conclusion. When the author makes claims, look for the evidence to support the claims. Know when the author is making suggestions for future research, when she is hypothesizing, and when she is drawing strong conclusions based upon substantial empirical evidence.

- Fifth, as you finish a section, write out the most concise definitions of the **key terms** that you can think of and answer the **guided review** questions. Take time to do this. You may think to yourself, "This is taking a long time, and I'm not getting very far in actually reading the chapter." That is exactly the point! By reading and thinking deeply about what you're reading, by defining the **key terms**, and by answering the **guided review** questions, you are cutting down on the amount of time that you'll have to spend reviewing later. Your first pass at the chapter should be an intense experience. You will only want to revisit the chapter for review later, and review only the essential details to remind yourself of what you know already, rather than learning it for the first time. The guided review questions will help you distinguish the important from less important information, as well as help you organize, comprehend, and assimilate the information. It is important to note that you do **not** necessarily need to write out the answers to the guided review questions. In fact, you should most definitely avoid writing out longwinded answers or answers that are straight out of the textbook. Rather, if you choose to write, stick to point-by-point answers or conceptual outlines. If you do not wish to write anything down, that is also fine. In that case, use the guided review questions to test your memory and comprehension of each chapter. Read each section, then put the book aside and answer the guided review questions out loud to yourself or in your head.

- Sixth, answer the questions for the **case example** after you've read the chapter (for the chapters that cover particular mental disorders). This will help your ability to apply the abstract concepts in the chapter to a particular instance. You will learn things that you didn't learn from reading and studying the chapter by making fine analytical distinctions and thinking in terms of a mental health professional.

- Seventh, take the **chapter test** in its entirety soon after reading the chapter, defining the **key terms**, answering the **guided review** questions, and answering the questions that accompany the **case example** (where relevant). You should take this practice test under exam conditions. Try **not** to look at your book, notes, or the relevant part of the study guide. Time yourself, giving yourself no more than 30 minutes for each chapter test. Do not get hung up on items that you think you should know if you do not recall them immediately, and do not get frustrated and start looking answers up. That defeats the purpose. Instead, be objective: test yourself, then check your answers against the answer key and check the essay questions against the text. Only by doing this will you be honestly finding out what you know and can feel confident about knowing as opposed to what you need more practice on. If you do need more practice, review the text, make more notes, and try to answer the guided review questions without looking at what you've written already.

- Eighth, when exam time comes around, you'll want to revisit the chapters again, not to re-read them in their entirety, but to remind yourself of what you already know. Try more now than ever to condense the information and remember things in terms of information clusters. Try to answer the **guided review** and chapter **test questions** without looking at your earlier answers. Do not make the mistake that many students make and write out several pages of notes. While writing notes is fine, you should limit them to only a few pages of the most essential details. Simply rewriting your notes or the textbook gets information only from one printed page to another, and your mind is lost in the middle. Initiate deliberate methods to grasp and retain the information by rehearsing, memorizing, and testing your ability to recall and articulate what you have learned.

GOOD LUCK!

Chapter 1: Looking at Abnormality

LEARNING OBJECTIVES
After reading and studying this chapter, you should be able to:

1. Discuss the factors that influence whether a behavior is regarded as normal or abnormal.

2. Summarize the different criteria for defining abnormality, and know the strengths and weaknesses of each criterion.

3. Describe the components of maladaptive behavior and how culture and gender may influence maladaptive behavior.

4. Distinguish among supernatural, natural, and psychological theories of abnormality, and discuss how each type of theory has led to different ways of treating mentally ill people throughout history.

5. Summarize how people from the Stone Age, the ancient Chinese, Egyptians, Greeks, and Hebrews thought about abnormality, and how each respective culture treated the mentally ill as a result.

6. Discuss the historical shift from the early asylums in Europe and America to the moral management and mental hygiene movements.

7. Identify some of the notable figures in psychology from the late nineteenth and early-to-mid twentieth centuries.

8. Discuss the professions within abnormal psychology and how they differ from one another.

ESSENTIAL IDEAS

I. Defining abnormality

    A. Cultural relativism is a perspective on abnormality that argues that the norms of a society must be used to determine the normality of a behavior.

    B. The unusualness criterion for abnormality suggest that unusual or rare behaviors should be labeled abnormal.

    C. The discomfort criterion suggests that only behaviors or emotions that an individual finds distressing should be labeled abnormal.

    D. The mental illness criterion for abnormality suggests that only behaviors resulting from mental illness or disease are abnormal.

E. The consensus among professionals in the mental health field is that behaviors that cause people to suffer distress or that prevent them from functioning in daily life are abnormal. Often these behaviors are referred to as *maladaptive* or *dysfunctional*.

II. Historical perspectives on abnormality

A. There are three types of theories that have influenced the definition and treatment of abnormality over the ages: the natural theories, the psychological theories, and the supernatural theories.

B. Stone Age people probably viewed mental disorders as the result of supernatural forces. They may have drilled holes in the skulls of sufferers – a procedure known as trephination – to release the evil forces causing the mental disorders.

C. Some of the earliest written references to mental disorders can be found in Chinese medical texts around 2674 B.C. and then in the papyri of Egypt and Mesopotamia, in the Old Testament, and in the writings of Greek and Roman philosophers and physicians. Mental disorders were often described as medical disorders in these ancient writings, although there is also evidence that they were viewed as due to supernatural forces.

D. The witch hunts began in the late Middle Ages. Some accused witches may have suffered from mental disorders.

E. Psychic epidemics have occurred throughout history. They were formerly explained as due to spirit possession, but are now seen as the result of the effects of the social context on people's self-perceptions.

F. In the eighteenth and nineteenth centuries, advocates of more gentle treatment of people with mental disorders began to establish asylums for these people.

G. The humanitarian movement focused on providing people with mental disorders with clean and safe living conditions and humane treatment.

III. The emergence of modern perspectives

A. Modern biological theories and therapies were greatly helped by the development of Kraepelin's classification scheme for mental disorders and the discovery that syphillis causes general paresis, a disease with symptoms including loss of touch with reality.

B. The roots of psychoanalytic theory can be found in the work of Mesmer and the suggestion that psychological symptoms could be relieved through hypnosis. Jean Charcot, Sigmund Freud, and Josef Breuer are among the founders of modern psychoanalytic theory, which focuses on the role of the unconscious in psychological symptoms.

C. Behavioral approaches to psychopathology began with the development of basic experimental techniques to study the effects of reinforcements and punishments in producing normal and abnormal behavior.

D. Cognitive approaches to abnormality did not emerge until the mid-nineteenth century, when theorists began arguing that the way people think about events in their environment determines their emotional and behavioral responses to those events.

IV. Professions within abnormal psychology

A. Psychiatry is a branch of medicine that focuses on mental disorders. Psychiatrists have a M.D. degree and can prescribe medications for the treatment of psychological problems.

B. Clinical psychologists typically have a Ph.D. in clinical psychology. They practice psychotherapy and do research into the causes and consequences of mental disorders.

C. Clinical social workers have a master's degree in social work and help people overcome social obstacles contributing to their problems.

D. Psychiatric nurses have a degree in nursing and specialize in the treatment of people with psychological problems.

KEY TERMS AND GUIDED REVIEW

<u>Key Terms</u>

psychopathology (p. 4):

Defining Abnormality

<u>Key Terms</u>

cultural relativism criterion (p. 5):

unusualness criterion (p. 7):

discomfort criterion (p. 8):

mental illness criterion (p. 8):

maladaptiveness criterion (p. 8):

1. Give an example of a behavior that would be considered abnormal in one context, but not in another context. (pp. 4-5)

2. If everyone agreed that cultural relativism were true and that no universal standards for labeling a behavior as abnormal existed, what positive and negative consequences might result? (pp. 5-6)

3. What is Thomas Szasz's view of cultural relativism? (p. 6)

4. How may gender roles influence the labeling of a behavior as abnormal? (pp. 5-7)

5. How are the cultural relativism criterion and the unusualness criterion related? (p. 7)

6. Give one advantage and one disadvantage of adopting the unusualness criterion as a standad for defining abnormal behavior. (p. 7)

7. Give one advantage and one disadvantage of adopting the discomfort criterion as a standard for defining abnormal behavior. (p. 8)

8. What is one problem with the mental illness criterion? (p. 8)

9. What are four components of the maladaptiveness criterion? (pp. 8-9)

10. What are four ways in which culture and gender may influence maladaptive behavior? (p. 9)

Historical Perspectives on Abnormality

Key Terms

natural theories (p. 10):

supernatural theories (p. 10):

psychological theories (p. 10):

trephination (p. 11):

psychic epidemic (p. 15):

moral treatment (p. 17):

mental hygiene movement (p. 21)

<u>Guided Review</u>

1. During the Stone Age, what was thought to cause abnormal behavior, and what was prescribed as a treatment? (pp. 10-11)

2. Summarize the concepts of "yin and yang" and "vital air" from ancient China. (pp. 11-12)

3. What did the Egyptians and Greeks believe was responsible for psychological problems? How did they attempt to treat these problems? (pp. 12-13)

4. What is the significance of the Papyrus Ebers? (p. 12)

5. Summarize the Hebrews' conception of abnormal behavior (as depicted in the Old Testament). (p. 12)

6. Summarize the views of Hippocrates on the causes and most appropriate treatments for mental disorders. How do these views differ from those of Plato? (pp. 12-13)

7. Describe the shift that occurred during the Middle Ages in which the causes of abnormal behavior came to be viewed differently. (pp. 13-14)

8. What was Saint Vitus' dance? What was tarantism? (p. 15)

9. Describe the harsh treatment of people with mental disorders during the eighteenth and nineteenth centuries in Europe and America. (pp. 16-17)

10. How did Dorothea Dix and Philippe Pinel contribute to the humane treatment of people with mental disorders? (pp. 17-18)

11. What led to the decline of the moral treatment movement? (p. 18)

12. Who was Clifford Beers, what happened to him, and how did he affect the public's view of mental illness? (pp. 20-21)

The Emergence of Modern Perspectives

<u>Key Terms</u>

general paresis (p. 19):

hysterical disorders (p. 20):

mesmerism (p. 20):

psychoanalysis (p. 22):

behaviorism (p. 24):

cognition (p. 24):

self-efficacy belief (p. 24):

<u>Guided Review</u>

1. What was Emil Kraepelin's contribution to our understanding of mental disorders? (p. 19)

2. What are two events that catapulted biological explanations of abnormality into accepted discourse? (p. 19)

3. What is the modern evidence that germs may cause some mental disorders? (p. 22)

4. According to Mesmer, what caused mental disorders and how could it be treated? How did Mesmer contribute to the development of psychoanalysis? (pp. 19-20)

5. What persuaded Charcot to believe that hysteria had psychological roots? (p. 21)

6. How did Breuer contribute to the development of psychoanalysis? (p. 22)

7. Summarize the contributions of Wundt, Witmer, Pavlov, Watson, Thorndike, and Skinner to the development of behaviorism. (p. 23)

8. Summarize the contributions of Bandura, Ellis, and Beck to the study of cognitive views of abnormality. (p. 24)

9. How do supernatural theories continue to affect the practice of psychotherapy? (p. 24)

Professions within Abnormal Psychology

<u>Guided Review</u>

1. What are the foci of psychiatrists, clinical psychologists, marriage and family therapists, clinical social workers, and psychiatric nurses? (p. 25)

CHAPTER TEST

A. <u>Multiple choice.</u> Choose the **best answer** to each question below.

1. People must suffer as a result of their behavior according to the _____, but not necessarily according to the _____.

    A. maladaptiveness criterion; cultural relativism criterion.
    B. mental illness criterion; discomfort criterion.
    C. cultural relativism criterion; unusualness criterion.
    D. discomfort criterion; unusualness criterion.

2. One problem with accepting the cultural relativism criterion is:

    A. Cultures may differ in how they define abnormal behavior.
    B. Some societies may label people or groups abnormal in order to justify controlling them.
    C. Some groups, such as gay men and lesbians, do not find their behavior distressing.
    D. Someone still has to decide how rare a behavior must be for it to be called abnormal.

3. The _____ criterion was responsible for _____.

    A. maladaptiveness; the imprisonment of Thomas Szasz.
    B. unusualness; the removal of homosexuality from the APA list of recognized psychological disorders.
    C. mental illness; the labeling of slaves who desired freedom as having drapetomania.
    D. discomfort; the removal of homosexuality from the APA list of recognized psychological disorders.

4. All of the following are components of the maladaptiveness criterion except:

    A. The behaviors are ones that the person wishes to be rid of.
    B. The behaviors are physically damaging to the individual.
    C. The behaviors suggest that the individual has lost touch with reality and cannot control his or her thoughts and behaviors.
    D. The behaviors interfere with the person's ability to function in daily life.

5. The idea that the flowing of "vital air" onto specific body organs was a _____ theory and was espoused by the:

    A. supernatural; Hebrews.
    B. psychological; Greeks.
    C. supernatural; Egyptians.
    D. natural; Chinese.

6. The idea that a woman's "wandering uterus" traveled around the female body, interfered with other organs, and caused _____, was held by which ancient culture(s)?

    A. hysteria; Hebrew and Egyptian.
    B. witchcraft and obscene behavior; European.
    C. hysteria; Greek and Egyptian.
    D. melancholia; Egyptian and Chinese.

7. Which of the following is true about a culture and its discovery?

    A. The Egyptians assigned mental functioning to the brain.
    B. The Greeks first drew the distinction between madness and witchcraft.
    C. The Chinese developed effective biological treatments for mental disorders.
    D. The Hebrews developed the first true systematic classification system of mental disorders.

8. Greek physicians believed that _____ caused psychological problems, and that the best type of treatment would involve _____.

    A. An imbalance of four humors (blood, phlegm, yellow bile, and black bile); physiological alterations or psychological treatments such as rest, relaxation, or change of lifestyle.
    B. Afflictions from the gods; trephination.
    C. Vital air blowing on specific body organs; restoration of the body to a more balanced state by rest, relaxation, and herbal medicine.
    D. Moral vice and sloth; a life of reason, rationality, and virtue.

9. Which of the following writings argued that many people accused of witchcraft actually suffered from mental illness?

    A. A Mind that Found Itself
    B. The Deception of Dreams
    C. Papyrus Ebers
    D. The Old Testament

10. What tends to characterize psychic epidemics and mass hysteria is:

    A. The fact that they can only occur in superstitious cultures.
    B. The fact that the participants are trying to express their emotions, yet lack an adaptive way to do this, and thus participate in psychic epidemics.
    C. The fact that they begin with one person, who then incites others to imitate the same behavioral symptoms.
    D. The fact that the participants suffer from psychological distress rather than an identifiable physical illness.

11. Which of the following people was associated with the moral treatment movement, and which statement best characterizes the beliefs of the movement?

   A. Clifford Beers; mental disorders result from blasphemy and the abandonment of religion: the purpose of treatment is to restore people's morality so that they might function again.
   B. Teresa of Avila; mental disorders result from natural causes and should be treated biologically.
   C. Dorothea Dix; mental illness resulted from the separation of people from nature and stresses resulting from rapid social changes.
   D. Philippe Pinel; hospitals should isolate mentally ill people to keep their immorality from afflicting the general populace.

12. At which location were mentally ill people provided with care, housing, and humane treatment?

   A. Gheel, Belgium
   B. Bedlam, London
   C. Hamburg, Germany
   D. Williamsburg, Virginia

13. All of the following contributed to the demise of the moral treatment movement toward the end of the nineteenth century except:

   A. Many patients failed to improve or got worse.
   B. The expansion of asylums created a shortage of personnel and resources.
   C. Biological treatments were developed and were more effective.
   D. An increasing number of asylum patients were from foreign countries.

14. The idea that all mental disorders were medical diseases and should be treated biologically was a cornerstone of the _____.

   A. moral treatment movement
   B. mental hygiene movement
   C. behaviorism movement
   D. cognitive revolution

15. A significant event that increased awareness that mental illness can have biological causes was:

   A. The publication of On the Psychical Mechanisms of Hysterical Phenomena.
   B. The discovery that untreated streptococcus can cause schizophrenia.
   C. The laboratory experiments of Kraepelin.
   D. The discovery that syphilis could cause general paresis.

16. _____ classified mental disorders into epilepsy, mania, melancholia, and brain fever.

    A. Kraepelin
    B. Hippocrates
    C. Freud
    D. Charcot

17. _____ is a technique used in _____.

    A. Mesmerism; classical conditioning
    B. Psychoanalysis; hypnosis
    C. Hypnosis; mesmerism
    D. Classical conditioning; psychoanalysis

18. _____ developed _____, which greatly influenced modern thinking.

    A. Anton Mesmer; psychoanalysis
    B. Emil Kraepelin; a classification system for mental disorders
    C. Willhelm Wundt; hypnosis
    D. Joseph Breuer; the first experimental psychology laboratory

19. Which of the following was instrumental in showing that behaviors followed by positive consequences were more likely to be repeated than behaviors followed by negative consequences?

    A. B.F. Skinner
    B. Ivan Pavlov
    C. Albert Ellis
    D. Lightner Witmer

20. When helping someone with a psychological disorder, which of the following would be most likely to focus on overcoming environmental conditions contributing to the person's problems, such as homelessness?

    A. Psychiatrists
    B. Psychiatric nurses
    C. Social workers
    D. Clinical psychologists

B. <u>True-False</u>. Select T (True) or F (False) below.

1. Supernatural theories no longer have any influence on the treatment of people with mental disorders by clinical psychologists.   T   F

2. In the early 1970s, homosexual men and women were found to experience more psychological distress than heterosexuals, and the diagnosis of homosexuality was removed in order to encourage a focus on the psychological problems of homosexuals, rather than the diagnosis itself.   T   F

3. People who do not consider their own behavior to be abnormal cannot be considered abnormal according to cultural relativism.   T   F

4. Culture and gender influence how likely it is that a given maladaptive behavior will be shown, as well as people's willingness to admit to certain kinds of maladaptive behaviors.
        T   F

5. Biological views have invariably led to more compassion for people afflicted with mental illness.   T   F

C. <u>Short Answer</u>.

1. List three criteria for defining abnormality. For each criterion, provide one argument in favor of the criterion and one argument against it.

2. What are four components of the maladaptiveness criterion?

3. Briefly discuss how "change came from within" to alter many people's views of those accused of being witches in the sixteenth century.

4. Give two historical examples of how a particular view of the cause(s) of abnormal behavior influenced views of the most appropriate treatment for the behavior.

5. What nineteenth century event provided strong evidence that some abnormal behavior has biological causes? Describe this event.

ANSWER KEY

<u>Multiple choice</u>
1. D
2. B
3. D
4. A
5. D
6. C
7. A
8. A
9. B
10. D
11. C
12. A
13. C
14. B
15. D
16. B
17. C
18. B
19. A
20. C

<u>True-False</u>
1. F
2. F
3. F
4. T
5. F

<u>Short Answer</u>
1. See pp. 5-9.
2. See pp. 8-9.
3. See pp. 14-15.
4. See pp. 10-19.
5. See p. 19.

<u>Additional Readings on Chapter 1 Topics</u>
Greenwood, J. D. (1999). Understanding the "cognitive revolution" in psychology. <u>Journal of the History of the Behavioral Sciences, 35,</u> 1-22.
Kraepelin, E. (1992). The manifestations of insanity. <u>History of Psychiatry, 3,</u> 509-529.
Wilson, K. (1997). Science and treatment development: Lessons from the history of behavior therapy. <u>Behavior Therapy, 28,</u> 547-558.

Chapter 2: Contemporary Theories of Abnormality

LEARNING OBJECTIVES

After reading and studying this chapter, you should be able to:

1. Distinguish between a biological approach and a psychosocial approach to abnormality. Also be able to discuss how these two approaches are not mutually exclusive, and know what the nature-nurture question, vulnerability-stress models, and feedback loops are.

2. Discuss three biological causes of abnormality. Summarize the processes involved in communication between neurons. Know three layers of the brain and what the HPA axis is. Summarize how researchers investigate genetic contributions to psychopathology and the shortcomings of these methods.

3. Describe the foundations of psychodynamic theory, and know each defense mechanism and Freud's stages of psychosexual development. Discuss the shortcomings of psychodynamic theory.

4. Know how various theorists have attempted to modify and extend psychodynamic theory (object relations theorists, Horney, Adler, and Erikson).

5. Summarize classical and operant conditioning, and give examples of each.

6. Discuss observational learning and modeling.

7. Distinguish among causal attributions, control beliefs, self-efficacy, and dysfunctional assumptions.

8. Discuss the elements of both humanistic and existential theories, and how they differ.

9. Discuss interpersonal, family systems, and social structural theories of abnormality.

ESSENTIAL IDEAS

I. Biological approaches

   A. The biological theories of psychopathology hold that psychological symptoms and disorders are caused by structural abnormalities in the brain, disordered biochemistry, or faulty genes.

   B. Structural abnormalities in the brain can be caused by injury or disease processes. The specific area of the brain damaged will influence the type of psychological symptoms shown.

   C. Most biochemical theories focus on neurotransmitters, the biochemicals that facilitate transmission of impulses in the brain. Some theories say that psychological symptoms are caused by too little or too much of a particular neurotransmitter in the synapses of the brain. Other theories focus on the number of receptors for neurotransmitters.

D. Some people may be genetically predisposed to psychological disorders. Most of these disorders are probably linked not to a single faulty gene but to the accumulation of a group of faulty genes.

E. Three methods of determining the heritability of a disorder are family history studies, twin studies, and adoption studies.

II. Psychological theories of abnormality

A. Psychoanalytic theories of psychopathology focus on unconscious conflicts that cause anxiety in the individual and result in maladaptive behavior.

B. The ways people handle their conflicts are defined by the types of defense mechanisms they use. Children can become fixated on certain needs or concerns if their transitions through psychosexual stages are not managed well.

C. More recent psychodynamic theories focused less on the role of unconscious impulses and more on the development of the individual's self-concept in the context of interpersonal relationships. They see a greater role for the environment in the shaping of personality and have more hope for change in personality during adulthood than Freud did.

D. The behavioral theories of abnormality focus only on the rewards and punishments in the environment that shape and maintain behavior.

E. Classical conditioning takes place when a previously neutral stimulus is paired with a stimulus that naturally creates a certain response; eventually the neutral stimulus will also elicit the response.

F. Operant conditioning involves rewarding desired behaviors and punishing undesired behaviors.

G. People also learn by imitating the behaviors modeled by others and by observing the rewards and punishments others receive for their behaviors.

H. Cognitive theories suggest that people's attributions for events, their perceptions of control and self-efficacy, and their beliefs about themselves and the world influence their behaviors and emotions in reaction to situations.

I. Humanist and existential theories suggest that all humans strive to fulfill their potential for good and to self-actualize. The inability to fulfill one's potential arises from the pressures of society to conform to others' expectations and values and from existential anxiety.

III. Sociocultural approaches

    A. The interpersonal theories assert that our self-concepts and expectations of others are based on our early attachments and relationships to caregivers.

    B. Family systems theories suggest that families form cohesive systems that regulate the behavior of each member in the system. Sometimes these systems support and enhance the well-being of their members and sometimes they do not.

    C. Social structural theories suggest that society contributes to psychopathology in some members by creating severe stresses for them, then allowing or encouraging them to cope with these stresses with psychological symptoms.

KEY TERMS AND GUIDED REVIEW

<u>Key Terms</u>

theoretical approach (p. 30):

biological approach (p. 30):

psychological approach (p. 30):

social approach (p. 30):

nature-nurture question (p. 30):

vulnerability-stress model (p. 31):

feedback loop (p. 31):

<u>Guided Review</u>

1. Give an example of how biological, psychological, and social factors can combine with stress to cause a disorder (pp. 30-31).

Biological Approaches

<u>Key Terms</u>

cerebrum (p. 35):

central core (p. 35):

hypothalamus (p. 35):

endocrine system (p. 35):

limbic system (p. 35):

neurotransmitters (p. 35):

synapse (p. 36):

reuptake (p. 36):

degradation (p. 36):

pituitary (p. 37):

behavior genetics (p. 38):

polygenic (p. 40):

predisposition (p. 40):

family history study (p. 40):

probands (p. 40):

monozygotic (MZ) twins (p. 41):

dizygotic (DZ) twins (p. 41):

twin study (p. 41):

concordance rate (p. 41):

adoption study (p. 41):

Guided Review

1. Describe the changes in Phineas Gage's behavior from before his accident to after his accident: what remained intact, and what changed about him? What nineteenth-century notion was shattered by the effects of Gage's injury on his behavior? (pp. 32-35)

2. What are the two parts of the cerebrum? (p. 35)

3. What are the functions of the hypothalamus? What role does the limbic system play with respect to the hypothalamus? (p. 35)

4. In a neuron, from where are neurotransmitters emitted? What space do they enter next? How do they stimulate the neuron on the other side of this space? (pp. 35-36)

5. What two natural processes govern the regulation of neurotransmitters in the synapse? What happens when each of these processes were inhibited? (p. 36)

6. Describe the HPA axis and the sequence of chemical events during a stress response. (pp. 37-38)

7. How are chromosomes, genes, and DNA related? (pp. 38-39)

8. Suppose that someone said to you, "My mother has a mental disorder, so I am inevitably going to develop it, too." Is this correct? Why or why not? (p. 40)

9. How is it possible for one son (or daughter) of a parent with schizophrenia to develop schizophrenia, but not the other son (or daughter)? Describe two ways in which this could occur. (p. 40)

10. How is a family history study conducted? What is a major limitation of family history studies? (p. 40)

11. Write the expected concordance rates for the following scenarios: a) a disorder is determined entirely by genetics; b) a disorder is determined partly by genetics; c) a disorder is not determined by genetics at all. (p. 41)

a. MZ = _____   DZ = _____
b. MZ = _____   DZ = _____
c. MZ = _____   DZ = _____

12. What is one limitation of twin studies? (p. 41)

13. How is an adoption study conducted? What is one limitation of these studies? (pp. 41-42)

14. What are some of the limitations of biological theories? Why does it seem that the general public has embraced them? (pp. 42-43)

Psychological Theories of Abnormality

Key Terms

psychodynamic theories (p. 43):

catharsis (p. 44):

repression (p. 44):

libido (p. 44):

id (p. 44):

pleasure principle (p. 44):

primary process thinking (p. 44):

ego (p. 44):

reality principle (p. 44):

secondary process thinking (p. 44):

superego (p. 45):

introject (p. 45):

unconscious (p. 45):

preconscious (p. 45):

conscious (p. 46):

defense mechanism (p. 46):

neurotic paradox (p. 46):

psychosexual stages (p. 46):

oral stage (p. 46):

anal stage (p. 48):

phallic stage (p. 48):

Oedipus complex (p. 48):

castration anxiety (p. 48):

Electra complex (p. 48):

penis envy (p. 48):

latency stage (p. 48):

genital stage (p. 48):

object-relations school (p. 49):

splitting (p. 49):

behavioral theories (p. 51):

classical conditioning (p. 51):

unconditioned stimulus (US) (p. 51):

unconditioned response (UR) (p. 51):

conditioned stimulus (CS) (p. 51):

conditioned response (CR) (p. 51):

law of effect (p. 51):

operant conditioning (p. 51):

continuous reinforcement schedule (p. 52):

partial reinforcement schedule (p. 52):

extinction (p. 52):

social learning theory (p. 52):

modeling (p. 52):

observational learning (p. 53):

cognitive theories (p. 53):

cognitions (p. 53):

causal attribution (p. 53):

control theory (p. 54):

learned helplessness (p. 54):

global assumptions (p. 54):

humanistic theory (p. 55):

existential theory (p. 55):

self-actualization (p. 56):

client-centered therapy (p. 56):

Guided Review

1. What early observations influenced Freud's thinking and the development of psychoanalysis? (p. 44)

2. From the perspective of psychodynamic theory, describe how the id, ego, and superego would interact given the following situation:

> A hungry young child sees an open cookie jar on the counter. His mother told him a few minutes ago not to have any snacks before dinner. He stares longingly at the cookie jar, but remembers what his mother has just told him.

At this moment, what is each system doing? What impulse or need would each attempt to satisfy, and within what constraints would each operate in this example? (pp. 44-46)

3. How does the ego prevent threatening material from reaching the conscious mind? (pp. 44-46)

4. What are Freud's five stages of psychosexual development? Describe each stage, and indicate what personality characteristics are thought to develop if each stage is not completed properly. (pp. 46-48)

5. How do boys and girls develop a value system, according to Freud? (p. 48)

6. According to the object relations school, what are the four steps in the development of a self-concept? What are two ways in which psychopathology may result from getting "stuck" at stages 2 or 3? (p. 49)

7. What are Horney's criticisms of Freudian theory? (pp. 50-51)

8. What are some of the limitations of Freudian theory? (pp. 50-51)

9. In the case study of the 2-year-old girl named Sarah, identify the unconditioned stimulus, unconditioned response, conditioned stimulus, and conditioned response. (pp. 51-52)

10. Suppose a man has a habit of buying flowers and giving them to female strangers spontaneously. What would be the difficulties inherent in attempting to extinguish this behavior, according to the tenets of operant conditioning? (pp. 51-52)

11. Give an example of how classical and operant conditioning can work in tandem to affect behavior. (p. 52)

12. According to social learning theory, what are two mechanisms of learning? Explain how both Bandura's social learning theory and Freud's theory of defense mechanisms would explain the behavior of a prisoner who began to act like the guards at his or her prison. (pp. 46-47, 52-53)

13. What is one strength and one weakness of behavioral theories? (p. 53)

14. Suppose that you attempted to run ten miles and did not succeed. How might the following two causal attributions for this failure affect you differently? (pp. 53-54)
        a. "It was too hot outside today to run that far."
        b. "I am no good at anything athletic."

15. According to Seligman (1975), what results from the continual experience of uncontrollable events (and what are these types of effects called)? (p. 54)

16. According to Bandura (1986), what type of person is most likely to persist in the face of difficult situations? (p. 54)

17. Give some examples of dysfunctional assumptions. (pp. 54-55)

18. What is one strength and one weakness of cognitive theories? (p. 55)

19. What leads to mental illness, according to humanistic theories? (pp. 55-57)

20. How do the existential theories differ from humanistic theories? (pp. 55-57)

21. What is one strength and one weakness of humanistic/existential theories? (p. 57)

Sociocultural Approaches

Key Terms

interpersonal theory (p. 57):

prototypes (p. 59):

family systems theory (p. 61):

homeostasis (p. 61):

social structural theory (p. 62):

Guided Review

1. How do the theories of Adler and Erikson differ from Freud's theory? (p. 59)

2. Describe Sullivan's (1953) theory. How does it differ from object relations theory and operant conditioning? (pp. 49, 51-52, 59)

3. What is Bowlby's (1980) theory, and how might it explain abnormal behavior in adults? (pp. 60-61)

4. What is a central assumption of family systems theories? Describe the following: 1) inflexible family; 2) enmeshed family; 3) disengaged family; and 4) pathological triangular relationships. (p. 61)

5. Describe some societal factors that may contribute to mental disorders in individuals. (pp. 62-63)

CHAPTER TEST

A. <u>Multiple Choice.</u> Choose the **best answer** to each question below.

1. The change in Phineas Gage's behavior following his accident showed which of the following at the time of the accident?

    A. Much of what determines a person's character is biological, as opposed to being solely a function of will and upbringing.
    B. The frontal cerebrum is involved in the production of rational decisions and control over inappropriate impulses.
    C. The frontal cerebrum is divided into two hemispheres, each of which performs separate functions.
    D. People who have head injuries can actually forget their injury if the brain area involved in long-term memory is damaged in the injury.

2. The _____ releases _____, which causes the _____ to release adrenocorticotrophic hormone.

    A. pituitary; growth hormone; hypothalamus
    B. hypothalamus; corticotrophin-releasing factor; pituitary
    C. pituitary; corticotrophin-releasing factor; adrenal gland
    D. cerebrum; serotonin; adrenal gland

3. Choose the correct order of the following steps involved in communication between neurons: 1) neurotransmitters bind to the dendrites of the receiving neuron; 2) a signal travels through the axon of the sending neuron; 3) neurotransmitter is released into the synapse; 4) the receiving neuron is stimulated to initiate an impulse; 5) the signal reaches the synaptic terminals of the sending neuron.

    A. 5,2,1,3,4
    B. 3,2,5,4,1
    C. 2,5,3,1,4
    D. 2,3,1,5,4

4. Inhibiting the process of reuptake in a neuron leads to:

    A. Compensation by means of increasing the frequency of degradation.
    B. A greater amount of neurotransmitter in the synapse.
    C. A lesser amount of neurotransmitter in the synapse.
    D. An increase in the number of dendrite receptors on the receiving neuron.

5. Judy has an anxiety disorder, but no one in her immediate family has ever had one, nor have any of her past relatives. How is this possible, according to what the chapter discussed about genetic transmission of mental disorders?

    A. Judy must have been adopted.
    B. Judy may have received enough abnormal genes from the chromosomes of her mother and father at birth to inevitably cause an anxiety disorder.
    C. Some of Judy's family members may actually carry a predisposition for an anxiety disorder, but may never have experienced an interaction among genetic, biological, and environmental factors sufficient to cause the disorder.
    D. The situation described is not possible according to what we know about genetics.

6. Investigators at the University of Planet Earth wanted to understand the biological roots of moon disorder, a condition in which individuals experience symptoms of depression and anxiety because they cannot live on the moon. They found a large sample of people who had moon disorder, and a large sample of people who did not have moon disorder. After analyzing the genetic history of these two groups, they found that significantly more relatives of the moon disorder group also had moon disorder, compared to the relatives of the group without moon disorder. Next, they examined the concordance rate of moon disorder among both monozygotic and dizygotic twins in the sample. The concordance rate of moon disorder was 43 percent among MZ twins, and was the same among DZ twins. What can the investigators conclude?

    A. There is substantial evidence that moon disorder is genetically transmitted.
    B. There is some evidence that moon disorder is genetically transmitted, but an adoption study would be necessary to tease apart genetic from environmental factors.
    C. There is no evidence that moon disorder is genetically transmitted, but there is some evidence that moon disorder occurs among people who share similar environments.
    D. There is no evidence that the rate of moon disorder is influenced either by genetic or environemental factors.

7. Leroy has just come home from a bad day at work. His boss ridiculed him at a group meeting when he did not have a report ready that had been due a week earlier. When he comes home, his dog comes running up to him, carrying its food dish in its mouth, wagging its tail excitedly. "You stupid mutt," he exclaims angrily, "you're always trying to torment me and remind me of what I forgot to do!" This is most likely an illustration of which defense mechanism?

    A. Reaction formation
    B. Rationalization
    C. Projection
    D. Displacement

8. According to Freud, _____ is responsible for _____

    A. castration anxiety; penis envy
    B. the supergo; channeling libido into activities that balance the demands of society and the moral conscience
    C. introjection; incorporation of the standards of others into one's own thinking
    D. the preconscious; holding desires, memories, and emotions of which we are not aware

9. A woman who is hungry for lunch, but who is stuck in a meeting until 1:30 p.m. and manages to avoid eating, is engaging in _____ which is controlled by the _____.

    A. primary process thinking; superego
    B. secondary process thinking; ego
    C. introjection; preconscious
    D. the reality principle; superego

10. According to object relations theory, in which of the following phases of self-concept development does the child see the self as either all-good or all-bad and others as either all-good or all-bad, and is able to distinguish between the self and others?

    A. separation-individuation
    B. symbiosis
    C. integration
    D. undifferentiated

11. The _____ stage lasts from _____, and if not resolved properly, an individual can be _____ as an adult.

    A. oral; 18 months to 3 years of age; stubborn, overcontrolling, and focused on orderliness
    B. anal; 6 years to puberty; have a deep mistrust of others and fear of abandonment
    C. phallic; 3 to 6 years of age; too self-aggrandizing or too self-deprecating
    D. latency; 3 to 6 years of age; riddled with hatred of the opposite sex

12. Which of the following is not one of Horney's criticisms of psychodynamic theory?

    A. Psychodynamic theory views males as prototypical human beings.
    B. Psychodynamic theory wrongly attempts to explain normal and abnormal behavior with similar processes.
    C. Psychodynamic theory overemphasizes sexual drives and anatomy in personality.
    D. Psychodynamic theory attempts to explain all human behavior based on a small sample.

13. Bill is running outside in his white tennis shoes when he looks down to see a snake slithering near his feet. Terrified, he yelps and half runs/half dances to get around the snake. The next morning, Bill experiences fear and anxiety when he goes to put on his shoes. The shoes are the:

    A. unconditioned stimulus.
    B. conditioned response.
    C. unconditioned response.
    D. conditioned stimulus.

14. To shape and maintain a behavior, the most efficient means would be _____, but if a behavior were learned by means of _____, then it would be _____ to extinguish.

    A. classical conditioning; operant conditioning; more difficult
    B. operant conditioning; classical conditioning; less difficult
    C. a continuous reinforcement schedule; a partial reinforcement schedule; more difficult
    D. a continuous reinforcement schedule; a partial reinforcement schedule; less difficult

15. A major problem for cognitive theories is:

    A. The fact that they are abstract and cannot be tested scientifically.
    B. The fact that they do not seem to recognize people's "free will."
    C. The fact that they have not shown convincingly that cognitions precede and cause disorders.
    D. The fact that they are studied in laboratories that do not resemble the real world.

16. Categorize the thought processes in the individual described below:

Maria is very upset, for she was supposed to start taking tennis lessons with her best friend Jane. Jane, however, decided to take lessons in another league that was closer to her home. (i) "Jane is so selfish," thought Maria, "and always thinks only of her own needs."
Maria started taking the tennis lessons anyway, but became very dismayed when she learned how much physical work was involved. (ii) "I should be able to do this with absolute perfection! It looks so simple and graceful when I watch other people; I should be able to do this correctly just like they do!"

    A. i. causal attribution; ii. dysfunctional assumption
    B. i. dysfunctional assumption; ii. control belief
    C. i. control belief; ii. self-efficacy expectation
    D. i. dysfunctional assumption; ii. learned helplessness

17. According to Maslow, needs for security and an absence of danger are called _____ and must be met _____ _____ needs.

        A. belongingness and love needs; after; aesthetic
        B. esteem needs; before; self-actualization
        C. safety needs; after; physiological
        D. physiological; before; cognitive

18. According to Erikson, individuals pass through a psychosocial crisis known as _____ when they are in early adulthood.

        A. identity vs. confusion
        B. integrity vs. despair
        C. initiative vs. guilt
        D. intimacy vs. isolation

19. The family system seeks to maintain _____, according to family systems theorists.

        A. strong attachments
        B. homeostasis
        C. adaptive scripts
        D. triangular relationships

20. A modern treatment for depression that involves magnetism is:

        A. magnetic resonance imaging.
        B. mesmerism.
        C. transcranial magnetic stimulation.
        D. left prefrontal photon enhancement.

B. <u>True-False.</u> Select T (True) or F (False) below.

1. The process of reuptake leads to a greater amount of neurotransmitter in the synapse.
      T   F

2. Neither family history studies nor twin studies can tease apart the influence of genes vs. the environment in shaping personality. T   F

3. Castration anxiety is responsible for resolution of the Oedipal complex in boys. T   F

4. According to object relations theory, symbiosis is the stage at which the infant cannot distinguish between self and other, but does distinguish between good and bad aspects of the self+other image.   T   F

5. B.F. Skinner's main contribution to psychology was the description and validation of observational learning as a learning mechanism.   T   F

C. Short Answer.

1. Describe the three types of studies used to test genetic hypotheses of mental disorders. What is one limitation of each method?

2. Summarize Freud's five stages of psychosexual development.

3. What are three problems with psychodynamic theory? Do behavioral and cognitive theories also suffer from these problems? Why or why not?

4. Who is Kay Redfield Jamison, and why is she noteworthy?

5. Summarize Bowlby's theory of normal and abnormal behavior.

ANSWER KEY

Multiple Choice
1. A
2. C
3. B
4. B
5. C
6. C
7. D
8. C
9. B
10. A
11. C
12. B
13. D
14. D
15. C
16. A
17. C
18. D
19. B
20. C

True-False
1. F
2. T
3. T
4. T
5. F

Short Answer
1. See pp. 40-42.
2. See pp. 46-48.
3. See pp. 50-55.
4. See p. 58.
5. See pp. 60-61.

Additional Readings on Chapter 2 Topics
    Bandura, A. (1986). Social foundations of thought and action: A social cognitive theory. New Jersey: Prentice Hall.
    Plomin, R. (1994). Nature, nurture, and social development. Social Development, 3, 37-53. (The same issue of this journal includes commentaries on this article.)
    Williams, J. M. G., Watts, F. N., MacLeod, C., Mathews, A. (1997). Cognitive psychology and the emotional disorders (2nd edition). New York: Wiley.

Chapter 3: The Research Endeavor

LEARNING OBJECTIVES
After reading and studying this chapter, you should be able to:

1. Discuss some of the difficulties inherent in psychological research.

2. Distinguish between a hypothesis and null hypothesis.

3. Distinguish between independent and dependent variables.

4. Explain the concept of operationalization.

5. Describe the elements of case, correlational, and experimental studies, as well as the strengths and weaknesses of each type of study.

6. Explain how one can improve internal and external validity and why this is important.

7. Discuss ways to rule out third variables.

8. Discuss statistical significance, how it is obtained, and what it means.

9. Distinguish among control groups, placebo control groups, wait list control groups, and experimental groups, and explain the circumstances in which each would be appropriate, and why (with regard to therapy outcome studies).

10. Discuss the ethical problems raised by human laboratory, therapy outcome, and animal studies, and ways in which researchers attempt to avoid these problems.

11. Discuss the challenges inherent in cross-cultural research.

12. Know the elements of each major section of a research paper in psychology.

ESSENTIAL IDEAS

I. The scientific method

    A. A hypothesis is a testable statement of what we expect to happen in a research study.

    B. A null hypothesis is the statement that the outcome of the study will contradict the primary hypothesis of the study. Usually, the null hypothesis is that the factors of interest (such as stress and depression) are unrelated to one another.

    C. A variable is a factor that can vary within individuals or between individuals.

    D. A dependent variable is the factor we try to predict in a study.

E. An independent variable is the factor we use to predict the dependent variable.

F. Operationalization is the way we measure or manipulate the variables of interest.

II. Case studies

A. Case studies are detailed histories of the experiences of individuals.

B. The advantages of case studies are their richness in detail, their attention to the unique experiences of individuals, their ability to focus on rare problems, and to generate new ideas.

C. The disadvantages of case studies are their lack of generalizability, their subjectivity, and difficulties in replication.

III. Correlational studies

A. A correlational study examines the relationship between two variables without manipulating either variable.

B. A correlation coefficient is an index of the relationship between two variables. It can range from -1.00 to $+1.00$. The magnitude of the correlation indicates how strong the relationship between the variables is. A positive correlation indicates that as values of one variable increase, values of the other variable increase. A negative correlation indicates that as values of one variable increase, values of the other variable decrease.

C. A result is said to be statistically significant if it is unlikely to have happened by chance. The convention in psychological research is to accept results for which there is a probability of less than 5 in 100 that they happened by chance.

D. A correlational study can show that two variables are related, but cannot show that one variable causes the other. All correlational studies suffer from the third variable problem—the possibility that variables not measured in the study actually account for the relationship between the variables measured in the study.

E. Continuous variable studies evaluate the relationship between two variables that vary along a continuum.

F. A sample is a subset of a population of interest. A representative sample is similar to the population of interest on all important variables. One way to generate a representative sample is to obtain a random sample.

G. Whereas cross-sectional studies assess a sample at one point in time, longitudinal studies assess the same sample at multiple points in time. A prospective longitudinal study assesses a sample that is expected to have some key event in the future both before and after the event, then examines changes that occurred in the sample.

H. Group comparison studies evaluate differences between key groups, such as a group that experienced a specific type of stressor and a comparison group that did not experience the stressor, but is matched on all important variables.

I. Other potential problems in correlational studies include the potential for bad timing and the expense of longitudinal studies.

IV. Experimental studies

A. Experimental studies attempt to control all variables affecting the dependent variable.

B. In human laboratory studies, the independent variable is manipulated and the effects on people participating in the study are examined. Control groups, in which participants have all the same experiences as the group of main interest in the study, except that they do not receive the key manipulation, are included to control for the effects of being in the experimental situation and the passage of time.

C. Demand characteristics are aspects of the experimental situation that cause participants to guess the purpose of the study and change their behavior as a result.

D. Disadvantages of human laboratory studies include their lack of generalizability and the ethical issues involved in manipulating people.

E. Therapy outcome studies assess the impact of an intervention designed to relieve symptoms. Simple control groups, wait list control groups, placebo control groups, are used to compare the effects of the intervention with other alternatives.

F. It can be difficult to determine what aspects of a therapy resulted in changes in participants. Therapy outcome studies also can suffer from lack of generalizability, and assigning people to control groups holds ethical implications.

G. Animal studies involve exposing animals to conditions thought to represent the causes of a psychopathology, and then measuring changes in the animals' behavior or physiology. The ethics of exposing animals to conditions that we would not expose humans to can be questionned, as can the generalizability of animal studies.

V. Cross-cultural research

A. Cross cultural research has expanded greatly in recent decades.

B. Some special challenges of cross cultural research include difficulty in accessing populations, in applying theories appropriate in one culture to other cultures, in translating concepts and measures across cultures, in predicting the responses of people in different cultures to being studied, and in demands to define "healthy" and "unhealthy" cultures.

KEY TERMS AND GUIDED REVIEW

<u>Guided Review</u>

1. What are some of the challenges faced by researchers in abnormal psychology? (p. 68)

The Scientific Method

<u>Key Terms</u>

scientific method (p. 69):

hypothesis (p. 69):

null hypothesis (p. 69):

variable (p. 69):

dependent variable (p. 69):

independent variable (p. 70):

operationalizations (p. 70):

<u>Guided Review</u>

1. What is the difference between a primary hypothesis and a null hypothesis? (p. 69)

2. If the results of a study do not support the primary hypothesis, why does this not disprove the theory upon which the primary hypothesis is based? (p. 69)

3. What is the difference between an independent and dependent variable? (pp. 69-71)

Case Studies

<u>Key Terms</u>

case study (p. 72):

generalizability (p. 73):

replicate (p. 73):

1. Suppose you wanted to test the hypothesis that a lack of aerobic exercise causes depression. How would you design a case study to test this hypothesis? (pp. 72-74)

2. What are some advantages and disadvantages of case studies? (pp. 72-74)

Correlational Studies

Key Terms

correlational study (p. 74):

continuous variable (p. 74):

group comparison study (p. 74):

cross-sectional study (p. 75):

longitudinal study (p. 75):

correlation coefficient (p. 75):

statistical significance (p. 76):

third variable problem (p. 76):

sample (p. 77):

representative sample (p. 77):

random sample (p. 77):

matching (p. 77):

external validity (p. 77):

Guided Review

1. What advantages and disadvantages do longitudinal studies have in comparison to cross-sectional studies? (pp. 74-75)

2. What is the difference between a positive and negative correlation? (p. 75)

3. How do researchers decide if a correlation is meaningful? (pp. 75-76)

4. Why does correlation <u>not</u> imply causation? (pp. 76-77)

5. Why is it important to have a representative sample? (p. 77)

6. In a correlational study, how can researchers protect against the third variable problem? (pp. 77-78)

7. What are some advantages and disadvantages of correlational studies? (pp. 77-78)

Experimental Studies

<u>Key Terms</u>

experimental study (p. 79):

human laboratory study (p. 79):

analogue study (p. 80):

internal validity (p. 80):

control group (p. 80):

experimental group (p. 80):

random assignment (p. 80):

demand characteristics (p. 80):

therapy outcome study (p. 82):

wait list control group (p. 82):

placebo control group (p. 82):

double-blind experiment (p. 82):

1. What is the difference between internal and external validity? (pp. 77-80)

2. How can researchers increase the internal validity of an experiment? (pp. 80-81)

3. How can researchers guard against demand characteristics? (pp. 80-81)

4. What are some advantages and disadvantages of human laboratory studies? (pp. 81-82)

5. Why would a researcher use a wait list control group instead of a regular control group? (pp. 82-83)

6. What are some advantages and disadvantages of placebo control groups? (pp. 82-83)

7. What are some advantages and disadvantages of therapy outcome studies? (pp. 82-83)

8. What are some advantages and disadvantages of animal studies? (pp. 84-85)

Cross-Cultural Research

Guided Review

1. Give an example of why researchers should be cautious in applying theories developed in one culture to individuals from another culture. (pp. 86-88)

2. What are some of the difficulties encountered by cross-cultural researchers? (pp. 86-88)

3. What are some advantages of conducting cross-cultural research? (pp. 86-88)

CHAPTER TEST

A. <u>Multiple Choice</u>. Choose the **best answer** to each question below.

1. If a researcher is studying the effects of humor on depression, depression is the:

    A. hypothesis.
    B. independent variable.
    C. dependent variable.
    D. operationalization.

Use the following study to answer questions 2 and 3:
Professor Llewellyn believes that depression is caused by experiences of loss (e.g., death of a loved one, or the breakup of a relationship). She administers questionnaires to people that ask about their experiences of loss and current depressive symptoms. She finds that depression and loss are not associated with one another in her study.

2. In this study, the questionnaires used to measure loss and depressive symptoms are the:

    A. independent and dependent variables.
    B. operationalization.
    C. primary hypothesis.
    D. null hypothesis.

3. The results of the study above fail to support the:

    A. primary hypothesis.
    B. null hypothesis.
    C. operationalization.
    D. variables.

4. Which of the following is <u>not</u> an advantage of case studies?

    A. They capture the uniqueness of an individual.
    B. They help generate new ideas and provide tentative support for those ideas.
    C. They are very likely to be replicated.
    D. They are sometimes the only way to study rare problems.

5. Researchers administer measures of memory and social skills to incoming college students during their orientation to a university. They predict that better social skills will be associated with better memory. This type of study is a:

    A. group comparison study.
    B. longitudinal study.
    C. continuous variable study.
    D. longitudinal group comparison study.

6. Researchers studying the relationship between success in college and frequency of alcohol use find that questionnaires measuring these variables are correlated -.45, p < .05. This means that:

    A. As alcohol use increases, success in college tends to decrease, and this finding is likely not due to chance alone.
    B. As alcohol use decreases, success in college tends to decrease, but this finding is likely due to chance alone.
    C. As success in college increases, alcohol use also increases, and these findings are likely not due to chance alone.
    D. There is no relationship between success in college and alcohol use, because the correlation is not statistically significant.

7. Which of the following is not an advantage of correlational studies?

    A. The fact that they can be cross-sectional or longitudinal.
    B. Their ability to establish that one variable causes another.
    C. Their external validity.
    D. The fact that they involve fewer ethical concerns than most experimental studies.

8. Professor Lozano wants to study the relationship between anger and aggression. She brings research participants into the laboratory and has one group of them watch an anger-inducing video, while the other group watches a neutral video about making cheesecake. She then gives participants the opportunity to punch an inflatable doll if they wish. Participants who watched the anger video punch the doll more than participants who watched the cheesecake video. A problem with the internal validity of this study is:

    A. The sample was not randomly drawn from the population.
    B. The level of generalizability to real-world conditions is questionable.
    C. There is no control group.
    D. Random assignment was not used.

9. An advantage of both human laboratory and therapy outcome studies is:

    A. They do not involve statistical significance tests.
    B. They have good internal validity.
    C. They involve very few ethical issues.
    D. They do not involve random assignment to condition.

10. Whether a correlation is statistically significant depends upon:

    A. The researcher's use of a random sample.
    B. The researcher's matching of experimental and control groups on important variables.
    C. Whether it is positive or negative.
    D. The size of the sample used by the researcher.

11. Filler measures and cover stories are used to:

   A. increase external validity.
   B. prevent demand effects.
   C. increase demand effects.
   D. increase internal validity.

12. Which of the following statements is <u>true</u>?

   A. If the results of a study fail to support the null hypothesis, then the primary hypothesis
      has been proven.
   B. If two variables are correlated .99, p < .05, then we know that one variable causes the
      other.
   C. Results that are not statistically significant support the null hypothesis.
   D. Variables must be operationalized before being defined.

13. Which of the following rankings of terms from most general to most specific (from left to
   right) is accurate?

   A. theory--hypothesis--operationalization
   B. operationalization--theory--hypothesis
   C. theory--operationalization--hypothesis
   D. hypothesis--theory--operationalization

14. Which of the following cannot establish causal relationships?

   A. longitudinal studies
   B. animal studies
   C. human laboratory studies
   D. therapy outcome studies

15. Which of the following is used to increase external validity?

   A. statistical significance tests
   B. random assignment
   C. random sampling
   D. matching

16. To rule out third variables, a researcher should:

   A. use statistical significance tests.
   B. conduct a longitudinal study.
   C. use random assignment.
   D. attempt to increase external validity.

17. To prevent demand effects, a researcher should:

    A. Conduct an analogue study.
    B. Use a process debriefing.
    C. Use a placebo control group.
    D. Conduct a double-blind experiment.

18. In writing a research paper, a detailed description of the participants in your study (their numbers, ages, genders, socioeconomic classes, racial/ethnic distribution) should appear in the:

    A. method section.
    B. results section.
    C. introduction.
    D. discussion.

19. Which of the following statements about Janice Egeland's study of the Amish is _true_?

    A. The Amish varied greatly in education and income status and were therefore difficult to study.
    B. The manifestations of depression and mania were different in the Amish.
    C. The Amish were poor candidates for genetic studies of mood disorders, although much was still learned by studying them.
    D. The researchers violated ethical guidelines by studying the Amish because they did not wish to be studied by outsiders.

20. The use of which of the following is most controversial in therapy outcome studies?

    A. matching
    B. placebo control groups
    C. random sampling
    D. demand characteristics

B. _True-False_. Select T (True) or F (False) below.

1. If intelligence and drug use are correlated -.70, $p > .05$, then we know that a statistically significant relationship exists between these variables.   T   F

2. When writing a research paper, one's hypothesis should first appear in the Method section.
    T   F

3. Low internal validity is a problem with case studies, cross-sectional studies, and longitudinal studies. T   F

4. If work efficiency and hours of sleep per night are correlated .60, $p < .05$, then we know that the probability that work efficiency is not related to hours of sleep is less than 5%.   T   F

5. Random assignment is important for establishing external validity, whereas random sampling is important for internal validity.   T   F

C. Short Answer.

1. What are some ethical issues involved in conducting human laboratory, therapy outcome, and animal studies?

2. Describe some difficulties in conducting cross-cultural research.

3. In what kinds of situations might it be important to maximize: 1) internal validity; and 2) external validity?

4. Why is it important to conduct statistical significance tests?

5. If the results of a study fail to support the primary hypothesis, why does this not prove that the null hypothesis is correct?

ANSWER KEY

<u>Multiple Choice</u>
1. C
2. B
3. A
4. C
5. C
6. A
7. B
8. D
9. B
10. D
11. B
12. C
13. A
14. A
15. C
16. C
17. D
18. A
19. B
20. B

<u>True-False</u>
1. F
2. F
3. T
4. F
5. F

<u>Short answer</u>
1. See pp. 81-85.
2. See pp. 85-90.
3. See pp. 77-80.
4. See p. 76.
5. See p. 69.

<u>Additional Readings on Chapter 3 Topics</u>

Faust, D., & Meehl, P. E. (1992). Using scientific methods to resolve questions in the history and philosophy of science: Some illustrations. <u>Behavior Therapy, 23,</u> 195-211.

Wampold, B. E., Davis, B., & Good, R. H. (1990). Hypothesis validity of clinical research. <u>Journal of Consulting and Clinical Psychology, 58,</u> 360-367.

Wilkinson, L. (1999). Statistical methods in psychology journals: Guidelines and explanations. <u>American Psychologist, 54,</u> 594-604.

Chapter 4: Assessing and Diagnosing Abnormality

LEARNING OBJECTIVES
After reading and studying this chapter, you should be able to:

1. Discuss the types of information that should be obtained during an assessment, why they are important, and the types of questions that may be asked to obtain the information.

2. Define and distinguish among the various psychometric properties (i.e., validity and reliability) that set the standard by which various assessment tools are evaluated.

3. Describe and give examples of each of the various tools (including biological, neuropsychological, and intelligence tests, clinical interviews, symptom questionnaires, personality inventories, observation, and projective tests) used by clinicians to gather information during an assessment.

4. Discuss the advantages and disadvantages of each assessment tool.

5. Discuss particular difficulties that can arise in the assessment of children.

6. Summarize how cultural biases may affect the assessment process and the issues involved in working with a client from a different culture.

7. Discuss the modern method for diagnosing mental disorders, the DSM-IV, and discuss its five axes.

8. Describe the changes in the DSM from its earliest version to its most recent version, and the factors that have influenced the changes.

9. Discuss the shortcomings of the DSM-IV.

10. Describe how culture and gender can influence the diagnostic process.

11. Present arguments both for and against diagnostic labels.

ESSENTIAL IDEAS

I. Gathering information

   A. Information concerning clients' symptoms and history is obtained in an assessment. This includes the details of their current symptoms, ability to function, coping strategies, self-concept, recent events, past history of psychological problems, and family history of psychological problems.

B. Clients' physiological and neurophysiological functioning are assessed as well. They may be asked to undergo a physical examination to detect medical conditions, questioned about their drug use, and tested for their cognitive functioning and intellectual abilities.

C. Clients' sociocultural background—including their social resources and cultural heritage—are important to ascertain in an assessment.

II. Assessment tools

A. Paper-and-pencil neuropsychological tests can help to identify specific cognitive deficits that may be tied to brain damage.

B. Intelligence tests can indicate a client's general level of intellectual functioning in verbal and analytic tasks.

C. Structured clinical interviews provide a standardized way to assess people's symptoms in an interview format.

D. Symptom questionnaires allow for mass screening of large numbers of people to determine self-reported symptoms.

E. Personality inventories assess stable personality characteristics.

F. Projective tests are used to uncover unconscious conflicts and concerns but are open to interpretive biases.

G. Behavioral observation and self-monitoring can help detect behavioral deficits and the environmental triggers for symptoms.

III. Problems in assessment

A. It is often difficult to obtain accurate information on children's problems because children are unable to report their thoughts and feelings. Parents and teachers may be relied upon for information about children, but can be biased in their own assessments of children's symptoms and needs.

B. When the clinician and client are from different cultures, language difficulties and cultural expectations can make assessment difficult. Interpreters can help in the assessment process but must be well-trained in psychological assessment.

IV. Diagnosis

A. The Diagnostic and Statistical Manual of Mental Disorders (DSM) provides criteria for diagnosing all psychological disorders currently recognized in the United States.

B. The first two editions of the DSM provided vague descriptions of disorder based on psychoanalytic theory, and thus the reliability of diagnoses made according to these manuals was low. More recent editions of the DSM contain more specific, observable criteria that are not as strongly based on theory for the diagnosis of disorders.

C. Five axes or types of information are specified in determining a DSM diagnosis. On Axis I, clinicians list all significant clinical syndromes. On Axis II, clinicians indicate if the client is suffering from a personality disorder or mental retardation. On Axis III, clinicians list the client's general medical condition. On Axis IV, clinicians list psychosocial and environmental problems the client is facing. On Axis V, clinicians indicate the client's global level of functioning.

D. Many critics of the DSM argue that it reflects Western, male perspectives on abnormality, and pathologizes the behavior of women and other cultures. The DSM-IV includes descriptions of culture-bound syndromes—groups of symptoms that appear to occur only in specific cultures.

E. Diagnoses can be misapplied for political or social reasons. The negative social implications of having a psychiatric diagnosis can be great. Having a standard diagnostic system helps in treatment and research, however.

KEY TERMS AND GUIDED REVIEW

Key Terms

assessment (p. 96):

diagnosis (p. 96):

Gathering Information

Key Terms

differential diagnosis (p. 98):

acculturation (p. 100):

Guided Review

1. In addition to finding out which symptoms a client has, what additional information should be gathered in an assessment? (pp. 96-100)

2. Why is it important to know about the client's concept of his or her symptoms? (p. 97)

3. What types of information are important to obtain when making a differential diagnosis? (p. 98)

4. In what way(s) can the use of biological tests inform an assessment? (pp. 98-99)

5. Why is it important to determine a client's level of acculturation? (pp. 99-100)

Assessment Tools

<u>Key Terms</u>

interview (p. 101):

unstructured interview (p. 101):

structured interview (p. 101):

resistance (p. 101):

validity (p. 102):

face validity (p. 103):

content validity (p. 103):

concurrent validity (p. 103):

predictive validity (p. 103):

construct validity (p. 103):

reliability (p. 103):

test-retest reliability (p. 103):

alternate form reliability (p. 104):

internal reliability (p. 104):

interrater reliability (p. 104):

neuropsychological test (p. 104):

intelligence test (p. 105):

computerized tomography (CT) (p. 105):

positron emission tomography (PET) (p. 105):

magnetic resonance imaging (MRI) (p. 106):

electroencephalogram (EEG) (p. 106):

event-related potential (ERP) (p. 106):

symptom questionnaire (p. 109):

personality inventory (p. 109):

projective test (p. 112):

behavioral observation (p. 114):

self-monitoring (p. 114):

Guided Review

1. What are the advantages of using a structured clinical interview, compared to using an unstructured one? (p. 101)

2. What are some of the shortcomings of clinical interviews? (p. 101)

3. What is the difference between validity and reliability? (pp. 102-104)

4. What are some reasons for using neuropsychological tests in assessment? (pp. 104-105)

5. How are CT, PET, MRI, and EEG/ERPs different from one another? (pp. 105-107)

6. What are some reasons for using intelligence tests in an assessment? (pp. 105-108)

7. What are some of the criticisms of intelligence tests? (pp. 108-109)

8. What are some reasons for using symptom questionnaires in an assessment? (p. 109)

9. What are some advantages and disadvantages of the MMPI? (pp. 110-112)

10. Give some examples of projective tests and what they are thought to measure. What is an important limitation of projective tests? (pp. 112-114)

11. What are some advantages and disadvantages of using behavioral observations in an assessment? (p. 114)

Problems in Assessment

<u>Guided Review</u>

1. When assessing a child, what are some reasons for obtaining information from people besides the child him/herself? (pp. 115-116)

2. What problems can result from using parents to assess a child's functioning? (pp. 115-116)

3. What problems can result from using teachers to assess a child's functioning? (pp. 115-116)

4. Why is it important for clinicians to take a client's culture into account? (pp. 116-117)

Diagnosis

<u>Key Terms</u>

syndrome (p. 118):

Diagnostic and Statistical Manual of Mental Disorders (DSM) (p. 118):

course (p. 120):

prevalence (p. 120):

point prevalence (p. 120):

lifetime prevalence (p. 120):

incidence (p. 121):

Guided Review

1. How do psychological syndromes differ from medical syndromes? (p. 118)

2. What are some of the ways in which the DSM changed from its first edition in 1952 through publication of its fourth edition in 1994? (pp. 118-124)

3. What are some reasons why the DSM does not have perfect reliability? (pp. 119-122)

4. Summarize the information that should appear on Axes I through V of the DSM. (pp. 122-124)

5. What are some of the criticisms of the DSM-IV? (pp. 121-129)

6. What are some of the advantages and disadvantages of using diagnostic labels? (pp. 124-129)

Bio-Psycho-Social Integration

Guided Review

1. How does the DSM-IV reflect a bio-psycho-social view of mental disorders? (p. 129)

CHAPTER TEST

A. <u>Multiple Choice</u>. Choose the **best answer** to each question below.

1. Clinicians do <u>not</u> use biological tests:

    A. To determine if a person is suffering from a medical condition that causes psychological symptoms.
    B. To determine if a patient has a brain injury or tumor.
    C. To identify gross structural or functional abnormalities in an individual patient.
    D. To perform a differential diagnosis between two disorders by comparing the PET scan of a client suspected of having a certain mental disorder with a PET scan of a different mental disorder.

2. All of the following are particularly important for making a differential diagnosis <u>except</u>:

    A. Recent events in the client's life.
    B. The client's past history of psychological problems.
    C. The client's self-concept and concept of his or her symptoms.
    D. The client's family history of psychological problems.

3. The extent to which a test yields the same results as other measures of the same behavior, thoughts, or feelings is referred to as:

    A. test-retest reliability.
    B. predictive validity.
    C. concurrent validity.
    D. construct validity.

4. Similarity in people's answers to different parts of the same test is referred to as:

    A. test-retest reliability.
    B. internal reliability.
    C. alternate form reliability.
    D. face validity.

5. Which of the following involves passing narrow X-ray beams through a person's head, determining the amount of radiation absorbed by each beam, and then constructing a computerized 3-D image of the person's brain?

    A. CT
    B. MRI
    C. PET
    D. EEG

6. An IQ score of 100 means that:

    A. The client's intellectual abilities are in the mentally retarded range.
    B. The client's intellectual abilities are in the gifted range.
    C. The client's intellectual abilities are in the average range.
    D. The IQ test is not appropriate for the client being tested.

7. Which of the following statements about the BDI is true?

    A. It can be used to diagnose depression.
    B. It discriminates clearly between the symptoms of depression and the symptoms of other disorders (e.g., anxiety disorders).
    C. It was developed empirically.
    D. It has cutoff scores that indicate moderate and severe levels of depression.

8. Which of the following includes validity scales that determine if a person is performing the test in a straightforward manner?

    A. Bender-Gestalt Test
    B. Minnesota Multiphasic Personality Inventory
    C. Stanford-Binet Intelligence Test
    D. Beck Depression Inventory

9. The reliability and validity of _____ has not proven to be strong in research.

    A. neuropsychological tests
    B. intelligence tests
    C. personality inventories
    D. projective tests

10. All of the following tests include data that define what is considered normal performance except the:

    A. Child Behavior Checklist (CBCL).
    B. Wechsler Intelligence Scale for Children - Third Edition (WISC-III).
    C. Minnesota Multiphasic Personality Inventory (MMPI).
    D. Thematic Apperception Test (TAT).

11. From DSM in 1952 to DSM-IV in 1994, the trend in diagnostic criteria has been:

   A. From vague, atheoretical classifications of disorders to theory-based criteria for each disorder.
   B. From not providing information about how long a person must display certain symptoms in order to qualify for a diagnosis to providing this information.
   C. From including prevalence information to concluding that cross-cultural differences make such information unsound.
   D. From requiring that symptoms either cause distress or interfere with functioning to requiring that unconscious conflicts play a role (in Axis I disorders).

12. Which of the following statements about assessing children is false?

   A. Children are typically able to differentiate among different types of emotions that they experience.
   B. Children with behavior problems often do not believe that they have problems.
   C. Parents' reports of child behavior may be affected by their own psychopathology.
   D. Teachers' assessments of children are often discrepant with the assessments given by parents and clinicians.

13. Which of the following statements about cultural biases in assessment is false?

   A. African Americans tend to be overdiagnosed with schizophrenia even when their symptoms actually fit the diagnosis of manic depression.
   B. When the clinician and client do not speak the same language, the clinician is highly likely to overdiagnose symptomatology rather than underdiagnose it.
   C. European Americans are more likely than members of other cultures to report feeling anxious or sad, whereas members of some other cultures tend to report symptoms as physical complaints.
   D. Members of non-European cultures may tend to be overdiagnosed with psychotic symptoms when they are really reporting on the beliefs of their culture.

14. Beginning with its third edition, the DSM was revamped due to:

   A. Problems with the validity of diagnostic criteria.
   B. Insufficient theory regarding the causes of disorders in earlier editions.
   C. Problems with the reliability of diagnostic criteria.
   D. The requirement (in earlier editions) that one's symptoms interfere with functioning.

15. If we measured the number of people who have an anxiety disorder today, we would be measuring the _____ of the anxiety disorder.

   A. course
   B. lifetime prevalence
   C. point prevalence
   D. incidence

16. The number of new cases of a disorder that develop during a specific period of time is referred to as:

    A. course.
    B. incidence.
    C. point prevalence.
    D. prevalence.

17. Mental retardation should be coded on:

    A. Axis I.
    B. Axis II.
    C. Axis III.
    D. Axis IV.

18. Problems such as housing or economic difficulties should be recorded on:

    A. Axis IV.
    B. Axis II.
    C. Axis V.
    D. Axis III.

19. A client whose Global Assessment of Functioning (GAF) is 90 would be regarded as having:

    A. Some danger of hurting self or others or gross impairment in communication.
    B. Moderate symptoms and difficulty in functioning.
    C. Serious symptoms and difficulty in functioning.
    D. Absent or minimal symptoms; good functioning in all areas.

20. The research conducted by Harris and colleagues (1992) illustrated:

    A. Sex bias in diagnosis.
    B. Cultural bias in diagnosis.
    C. Negative implications of diagnostic labels.
    D. The low reliability of diagnostic labels.

B. <u>True-False</u>. Select T (True) or F (False) below.

1. Construct validity is the extent to which a test assesses all the important aspects of a phenomenon that it purports to measure.   T   F

2. Alternate form reliability is an index of how consistent the results of a test are over time.   T   F

3. The Bender-Gestalt Test is an example of a projective test.   T   F

4. Magnetic Resonance Imaging (MRI) does not require exposing a patient to any form of radiation, but Positron Emission Tomograpy (PET) does.   T   F

5. The Beck Depression Inventory (BDI) cannot establish a diagnosis of depression.
        T   F

C. Short Answer.

1. Identify five areas that are important to assess during a clinical interview. For each area, briefly explain why it is important to assess and give an example of how you might assess it.

2. Discuss the appropriate and inappropriate uses of biological tests in assessing mental disorders.

3. Discuss how cultural biases can affect the assessment process. Give some examples from the chapter.

4. What are some of the shortcomings of the DSM-IV? How does the DSM-IV represent an improvement over earlier versions of the DSM?

5. What are the advantages and disadvantages of using diagnostic labels?

ANSWER KEY

<u>Multiple Choice</u>
1. D
2. C
3. C
4. B
5. A
6. C
7. D
8. B
9. D
10. D
11. B
12. A
13. B
14. C
15. C
16. B
17. B
18. A
19. D
20. C

<u>True-False</u>
1. F
2. F
3. F
4. T
5. T

<u>Short Answer</u>
1. See pp. 96-101.
2. See pp. 98-99, 105-107.
3. See pp. 99-100, 108-109, 116-117.
4. See pp. 118-122.
5. See pp. 124-129.

<u>Additional Readings on Chapter 4 Topics</u>

Cipolotti, L., & Warrington, E. K. (1995). Neuropsychological assessment. <u>Journal of Neurology, Neurosurgery, and Psychiatry, 58,</u> 655-664.

Garb, H. N. (1997). Race bias, social class bias, and gender bias in clinical judgment. <u>Clinical Psychology: Science and Practice, 4,</u> 99-120.

Widiger, T. A., & Trull, T. J. (1991). Diagnosis and clinical assessment. <u>Annual Review of Psychology, 42,</u> 109-133.

Chapter 5: Treatments for Abnormality

LEARNING OBJECTIVES

After reading and studying this chapter, you should be able to:

1. Give examples of antipsychotic, antidepressant, mood stabilizing, and antianxiety drugs and know their appropriate uses and limitations.

2. Distinguish among MAO inhibitors, tricyclic antidepressants, and SSRIs.

3. Identify the appropriate and inappropriate uses of ECT and psychosurgery.

4. Describe the components of psychodynamic therapy and how it is thought to work.

5. Describe humanistic therapy and how it is conducted.

6. Describe techniques used in behavior therapy.

7. Describe the elements of cognitive therapy and how it is similar to behavior therapy.

8. Discuss IPT and how it is both similar to and different from psychodynamic therapy.

9. Discuss alternatives to individual therapy (i.e., family and group therapy).

10. Describe how mental health treatment may be carried out in a community.

11. Discuss how cultural issues may affect treatment and the extent to which research suggests that these issues should affect therapist-client matching.

12. Discuss some of the problems with therapy outcome research.

13. Summarize the common components of successful therapies.

14. Discuss the special issues that can arise when treating children.

ESSENTIAL IDEAS

I. Biological treatments

    A. Antipsychotic drugs such as the phenothiazines and butyrophenone help to reduce symptoms of psychosis.

B. Antidepressant drugs, including the monoamine oxidase inhibitors, the tricyclic antidepressants, the selective serotonin reuptake inhibitors, and substance P receptor antagonists help reduce symptoms of depression.

C. Lithium is used to treat the symptoms of mania.

D. Anticonvulsant drugs and calcium channel blockers also help to treat mania.

E. Antianxiety drugs include the bartiturates and the benzodiazepines.

F. Electroconvulsive therapy is useful in the treatment of severe depression.

G. Psychosurgery is used on rare occasions to help people with severe psychopathology that is not affected by drugs or other treatments.

II. Psychological therapies

A. Psychodynamic therapies focus on uncovering unconscious motives and concerns behind psychopathology through free association and analysis of transferences and dreams.

B. Humanistic or client-centered therapy attempts to help clients find their own answers to problems by supporting them and reflecting back these concerns so they can self-reflect and self-actualize.

C. Behavioral therapies focus on the reinforcements and punishments people receive for maladaptive behavior, and altering these. Behavioral therapists also help clients learn new behavioral skills.

D. Cognitive therapy focuses on the changing maladaptive cognitions behind distressing feelings and behaviors.

III. Sociocultural approaches

A. Interpersonal therapy is a short-term therapy that focuses on clients' current relationships and concerns, but explores the roots of their problems in past relationships.

B. Family systems therapists focus on changing maladaptive patterns of behavior within family systems to reduce psychopathology in individual members.

C. In group therapy, people who share a problem come together to support each other, learn from each other, and practice new skills. Self-help groups are a form of group therapy that does not involve a mental health professional.

D. The community mental health movement was aimed at deinstituionalizing people with mental disorders, and treating them through community mental health centers, halfway houses, and day treatment centers. The resources for these community treatment centers have never been adequate, however, and many people do not have access to mental health care.

E. Primary prevention programs aim to stop the development of disorders before they start. Secondary prevention programs provide treatment to people in the early stages of their disorders in hope of reducing the development of the disorders.

F. Values inherent in most psychotherapies that can clash with the values of certain cultures include the focus on the individual, the expression of emotions and disclosure of personal concerns, and the expectation that clients take initiative.

G. People from minority groups may be more likely to remain in treatment if matched with a therapist from their own cultural group, but there are large individual differences in these preferences.

H. There are a number of culturally specific therapies designed by cultural groups to address psychopathology within the traditions of that culture.

IV. Evaluating treatments

A. Some reviews of studies of the effectiveness of psychosocial treatments find they are all equally effective and others suggest that certain treatments are more effective than others in the treatment of specific disorders.

B. Methodological and ethical problems make doing good research on the effectiveness of therapy difficult.

C. Most therapies involve a positive relationship between a therapist and client, provide an explanation or interpretation to the client, and encourage clients to confront painful emotions.

D. Many therapists are eclectic, combining different techniques from various therapeutic approaches.

V. Special issues in treating children

A. Treatments for children must take into account their cognitive skills and developmental levels and adapt to their ability to comprehend and participate in therapy.

B. There are reasons to be concerned about the possible toxic effects of drugs on children.

C. Often, a child's family must be brought into therapy, but the child or the family may object.

D. Most children who enter therapy do not seek it out themselves but are brought by others, raising issues about children's willingness to participate in therapy.

KEY TERMS AND GUIDED REVIEW

<u>Key Terms</u>

medications (p. 134):

psychotherapy (p. 134):

Biological Treatments

<u>Key Terms</u>

chlorpromazine (p. 137):

phenothiazines (p. 137):

neuroleptic (p. 137):

butyrophenone (p. 138):

antipsychotic drugs (p. 138):

antidepressants (p. 138):

monoamine oxidase inhibitors (MAOIs) (p. 138):

tricyclic antidepressants (p. 138):

selective serotonin reuptake inhibitor (SSRI) (p. 139):

substance P (p. 140):

lithium (p. 140):

anticonvulsants (p. 140):

calcium channel blockers (p. 140):

barbiturates (p. 140):

benzodiazepines (p. 140):

electroconvulsive therapy (ECT) (p. 141):

prefrontal lobotomies (p. 141):

psychosurgery (p. 141):

<u>Guided Review</u>

1. Describe some of the differences between MAOIs and tricyclic antidepressants. (pp. 138-139)

2. What are some reasons why SSRIs have become so popular? (pp. 139-140)

3. List the side effects of MAOIs, tricyclic antidepressants, SSRIs, barbiturates, and benzodiazepines. (pp. 138-141)

4. In general, how were most of the drugs described in this section discovered? Give examples. (pp. 137-141)

5. What are some advantages and disadvantages of biological therapies? (pp. 142-144).

Psychological Therapies

<u>Key Terms</u>

psychodynamic therapies (p. 145):

free association (p. 145):

resistance (p. 145):

transference (p. 146):

working through (p. 146):

catharsis (p. 146):

therapeutic alliance (p. 147):

psychoanalysis (p. 147):

humanistic therapy (p. 147):

person-centered therapy (p. 147):

client-centered therapy (p. 148):

unconditional positive regard (p. 148):

reflection (p. 148):

behavior therapies (p. 148):

behavioral assessment (p. 148):

role play (p. 148):

systematic desensitization (p. 149):

modeling (p. 150):

in vivo exposure (p. 150):

flooding (implosive therapy) (p. 150):

token economy (p. 150):

response shaping (p. 150):

social skills training (p. 150):

cognitive therapies (p. 151):

behavioral assignments (p. 153):

Guided Review

1. What are the main components of psychodynamic therapy, and how does it work? (pp. 145-147)

2. What is the difference between psychoanalysis and psychodynamic therapy? (p. 147)

3. What are some limitations of psychodynamic therapy? (p. 147)

4. What are the main components of client-centered therapy, and how does it work? (pp. 147-148)

5. Describe how a behavior therapist might go about reducing unwanted behaviors in a client. (pp. 148-150)

6. What are some differences between behavior therapy and psychodynamic therapy? (pp. 145-151)

7. Describe how a behavior therapist might go about increasing positive behaviors in a client. (pp. 150-151)

8. What are some goals of cognitive therapy? (pp. 151-153)

9. Describe some techniques used by cognitive therapists. (pp. 151-153)

Sociocultural approaches

Key Terms

interpersonal therapy (IPT) (p. 154):

family systems (p. 156):

group therapy (p. 157):

self-help groups (p. 157):

community mental health movement (p. 158):

deinstitutionalization (p. 158):

community mental health centers (p. 158):

halfway houses (p. 158):

day treatment centers (p. 158):

primary prevention (p. 159):

secondary prevention (p. 159):

<u>Guided Review</u>

1. What are some of the differences between IPT and traditional psychodynamic therapy? (pp. 154-156)

2. What are some similarities and differences between Minuchin's Structural Family Therapy and Satir's Conjoint Family Therapy? (pp. 156-157)

3. What advantages might group therapy have over individual therapy? (pp. 157-158)

4. Give examples of some alternatives to institutionalization of mental health patients. (pp. 158-159)

5. What is the difference between primary and secondary prevention? (p. 159)

6. What are some ways in which non-Western cultural norms can clash with assumptions of psychotherapy? (pp. 160-161)

7. Give some examples of culturally specific therapies. (pp. 162-163)

Evaluating Treatments

<u>Key Terms</u>

Dodo bird verdict (p. 163):

<u>Guided Review</u>

1. What are some of the difficulties faced in therapy outcome research? (pp. 164-165)

2. What appear to be some common components of successful therapies? (pp. 165-166)

Special Issues in Treating Children

<u>Guided Review</u>

1. Give an example of how a therapy developed for adults may be applied differently with children. (pp. 166-170)

2. What are some safety issues that arise when treating a child's psychopathology with drugs? (p. 170)

3. What are some difficulties that arise when treating children using psychotherapy? (pp. 170-171)

CHAPTER TEST

A. <u>Multiple Choice</u>. Choose the **best answer** to each question below.

1. Haloperidol belongs to the group of drugs known as:

    A. Tricyclic antidepressants.
    B. Monoamine oxidase inhibitors.
    C. Phenothiazines.
    D. Butyrophenones.

2. Tardive dyskinesia is a side effect that may be caused by:

    A. Tricyclic antidepressants.
    B. Phenothiazines.
    C. Lithium.
    D. Benzodiazepines.

3. Inhibiting monoamine oxidase:

    A. Leads to lower levels of dopamine in the synapse.
    B. Inhibits the reuptake of norepinephrine.
    C. Leads to higher levels of norepinephrine in the synapse.
    D. Increases levels of substance P.

4. One important reason that selective serotonin reuptake inhibitors (SSRIs) became very popular soon after their development was:

    A. They were shown to be more effective than tricyclic antidepressants.
    B. They were shown to be more effective than MAO inhibitors.
    C. They were found to be specific to depression and not other problems.
    D. Their side effects were more easily tolerated by many people.

5. _____ may be prescribed to treat mania, whereas _____ may be prescribed to treat depression.

    A. Calcium channel blockers; electroconvulsive therapy
    B. Anticonvulsants; neuroleptics
    C. Barbiturates; substance P
    D. MAO inhibitors; lithium

6. Analyzing a client's transference toward the therapist would most likely occur in:

    A. Behavior therapy.
    B. Psychodynamic therapy.
    C. Cognitive therapy.
    D. Client-centered therapy.

7. Exposing clients to feared stimuli or situations to an excessive degree while preventing them from avoiding the stimuli or situation is known as:

    A. Modeling.
    B. Systematic desensitization.
    C. Response shaping.
    D. Flooding.

8. Which of the following is designed to be short term (one or two sessions per week for 12 to 20 weeks)?

    A. Cognitive therapy
    B. Humanistic therapy
    C. Psychodynamic therapy
    D. Family therapy

9. Techniques such as fantasized consequences and guided association are used in:

    A. Psychoanalytic therapy.
    B. Cognitive therapy.
    C. Interpersonal therapy.
    D. Psychodynamic therapy.

10. A key technique used by humanistic therapists is:

    A. Allowing a client to freely convey his or her thoughts and feelings in an unstructured manner, collecting bits of information from these thoughts, and eventually voicing an interpretation about the client's problems.
    B. Changing the client's tendency to automatically assume that his or her negative thoughts are true by identifying and challenging them.
    C. Communicating to the client that the therapist is a real person like the client, and can empathize with the client's concerns in a nondirective way.
    D. Focusing on the client's relationships as the source of his or her distress while voicing interpretations and directing the client toward changing these relationships.

11. A therapy that focuses on pointing out dysfunctional communication patterns in families and teaching family members to communicate better is known as:

   A. Interpersonal therapy (IPT).
   B. Satir's conjoint family therapy.
   C. Yalom's group therapy.
   D. Minuchin's structural family therapy.

12. A place where people with long-standing mental health problems may live in a structured, supportive environment is known as a:

   A. Community mental health center.
   B. Halfway house.
   C. Day treatment program.
   D. Homebuilders program.

13. Research on sociocultural factors has not shown that:

   A. Matching therapist and client on ethnicity or race leads to better outcomes for the client.
   B. People from Latino, Asian, and Native American cultures are more comfortable with structured and action-oriented therapies than with less structured therapies.
   C. People from ethnic minority groups in the U.S. are more likely to drop out of psychotherapy.
   D. Men and women report that they prefer a therapist of the same gender.

14. All of the following have been found to be common components of successful therapies except:

   A. A positive relationship with the therapist.
   B. An explanation or interpretation of why the client is suffering.
   C. Short-term, structured therapy sessions.
   D. Confrontation of negative emotions.

15. In 1952, Hans Eysenck concluded that:

   A. Psychotherapy was effective for a wide variety of problems.
   B. Behavior therapies were superior to psychodynamic therapies for most disorders.
   C. All therapies were about equally effective.
   D. Psychotherapy did not work.

16. The Dodo bird verdict states that:

     A. All psychotherapies have not been shown to be effective.
     B. Drug therapies are equivalent to psychotherapies in their effectiveness.
     C. No psychotherapy has been convincingly shown to be more effective than another.
     D. All psychotherapies have been shown to be effective.

17. Which of the following is not a problem in therapy outcome research?

     A. Defining what constitutes a good outcome.
     B. Finding people who suffer from more than one disorder to participate in studies.
     C. Defining an appropriate no-treatment control group.
     D. Finding therapists who are well-trained enough to conduct the therapies being studied.

18. An eclectic therapist:

     A. Practices only those techniques that have been shown to be effective.
     B. Believes that drug therapies should be the treatment of choice for most disorders.
     C. Uses techniques of different therapies depending on the specific issues needing to be addressed.
     D. Receives extensive training in one therapy from an expert and practices only that form of therapy.

19. Which of the following is not a problem in treating children?

     A. Children cannot participate meaningfully in talking therapies, such as cognitive therapy.
     B. Studies of the long-term impact of drugs on child development have not been done.
     C. Children often do not seek therapy themselves.
     D. There is more variability in the proper dosage of a drug among children than there is among adults.

20. Which of the following appears to be an effective treatment for mild to moderate depression?

     A. Hypericum perforatum.
     B. Rauwolfia serpentina.
     C. Valeriana officinalis.
     D. Gingko biloba.

B. True-False. Select T (True) or F (False) below.

1. Most antipsychotic drugs are thought to work by increasing norepinephrine levels or influencing receptors for norepinephrine in the brain.   T   F

2. Chlorpromazine is both a neuroleptic and a phenothiazine.   T   F

3. Anticonvulsants and calcium channel blockers are effective treatments for depression.
      T   F

4. The notion of unconditional positive regard was introduced by Freud.   T   F

5. Both interpersonal therapy and cognitive therapy are designed to be short-term treatments.
      T   F

C. Short Answer.

1. How does the role of the therapist differ in psychodynamic therapy, compared to client-centered therapy and cognitive therapy?

2. Why are SSRIs preferred over MAOIs and tricyclic antidepressants?

3. What are some common components of successful therapies?

4. What are some reasons that therapies developed in Western cultures may be hard to practice with individuals from different cultures?

5. What are some problems with therapy outcome research?

ANSWER KEY

<u>Multiple Choice</u>
1. D
2. B
3. C
4. D
5. A
6. B
7. D
8. A
9. B
10. C
11. B
12. B
13. A
14. C
15. D
16. C
17. B
18. C
19. A
20. A

<u>True-False</u>
1. F
2. T
3. F
4. F
5. T

<u>Short Answer</u>
1. See pp. 145-153.
2. See pp. 138-140.
3. See pp. 164-166.
4. See pp. 160-161.
5. See pp. 163-165.

<u>Additional Reading on Chapter 5 Topics</u>
Elkin, I. A. (1999). A major dilemma in psychotherapy outcome research: Disentangling therapists from therapies. <u>Clinical Psychology: Science and Practice, 6,</u> 10-32.

Nathan, P. E., & Gorman, J. M. (1998). <u>A guide to treatments that work</u>. New York: Oxford University Press.

Prochaska, J. O., & DiClemente, C. C. (1982). Transtheoretical therapy: Toward a more integrative model of change. <u>Psychotherapy: Theory, Research, and Practice, 19,</u> 276-288.

Chapter 6: Anxiety Disorders: Panic, Phobias, and Generalized Anxiety

LEARNING OBJECTIVES
After reading and studying this chapter, you should be able to:

1. Identify and give examples of the four types of symptoms that constitute anxiety.

2. Know the differences between adaptive fear and maladaptive anxiety.

3. Identify the brain areas and physiological changes that are active in the fight-or-flight response.

4. Know the key features of panic disorder and the biological and psychological theories that attempt to explain it.

5. Identify the treatments available for panic disorder as well as their advantages and disadvantages.

6. Know the key features of agoraphobia.

7. Identify the four main types of specific phobias.

8. Discuss the biological and psychological theories of phobias.

9. Discuss the effective behavioral treatments for phobias.

10. Discuss the key features of GAD and the theories that attempt to explain it.

11. Identify treatments used for GAD.

12. Describe how the anxiety disorders discussed in this chapter vary between the sexes and across cultures.

ESSENTIAL IDEAS

I. Panic disorder

    A. Panic disorder is characterized by sudden bursts of anxiety symptoms, a sense of loss of control or unreality, and the sense that one is dying.

    B. Several neurotransmitters, including norepinephrine, serotonin, GABA, and CCK have been implicated in panic disorders.

C. The kindling model of panic disorders suggests that dysregulation of the locus ceruleus causes panic attacks, and also kindles the limbic system, lowering the threshold for chronic anxiety. This chronic anxiety then increases a person's risk of a new panic attack.

D. The suffocation false alarm theory suggests that people with panic attacks are hypersensitive to increases in levels of carbon dioxide in the brain, which sends them into frequent fight-or-flight responses.

E. There is some evidence that genetics play a role in panic disorders.

F. The cognitive model suggests that people with panic disorder are hypersensitive to bodily symptoms and tend to catastrophize these symptoms.

G. The vulnerability-stress model suggests that people who develop panic disorder are born with a biological predisposition to an overactive fight-or-flight response, but don't develop the disorder unless they also tend to catastrophize their bodily symptoms.

H. Tricyclic antidepressants, serotonin reuptake inhibitors and benzodiazepines can be helpful in reducing symptoms but these symptoms tend to recur once the drugs are discontinued.

I. Cognitive-behavioral therapy has proven very useful in reducing and preventing relapse in panic disorder.

II. Phobias

A. People with agoraphobia fear a wide variety of situations in which they might have an emergency but not be able to escape or get help. Many people with agoraphobia also suffer from panic disorder.

B. The specific phobias include animal type phobias, natural environment type phobias, situational type phobias, and blood-injection-injury type phobias.

C. People with social phobia fear social situations in which they might be embarrassed or judged by others.

D. Psychodynamic theories of phobias suggest that they represent unconscious anxiety that has been displaced.

E. Behavioral theories of phobias suggest that they develop through classical and operant conditioning. Humans may be evolutionarily prepared to develop some types of phobias more easily than others.

F. Biological theories of phobias attribute their development to heredity.

G. Behavioral treatments for phobias include systematic desensitization, modeling, and flooding.

H. Cognitive techniques are sometimes used to help clients identify and challenge negative, catastrophizing thoughts they have when anxious.

I. The benzodiazepines and antidepressant drugs can help to quell anxiety symptoms, but people soon relapse into phobias after they are discontinued.

III. Generalized anxiety disorder

A. Generalized anxiety disorder is characterized by chronic symptoms of anxiety across most situations.

B. Freud suggested that GAD develops when people cannot find ways to express their impulses and fear the expression of these impulses. Newer psychodynamic theories suggest that children whose parents are not sufficiently warm and nurturing develop images of the self as vulnerable and images of others as hostile, which results in chronic anxiety.

C. Humanistic theories suggest generalized anxiety results in children who develop a harsh set of self-standards they feel they must achieve in order to be acceptable.

D. Existential theories attribute generalized anxiety to existential anxiety, a universal fear of the limits and responsibilities of one's existence.

E. Cognitive theories suggest that both the conscious and unconscious thoughts of people with GAD are focused on threat.

F. Biological theories suggest that people with GAD have a deficiency in GABA or GABA receptors. They may also have a genetic predisposition to generalized anxiety.

G. Cognitive-behavioral treatments for people with GAD focus on helping them confront their negative thinking.

H. Drug therapies have included the use of benzodiazepines and a newer drug called buspirone.

IV. Sociocultural approach to the anxiety disorders

A. Sociocultural perspectives on anxiety disorders suggest that group differences are tied to environmental pressure and to social and cultural norms.

B. Women are more susceptible than men to panic disorder, phobias, and generalized anxiety disorder. This difference may be tied to women's role in society and to gender roles. Some biological explanations have also been offered.

C. The manifestation of anxiety may differ across cultures. As examples, Hispanic cultures have *ataque de nervios* and Japanese culture has *taijin kyofu-sho*, which may represent culturally acceptable forms of panic attacks and social phobia, respectively, or may be true culture-bound syndromes.

KEY TERMS AND GUIDED REVIEW

Key Terms

fight-or-flight response (emergency reaction) (p. 178):

hypothalamus (p. 178):

sympathetic division of the autonomic nervous system (p. 178):

adrenal-cortical system (p. 178):

cortisol (p. 179):

neurosis (p. 180):

Guided Review

1. Give examples of a somatic, emotional, cognitive, and behavioral symptoms of anxiety. (pp. 178-179)

2. What happens in our bodies during the fight-or-flight response? (pp. 178-179)

3. Discuss the functions of the hypothalamus during the fight-or-flight response and the ways it affects other brain areas. (pp. 178-179)

4. Summarize the differences between adaptive fear and maladaptive anxiety. (pp. 179-180)

5. What does the term "neurosis" refer to in modern times? (p. 180)

Panic Disorder

<u>Key Terms</u>

panic attacks (p. 181):

panic disorder (p. 181):

norepinephrine (p. 182):

locus ceruleus (p. 182):

limbic system (p. 183):

suffocation false alarm theory (p. 184):

anxiety sensitivity (p. 185):

tricyclic antidepressants (p. 186):

selective serotonin reuptake inhibitors (p. 186):

benzodiazepines (p. 187):

systematic desensitization (p. 191):

<u>Guided Review</u>

1. What is required for someone to be diagnosed with panic disorder? (p. 181)

2. What kinds of problems do people with panic disorder often experience (besides panic disorder itself)? (pp. 181-182)

3. What is the evidence that norepinephrine is involved in panic attacks? (pp. 182-183)

4. What is the evidence that serotonin is involved in panic attacks? (pp. 183, 186-187)

5. How might hormones contribute to panic attacks in women? (p. 183)

6. Summarize the kindling model proposed by Gorman and colleagues. (pp. 183-184)

7. What are some ways in which panic attacks can be induced in people with panic disorder? (pp. 183-184)

8. What is the main idea of suffocation false alarm theory? (p. 184)

9. What is the evidence that genetics play a role in panic disorder? (pp. 184-185)

10. Summarize the cognitive model of panic disorder. (p. 185)

11. What is the evidence that anxiety sensitivity is important in panic disorder? (p. 185)

12. Describe the vulnerability-stress model of panic disorder. (pp. 185-186)

13. What are the advantages and disadvantages of using tricyclic antidepressants, SSRIs, and benzodiazepines to treat panic disorder? (pp. 186-187)

14. Describe cognitive-behavioral therapy for panic disorder. (pp. 187-191)

15. What is the evidence that cognitive-behavioral therapy is effective? (pp. 191-192)

Phobias

Key Terms

agoraphobia (p. 192):

specific phobias (p. 194):

animal type phobias (p. 194):

natural environment type phobias (p. 195):

situational type phobias (p. 195):

blood-injection injury type phobias (p. 195):

social phobia (p. 195):

safety signal hypothesis (p. 199):

prepared classical conditioning (p. 200):

applied tension technique (p. 202):

modeling (p. 202):

flooding (p. 202):

<u>Guided Review</u>

1. What are the primary sources of anxiety for people with agoraphobia? (pp. 192-193)

2. Identify and describe the four main types of specific phobias. (pp. 194-195)

3. How does social phobia differ from specific phobias? (pp. 195-196)

4. What is Freud's theory of phobias? (p. 197)

5. Explain how phobias might develop through classical conditioning. (pp. 197-199)

6. How can classical and operant conditioning work together to maintain a phobia? (pp. 198-199)

7. What is the evidence that people are predisposed by evolution to develop certain fears? (p. 200)

8. Describe some of the behavioral therapies for phobias. (pp. 201-202)

Generalized Anxiety Disorder

<u>Key Terms</u>

generalized anxiety disorder (GAD) (p. 204):

realistic anxiety (p. 205):

neurotic anxiety (p. 205):

moral anxiety (p. 205):

conditions of worth (p. 205):

existential anxiety (p. 205):

GABA (p. 208):

Guided Review

1. Summarize the main features of GAD. How does it differ from other anxiety disorders? (pp. 204-205)

2. How do psychodynamic theories attempt to explain GAD? (p. 205)

3. Describe Carl Rogers' theory of GAD. (p. 205)

4. What maladaptive cognitive processes appear to be operating in GAD? (pp. 207-208)

5. What is the evidence that biological factors play a role in GAD? (p. 208)

6. What treatments are effective for GAD? (p. 208)

Sociocultural Approach to the Anxiety Disorders

Guided Review

1. What are some reasons that women may experience anxiety disorders more so than men? (pp. 209-210)

2. Give an example of an anxiety-related problem that occurs in another culture. (p. 210)

CASE EXAMPLE

Read the following description and answer the questions below:

Stan's father died three months ago after a protracted illness. On the day of his father's funeral, Stan experienced an episode of dizziness, sweating, and had a sense that his limbs were not attached to his body. This lasted for about an hour, then disappeared. Over the next several months, however, these sensations came more frequently.

When interviewed by a therapist, Stan was tense, worried, and frightened. He sat on the edge of his chair and fidgeted constantly. He reported that for the last month, he has had a chronic sense of edginess, and an inability to maintain his concentration on anything for very long. He frequently has periods in which he feels his heart racing, he is dizzy, his ears ring, and he feels he may faint. "I think I'm going crazy!" he says. He has been thoroughly examined by his physician, and no medical causes of his symptoms can be found.

Stan's inability to concentrate interferes with his performance on the job to such an extent that his supervisor told him to get some help or he was at risk of losing his job. Stan is constantly vigilant for signs that he is having another "attack." He worries constantly about his physical and mental condition, and the possibility that he might lose his job.

1. What two anxiety disorders might Stan be suffering from, and why?

2. How would you determine which of these two diagnoses should be considered the "primary" or predominant diagnosis?

3. What is the prognosis for successful treatment of Stan's symptoms? Does it depend on which diagnosis he has?

4. What course of treatment might be most useful for Stan?

CHAPTER TEST

A. <u>Multiple Choice</u>. Choose the **best answer** to each question below.

1. Which of the following first activates the sympathetic nervous system during the fight-or-flight response?

    A. Epinephrine.
    B. The adrenal glands.
    C. The hypothalamus.
    D. The pituitary gland.

2. Which of the following stimulates the adrenal cortex to release stress hormones?

    A. The hypothalamus.
    B. Cortisol.
    C. The sympathetic nervous system.
    D. Adrenocorticotrophic hormone.

3. Which of the following statements about panic disorder is <u>false</u>?

    A. About 40% of people will develop panic disorder at some time in their lives.
    B. Panic disorder tends to be chronic once it begins.
    C. About one-third to one-half of people with panic disorder develop agoraphobia.
    D. Panic disorder typically develops between late adolescence and the mid-30s.

4. People with panic disorder may have poorly regulated levels of _____, which is concentrated in a brain area called _____.

    A. norepinephrine; locus ceruleus
    B. serotonin; locus ceruleus
    C. epinephrine; periaqueductal gray
    D. GABA; basal ganglia

5. Which of the following neurotransmitters has <u>not</u> been implicated in panic disorder?

    A. Serotonin.
    B. Norepinephrine.
    C. GABA.
    D. Acetylcholine.

6. Animal studies suggest that increases in _____ in the _____ reduce panic-like responses in animals.

    A. norepinephrine; amygdala
    B. serotonin; periaqueductal grey
    C. serotonin; amygdala
    D. epinephrine; adrenal cortex

7. The kindling model of panic disorder suggests that _____ is involved in the production of panic attacks whereas _____ is involved in diffuse, anticipatory anxiety.

    A. serotonin; norepinephrine
    B. locus ceruleus; the limbic system
    C. the limbic system; locus ceruleus
    D. sodium lactate; the periaqueductal grey

8. Which of the following is not a common side effect of tricyclic antidepressants?

    A. Anticholinergic effects.
    B. Hypotension and dizziness.
    C. Sexual dysfunction.
    D. Addiction.

9. One main limitation of using SSRIs to treat panic disorder is that:

    A. The side effects of SSRIs are usually worse than those of tricyclic antidepressants.
    B. People experience unpleasant withdrawal symptoms when they are not using SSRIs.
    C. Many people relapse after they quit using SSRIs.
    D. The SSRIs often interfere with cognitive and motor functioning.

10. Which of the following statements about agoraphobia is false?

    A. To be diagnosed with agoraphobia, a person must also have panic attacks.
    B. Agoraphobia tends to develop before the age of 25.
    C. Agoraphobia tends to develop within one year after a person experiences frequent anxiety symptoms.
    D. People with agoraphobia fear both wide-open and enclosed spaces.

11. People with _____ phobia experience significant drops in heart rate and blood pressure when confronted with their feared stimulus:

    A. animal type
    B. natural environment type
    C. blood-injection-injury
    D. situational type

12. Which of the following statements is _false_?

    A. About 8% of people meet criteria for social phobia in a 12-month period.
    B. Most people who develop social phobia seek treatment for their symptoms since it is such a debilitating problem.
    C. Social phobia tends to develop during the adolescent years.
    D. Social phobia is often comorbid with antisocial personality disorder.

13. Which of the following statements is _false_?

    A. According to behavioral theories, phobias develop through operant conditioning but are maintained by classical conditioning.
    B. Evolution may have prepared us biologically to learn certain associations quickly, such as a fear of spiders.
    C. Phobias do not appear to be completely learned behavior: there is some evidence for a genetic contribution.
    D. According to the safety signal hypothesis, people remember the places in which they have had panic attacks and associate these places with their symptoms.

14. The applied tension technique is an effective treatment for:

    A. Animal type phobia.
    B. Natural environment type phobia.
    C. Social phobia.
    D. Blood-injection-injury type phobia.

15. Which of the following statements about GAD is _false_?

    A. About 4% of the U.S. population experiences GAD in any 6-month period.
    B. The majority of people with GAD also have another anxiety disorder.
    C. People with GAD report feeling restless most of the time and becoming tired only rarely.
    D. People with GAD tend to worry about many things instead of focusing on one issue or concern.

16. According to Freud, ___A___ anxiety occurs when we have been punished for expressing our id impulses.

    A. moral
    B. neurotic
    C. realistic
    D. generalized

17. Current biological theories of generalized anxiety disorder (GAD) implicate _____, which is an _____ neurotransmitter.

       A. norepinephrine; excitatory
       B. GABA; inhibitory
       C. GABA; excitatory
       D. serotonin; inhibitory

18. *Taijin-kyofu-sho* is not:

       A. More common in women than in men.
       B. An intense fear of interpersonal relations.
       C. A fear of blushing, smelling bad, and/or irritating others.
       D. A syndrome encountered in Japan.

19. Which of the following groups of people is not more likely to develop anxiety disorders?

       A. Women.
       B. Members of minority groups.
       C. People with higher levels of education.
       D. People in higher socioeconomic groups.

20. Which of the following is not a characteristic of *ataque de nervios*?

       A. Falling to the ground and convulsing.
       B. Becoming unable to speak.
       C. Difficulty breathing.
       D. Difficulty moving limbs.

B. True-False. Select T (True) or F (False) below.

1. The DSM-IV assumes that anxiety underlies depression, hypochondriasis, and many other forms of psychopathology.   T   F

2. People treated with cognitive-behavioral therapy are less likely to reexperience panic attacks than people treated with medication for panic disorder.   T   F

3. Anticholinergic effects can result from the use of tricyclic antidepressants.   T   F

4. Panic disorder tends to be chronic because few effective treatments are available for it.
     T   F

5. Most people with GAD have another anxiety disorder, too.   T   F

C. <u>Short Answer</u>.

1. What are the advantages and disadvantages of prescribing medications for people with panic disorder?

2. Describe two theories (one biological, one psychological) of panic disorder. What <u>evidence</u> supports each theory?

3. What commonalities are present in cognitive and/or behavioral therapies for panic disorder and phobias?

4. How do phobias develop, according to behavioral theories?

5. How is adaptive fear different from maladaptive anxiety?

ANSWER KEY

<u>Case Example</u>

1. Panic disorder: episodes of dizziness, sweating, sense of limbs not attached to body, heart racing, thoughts of going crazy, worries about future attacks; generalized anxiety disorder: chronic symptoms of tension, worry, edginess, problems in concentrating that interfere with his job.

2. If Stan's anxiety is primarily about having a panic attack, then panic disorder is the primary diagnosis. If his anxiety is about a number of events and activities, then generalized anxiety disorder is a more appropriate diagnosis.

3. The prognosis for the successful treatment of panic disorder is quite good; for generalized anxiety disorder it is not as good.

4. Cognitive-behavioral treatments have been effective in treating symptoms like Stan's. Antidepressant drugs can also be helpful.

<u>Multiple Choice</u>

1. C
2. D
3. A
4. A
5. D
6. B
7. B
8. D
9. C
10. A
11. C
12. B
13. A
14. D
15. C
16. A
17. B
18. A
19. C
20. B

<u>True-False</u>

1. F
2. T
3. T
4. F
5. T

Short Answer
1. See pp. 186-187.
2. See pp. 182-186.
3. See pp. 187-192, 202-204.
4. See pp. 197-200.
5. See pp. 179-180.

Additional Readings on Chapter 6 Topics

Coplan, J. D., & Lydiard, R. B. (1998). Brain circuits in panic disorder. Biological Psychiatry, 44, 1264-1276.

Foa, E. B., & Kozak, M. J. (1986). Emotional processing of fear: Exposure to corrective information. Psychological Bulletin, 99, 20-35.

Wells, A. (1999). A cognitive model of generalized anxiety disorder. Behavior Modification, 23, 526-555.

Chapter 7: Anxiety Disorders: Posttraumatic Stress Disorder and Obsessive-Compulsive Disorder

LEARNING OBJECTIVES
After reading and studying this chapter, you should be able to:

1. Summarize the symptoms of PTSD, acute stress disorder, and OCD.

2. Discuss the types of events that can contribute to PTSD.

3. Discuss cross-cultural differences in the presentation and treatment of PTSD.

4. Discuss the sociocultural, psychological, and biological factors associated with increased risk of PTSD.

5. Describe how cognitive-behavioral therapy for PTSD and OCD is conducted.

6. Discuss the effectiveness of biological therapies for PTSD and OCD.

7. Define obsessions and compulsions and give examples of each.

8. Summarize the biological, psychodynamic, and cognitive-behavioral theories of OCD.

ESSENTIAL IDEAS

I. Posttraumatic stress disorder

    A. People with posttraumatic stress disorder repeatedly reexperience the traumatic event, avoid situations that might arouse memories of their trauma, and they are hypervigilant and chronically aroused.

    B. PTSD may be most likely to occur following traumas that shatter people's assumptions
that they are invulnerable, that the world is a just place, and that bad things do not happen to good people.

    C. People who experience severe and long-lasting traumas, who have lower levels of social support, who experience socially stigmatizing traumas, who were already depressed or anxious before the trauma, or have maladaptive, ruminative coping styles may be at increased risk for PTSD.

    D. People who are unable to somehow make sense of a trauma appear more likely to have chronic PTSD symptoms.

E. PTSD sufferers show greater physiological reactivity to stressors, and greater activity in areas of the brain involved in emotion and memory, but blunted resting cortisol levels. The meaning of these neurobiological abnormalities is not yet clear.

F. The most effective treatment for PTSD involves exposing the person to his or her memories of the trauma through systematic desensitization and flooding, to extinguish his or her anxiety over these memories.

G. Some people cannot tolerate such exposure, however, and may do better with supportive therapy focused on solving current interpersonal difficulties and life problems.

H. Benzodiazepines and antidepressant drugs can quell some of the symptoms of PTSD, but these symptoms tend to recur when the drugs are discontinued.

I. Clinicians treating people with anxiety disorders must be sensitive to the extraordinary circumstances that may have lead to these disorders and to cultural norms for what is appropriate to discuss outside one's immediate family or culture.

II. Obsessive-compulsive disorder

A. Obsessions are thoughts, images, ideas, or impulses that are persistent, intrusive, and cause distress. They commonly focus on contamination, sex, violence, and repeated doubts.

B. Compulsions are repetitive behaviors or mental acts that the individual feels he or she must perform to somehow erase his or her obsessions.

C. Biological theories of OCD speculate that areas of the brain involved in the execution of primitive patterns of behavior, such as washing rituals, may be impaired in people with OCD. These areas of the brain are rich in the neurotransmitter serotonin, and drugs that regulate serotonin have proven helpful in the treatment of OCD.

D. Psychodynamic theories of OCD suggest that the obsessions and compulsions symbolize unconscious conflicts or impulses and that the proper therapy for OCD involves uncovering these unconscious thoughts.

E. Cognitive-behavioral theories suggest that people with OCD are chronically distressed, think in rigid and moralistic ways, judge negative thoughts as less acceptable than other people do, and feel more responsible for their thoughts and behaviors. This makes them unable to turn off the negative, intrusive thoughts that most people have occasionally.

F. Compulsive behaviors develop through operant conditioning; people are reinforced for compulsive behaviors by the fact that they reduce anxiety.

KEY TERMS AND GUIDED REVIEW

Posttraumatic Stress Disorder

<u>Key Terms</u>

posttraumatic stress disorder (p. 216):

acute stress disorder (p. 218):

dissociative symptoms (p. 218):

systematic desensitization (p. 229):

stress-management interventions (p. 230):

<u>Guided Review</u>

1. What three types of symptoms must be present for someone to be diagnosed with PTSD? (pp. 216-217)

2. What are some ways in which children may manifest PTSD differently than adults? (p. 218)

3. What are some of the differences between PTSD and acute stress disorder? (p. 218)

4. Describe some of the events that tend to be associated with PTSD? (pp. 218-223)

5. What are some of the sociocultural factors that increase one's risk of developing PTSD? (pp. 223-225)

6. Which personal assumptions, if shattered by a trauma, increase one's risk of developing PTSD? (p. 225)

7. What coping styles increase one's risk of developing PTSD? (pp. 226-227)

8. Which brain areas may be overactive in PTSD? Which brain area may be damaged? (pp. 227-229)

9. What is the role of cortisol in PTSD? (p. 228)

10. Describe how cognitive-behavioral therapy for PTSD is conducted. (pp. 229-231)

11. How does the presentation and treatment of PTSD differ across cultures? (pp. 232-234)

Obsessive-Compulsive Disorder

Key Terms

obsessions (p. 234):

compulsions (p. 234):

obsessive-compulsive disorder (OCD) (p. 234):

caudate nucleus (p. 239):

Guided Review

1. What are the symptoms of OCD? (pp. 234-236)

2. What are some common foci of obsessions? (p. 236)

3. Describe the prevalence of OCD. (p. 236)

4. What brain circuit is hypothesized to be involved in OCD? (pp. 239-240)

5. According to cognitive-behavioral theory, how do people with OCD differ from people without OCD? (pp. 241-242)

6. How do compulsions develop, according to cognitive-behavioral theory? (pp. 241-242)

7. What appears to be the most promising biological treatment for OCD? (p. 242)

8. Describe cognitive-behavioral therapy for OCD. (p. 243)

CASE EXAMPLE

Read the following description and answer the questions below:

Phil saw his psychologist for treatment of depression for six months before he finally had the courage to bring up his other "secret" problem. Since childhood, he had a compulsion to count things. He felt a sense of tremendous pressure to count things and would feel nauseated and anxious if he were prevented from counting. He had to count the letters in words and in people's names. If the letters added up to any number except nine he felt a sense of release and could stop counting. He knew it was silly, but nevertheless he had a fear that if he did not do this something bad could happen to his mom or dad. He constantly tried not to count, but seemed unable to stop. He did poorly in school because he was distracted by his secret compulsion to count letters when he should have been paying attention to the teacher's lessons. He was later bothered as a teenager by upsetting sacrilegious mental images when he was in church. Having these sacrilegious images made him feel that he lost his soul for eternity.

In addition to these two problems, he was having trouble driving. When he felt a bump as his tire rolled over a little stone, he would think he may had accidentally run over a pedestrian. He would instantly check his rearview mirror for the injured person he feared was lying on the road. Relieved to not see an injured person, he would start to drive forward. Obsessing that the injured person might have been flung entirely off the road by the impact, he would then stop, and back up his car to the scene, and search the ditch and weeds. These obsessions and compulsions were taking over his life but he was too embarrassed to tell anyone about them, even his psychologist, until now (Adapted from the National Anxiety Foundation, 2000).

1. Describe the symptoms of OCD that Phil is experiencing.

2. How would biological and cognitive-behavioral theories explain Phil's problems?

3. What treatments might be effective for Phil?

CHAPTER TEST

A. <u>Multiple Choice</u>. Choose the **best answer** to each question below.

1. Which of the following is not required for a diagnosis of PTSD?

    A. Reexperiencing of the traumatic event.
    B. Emotional numbing and detachment.
    C. Hypervigilance and chronic arousal.
    D. Persistent and uncontrollable worry.

2. Which of the following statements is <u>true</u> about acute stress disorder?

    A. It includes symptoms of emotional numbing as well as hyperarousal.
    B. It must occur within 1 week of exposure to a stressor.
    C. It lasts longer than 4 weeks.
    D. It does not include dissociative symptoms.

3. Which of the following statements is <u>false</u>?

    A. About 95% of rape survivors meet criteria for PTSD within the first 2 weeks after the rape, but only 50% still qualify for a diagnosis at 3 months after the rape.
    B. About 90% of childhood rape survivors develop PTSD at some time in their lives.
    C. Only 13% of Persian Gulf War veterans were suffering from PTSD in the year after the war.
    D. Among Vietnam veterans, Hispanics have the highest rates of PTSD.

4. Which of the following is <u>not</u> a risk factor for PTSD?

    A. Low social support.
    B. Having low stress before the trauma hits.
    C. Detaching from the trauma and ongoing events.
    D. Ruminating about one's symptoms.

5. While imagining combat scenes, combat veterans with PTSD show increased blood flow in the:

    A. Hippocampus.
    B. Hypothalamus.
    C. Amygdala.
    D. Frontal lobe.

6. Which of the following statements is <u>true</u> about treatment for PTSD?

    A. Some clients are most helped by being exposed to memories of the trauma, whereas others are most helped by avoiding memories or thoughts about the trauma.
    B. Repeated exposure to one's memories of the trauma significantly reduces PTSD symptoms, but does not protect against relapse.
    C. To be effective, treatment for PTSD should be focused on the trauma rather than the client's other problems, such as marital problems.
    D. Systematic desensitization is effective for phobias but not PTSD.

7. Which of the following has been found to significantly decrease PTSD symptoms and help prevent relapse?

    A. Serotonin reuptake inhibitors.
    B. Benzodiazepines.
    C. Exposure therapy.
    D. Tricyclic antidepressants.

8. Some people with PTSD have damage to the:

    A. Hypothalamus.
    B. Frontal lobes.
    C. Hippocampus.
    D. Adrenal cortex.

9. Which of the following statements is <u>false</u> about obsessive-compulsive disorder?

    A. Compulsions can be either repetitive behaviors or mental acts.
    B. Men are more likely to develop OCD than are women.
    C. The prevalence of OCD does not differ across cultures.
    D. People with OCD are aware of how irrational their thoughts and behaviors are.

10. The most common focus of obsessive thoughts is:

    A. Sexual impulses.
    B. Aggressive impulses.
    C. Dirt and contamination.
    D. Repeated doubts.

11. Biological theories of OCD propose that impulses arise in the _____ and are carried to the _____.

    A. caudate nucleus; thalamus
    B. orbital frontal cortex; caudate nucleus
    C. thalmus; orbital frontal cortex
    D. orbital frontal cortex; hypothalamus

12. Which of the following is not a reason why people with OCD have trouble turning off their negative thoughts?

    A. People with OCD may have a tendency toward rigid, moralistic thinking.
    B. People with OCD are often depressed or anxious much of the time.
    C. People with OCD equate having negative thoughts with actually engaging in the behaviors.
    D. People with OCD do not believe they should be able to control their thoughts.

13. A neurotransmitter involved in the production of OCD symptoms and which, when treated, leads to improvement in symptoms, is:

    A. Norepinephrine.
    B. GABA.
    C. Epinephrine.
    D. Serotonin.

14. The failure of which type of drug to treat OCD effectively provided a clue that OCD was different from the other anxiety disorders?

    A. Serotonin reuptake inhibitors.
    B. Tricyclic antidepressants.
    C. Benzodiazepines.
    D. Barbiturates.

15. Which of the following is not a diagnostic criterion for PTSD?

    A. Three or more dissociative symptoms.
    B. Reexperiencing the event.
    C. Emotional numbing and detachment.
    D. Exaggerated startle response.

16. Which of the following is <u>not</u> a diagnostic criterion for OCD?

   A. The person recognizes that the obsessional thoughts, impulses, or images are a product of his or her own mind.
   B. The person must experience both obsessions and compulsions.
   C. The thoughts, impulses, or images are not simply excessive worries about real-life problems.
   D. The person attempts to ignore or suppress the intrusive thoughts, impulses, or images, or to neutralize them with some other thought or action.

17. Which of the following is a commonality between PTSD and OCD?

   A. Both are more likely to occur in women than men.
   B. Both appear to involve damage to the hippocampus.
   C. Both can be treated effectively with benzodiazepines.
   D. Both can be treated effectively with exposure therapy.

18. Which of the following statements is <u>true</u>?

   A. People with OCD have reduced activity in the primitive brain circuit thought to be important in the disorder.
   B. The neurotransmitter GABA plays an important role in this primitive brain circuit.
   C. OCD patients who respond to drug therapy show increased activity in this brain circuit.
   D. OCD patients who respond to behavior therapy show decreased activity of the caudate nucleus and thalamus.

19. Which of the following is <u>not</u> a cultural difference in the presentation of PTSD among Southeast Asians?

   A. Southeast Asians do not tend to experience dissociative symptoms.
   B. Southeast Asians tend to present with somatic complaints rather than psychological complaints.
   C. Southeast Asians do not feel that their experiences of trauma are worth mentioning to a physician.
   D. Southeast Asians often steadfastly avoid talking or thinking about the traumas they have experienced.

20. Which of the following contributes to both the development of compulsions in OCD and the maintenance of phobias?

    A. Classical conditioning.
    B. Observational learning.
    C. Operant conditioning.
    D. Magical thinking.

B. <u>True-False</u>. Select T (True) or F (False) below.

1. To be diagnosed with PTSD, an individual must be reexperiencing the traumatic event, exhibit dissociative symptoms, and experience hypervigilance and chronic arousal.   T   F

2. The hippocampus appears to be damaged in some PTSD patients.   T   F

3. In OCD, compulsions are always logically tied to an individual's specific obsessions (e.g., obsessions about contamination lead people to wash their hands).   T   F

4. Having negative, intrusive thoughts is central to OCD, as only 10% of normal people experience them.   T   F

5. People who are distressed before a trauma occurs are more likely to develop PTSD than people who were not distressed.   T   F

C. <u>Short Answer</u>.

1. What are some factors that increase one's risk of developing PTSD following a trauma?

2. How do people with OCD differ from people without OCD, according to cognitive-behavioral theory?

3. How do biological theories attempt to explain OCD?

4. Describe how a cognitive-behavioral therapist might treat someone with PTSD. Would the therapist treat each PTSD patient in the same way? Why or why not?

5. What are some differences between acute stress disorder and PTSD?

ANSWER KEY

Case Example

1. Obsessions (that something bad would happen to his parents, that he lost his soul for eternity, that he may have run over someone); and compulsions (counting, checking).
2. Biological: low serotonin levels, genetics, dysfunction of the orbital frontal cortex, caudate nucleus, and thalamus. Cognitive-behavioral: Like people without OCD, Phil has intrusive thoughts, but he catastrophizes them. He also has depression and may be distressed in general. He may feel more responsible for his thoughts, and/or equate having "bad" thoughts with engaging in negative actions. His compulsions may develop through operant conditioning: he finds that counting, for example, reduces his anxiety, which then reinforces the compulsion.
3. Selective serotonin reuptake inhibitors and/or cognitive-behavioral therapy with an emphasis on exposure and ritual prevention.

Multiple Choice

1. D
2. A
3. B
4. B
5. C
6. A
7. C
8. C
9. B
10. C
11. B
12. D
13. D
14. C
15. A
16. B
17. D
18. D
19. A
20. C

True-False

1. F
2. T
3. F
4. F
5. T

Short Answer
1. See pp. 223-229.
2. See pp. 241-242.
3. See pp. 239-240.
4. See pp. 229-231.
5. See p. 218.

Additional Readings on Chapter 7 Topics

Foa, E. B., & Meadows, E. A. (1997). Psychosocial treatments for posttraumatic stress disorder: A critical review. Annual Review of Psychology, 48, 449-480.

Salkovskis, P. M. (1999). Understanding and treating obsessive-compulsive disorder. Behaviour Research and Therapy, 37 (Suppl 1), S29-S52.

Tallis, F. (1997). The neuropsychology of obsessive-compulsive disorder: A review and consideration of clinical implications. British Journal of Clinical Psychology, 36, 3-20.

Chapter 8: Mood Disorders

LEARNING OBJECTIVES
After reading and studying this chapter, you should be able to:

1. Distinguish between unipolar and bipolar depression, and know the diagnostic criteria for the disorders that fall under each category: major depression (and its associated subtypes), dysthymic disorder, double depression, Bipolar I Disorder, Bipolar II Disorder, cyclothymic disorder, and rapid cycling bipolar disorder.

2. Explain how depression affects the whole person, i.e., cognitively, emotionally, behaviorally, and physiologically.

3. Discuss how rates of unipolar depression vary as a function of age, gender, and culture, as well as the proposed explanations for these differences.

4. Summarize the evidence for the idea that bipolar disorder is linked to creativity.

5. Summarize the evidence for and against the idea that genetics partially determine who will develop a mood disorder.

6. Discuss the monoamine theory of depression.

7. Discuss the neuroendocrine and neurophysiological abnormalities in depression.

8. Discuss drugs used to treat bipolar disorder.

9. Discuss how tricyclic antidepressants, monoamine oxidase inhibitors, and selective serotonin reuptake inhibitors work, their side effects, and their effectiveness for treating depression.

10. Discuss the type of patient most likely to receive electroconvulsive therapy, what the therapy entails, and how it might work.

11. Explain how light therapy for seasonal affective disorder might work.

12. Discuss the behavioral, psychodynamic, learned helplessness, reformulated learned helplessness, cognitive, and sociocultural theories of depression.

13. Describe interpersonal therapy for depression.

14. Discuss research on the relationship between depression and hormone levels in women.

ESSENTIAL IDEAS

I. Syndromes, diagnosis, and prognosis

        A. Depression includes disturbances in emotion (sadness, loss of interest), bodily functions (loss of sleep, appetite, and sexual drive), behaviors (retardation or agitation), and thoughts (worthlessness, guilt, suicidality).

        B. The two primary categories of unipolar depressive disorders are major depression and dysthymic disorder; in addition, there are several subtypes of major depression.

        C. Young and middle-aged adults have the highest rates of depression.

        D. Many people who become depressed remain so for several months or more and have multiple relapses over their lifetime.

        E. The two major diagnostic categories of bipolar mood disorders are bipolar disorder and cyclothymic disorder.

        F. Bipolar mood disorders are less common than depressive disorders, but are equally common in men and women.

        G. The onset of bipolar disorders is most often in late adolescence or early adulthood. Most people with bipolar disorder have multiple episodes.

II. Biological theories of mood disorders

        A. Genetics clearly play a role in bipolar disorder, although it is somewhat less clear what role genetics play in many forms of unipolar depression.

        B. The neurotransmitter theories suggest that imbalances in levels of norepinephrine or serotonin or dysregulation of receptors for these neurotransmitters contributes to depression, and dysregulation of norepinephrine, serotonin, or dopamine is involved in bipolar disorder.

        C. Some depressed people have unusual EEG patterns, disrupted sleep patterns, and abnormalities detectable on CT, PET, and MRI scans.

        D. Depressed people have chronic hyperactivity of the hypothalamic-pituitary-adrenal axis, which helps to regulate the body's response to stress.

III. Psychological theories of mood disorders

    A. The behavioral theories of depression suggest that stress can induce depression by reducing the number of reinforcers available to people.

    B. The learned helplessness theory of depression says that uncontrollable events can lead people to believe that important outcomes are outside of their control and thus to develop depression.

    C. The cognitive theories of depression argue that depressed people think in distorted and negative ways, and this leads them to become depressed, particularly in the face of negative events.

    D. The psychodynamic theories posit that depressed people are overly dependent on the evaluations and approval of others for their self-esteem, as a result of poor nurturing by parents.

IV. Sociological perspectives on mood disorders

    A. The interpersonal theories of depression suggest that poor attachment relationships early in life can lead children to develop expectations that they must be or do certain things in order to win the approval of others, which puts them at risk for depression.

    B. More recent generations appear to be at higher risk for depression than earlier generations, perhaps because of historical changes in values and social structures related to depression.

    C. People of lower social status tend to have higher rates of depression. Women's greater vulnerability to depression may be tied to their lower social status, and the risks of abuse that accompany this social status.

    D. Less industrialized cultures may have lower rates of depression than more industrialized cultures. Some studies suggest that the manifestation of depression and mania may be different across cultures.

V. Mood disorders treatments

    A. Tricyclic antidepressants are effective in treating depression but have some side effects and can be dangerous in overdose.

    B. The monoamine oxidase inhibitors also are effective treatments for depression but can interact with certain medications and foods.

C. The selective serotonin reuptake inhibitors are effective treatments for depression and have become popular because they are less dangerous and have more tolerable side effects than other drug treatments.

D. Electroconvulsive therapy involves inducing seizures in depressed people; it can be quite effective but is controversial.

E. Lithium is useful in the treatment of mood disorders but requires careful monitoring to prevent dangerous side effects.

F. Anticonvulsants, antipsychotics, and calcium channel blockers can also help to relieve mania.

G. Behavioral treatment focuses on increasing positive reinforcers and decreasing aversive events by helping clients change their environments, learn social skills, and learn mood-management skills.

H. Cognitive-behavioral treatment combines the techniques of behavioral therapy with techniques to identify and challenge depressive thinking patterns.

I. Psychodynamic therapy focuses on uncovering unconscious hostility and fears of abandonment through the interpretation of transference, memories, dreams, and resistance.

J. Interpersonal therapy seeks to identify and overcome problems with grief, role transitions, interpersonal role disputes, and deficits in interpersonal skills that contribute to depression.

K. Community-based programs such as the D/ART program attempt to educate health care professionals and the lay public about depression in hopes of getting depressed people into more effective therapy.

L. Some research suggests that interventions targeting high risk groups can help to prevent or delay first onsets of depression.

KEY TERMS AND GUIDED REVIEW

Key Terms

bipolar disorder (p. 248):

mania (p. 248):

depression (p. 248):

unipolar depression (p. 248):

Guided Review

1. What is the difference between unipolar and bipolar depression? (p. 248)

Symptoms, Diagnosis, and Prognosis

Key Terms

catatonia (p. 249):

catalepsy (p. 249):

delusions (p. 250):

hallucinations (p. 250):

major depression (p. 250):

dysthymic disorder (p. 250):

double depression (p. 251):

seasonal affective disorder (SAD) (p. 251):

bipolar I disorder (p. 256):

bipolar II disorder (p. 256):

hypomania (p. 256):

cyclothymic disorder (p. 256):

rapid cycling bipolar disorder (p. 257):

Guided Review

1. What are the emotional, behavioral, physiological, and cognitive symptoms of depression? (pp. 248-250)

2. What are the differences between major depression and dysthymia? (pp. 250-251)

3. Describe the subtypes of depression. (p. 251)

4. Discuss how the prevalence of depression varies with age, and why it might vary. (pp. 252-253)

5. What are some of the long-term effects of depression among both children and adults? (pp. 253-254)

6. Does depression appear to be "masked" in children? Why or why not? (pp. 253-254)

7. How does puberty affect boys and girls differently with respect to depression? (p. 254)

8. What are the symptoms of mania? (pp. 255-256)

9. How does mania differ from hypomania? (p. 256)

10. How does bipolar I disorder differ from bipolar II disorder? (p. 256)

11. How common in bipolar disorder? (p. 257)

12. What are some long-term effects of bipolar disorder? (p. 257)

13. What are some ways in which creativity and bipolar disorder are related? (pp. 257-259)

Biological Theories of Mood Disorders

Key Terms

monoamines (p. 262):

norepinephrine (p. 262):

serotonin (p. 262):

dopamine (p. 262):

monoamine theories (p. 263):

glutamate (p. 263):

substance P (p. 263):

hypothalamic-pituitary-adrenal (HPA) axis (p. 266):

cortisol (p. 266):

premenstrual dysphoric disorder (p. 267):

Guided Review

1. What are some clues that mood disorders have biological underpinnings? (pp. 259-260)

2. What is the evidence that mood disorders have a genetic basis? (pp. 260-262)

3. What neurotransmitters appear to be involved in mood disorders, and what kind of abnormalities appear to be present in the mood disorders? (pp. 262-264)

4. Describe the kindling-sensitization model. (pp. 263-264)

5. What are some of the neurophysiological abnormalities that can occur in depression? (pp. 264-265)

6. What is the HPA axis, and how is it altered in depression? (pp. 265-266)

7. What is the evidence that women experience more depression during the postpartum period and menopause? (pp. 266-267)

Psychological Theories of Mood Disorders

<u>Key Terms</u>

behavioral theory of depression (p. 268):

learned helplessness theory (p. 269):

learned helplessness deficits (p. 269):

rumination (p. 269):

reformulated learned helplessness theory (p. 270):

causal attribution (p. 270):

depressive realism (p. 271):

introjected hostility (p. 272):

<u>Guided Review</u>

1. What is Lewinsohn's behavioral theory of depression? (pp. 268-269)

2. What is learned helplessness theory and what evidence supports it? (p. 269)

3. What coping styles may contribute to depression? (pp. 269-270)

4. What is the reformulated learned helplessness theory and what evidence supports it? (pp. 270-271)

5. What is the psychodynamic theory of depression and what evidence supports it? (pp. 272-275)

Sociocultural Perspectives on Mood Disorders

<u>Key Terms</u>

interpersonal theories of depression (p. 275):

contingencies of self-worth (p. 275):

1. What is the interpersonal theory of depression and what evidence supports it? (pp. 275-276)

2. What is a cohort effect and how might such an effect account for age differences in depression? (p. 276)

3. What are the relationships among social status, gender, and depression? (p. 276)

4. Give some examples of how depression may differ across cultures. (pp. 276-278)

Mood Disorders Treatments

Key Terms

tricyclic antidepressant drugs (p. 279):

monoamine oxidase inhibitors (MAOIs) (p. 280):

selective serotonin reuptake inhibitors (SSRIs) (p. 280):

electroconvulsive therapy (ECT) (p. 281):

light therapy (p. 283):

lithium (p. 284):

anticonvulsant drugs (p. 284):

antipsychotic drugs (p. 284):

calcium channel blockers (p. 284):

behavioral therapy (p. 285):

cognitive-behavioral therapy (p. 286):

psychodynamic therapy (p. 289):

interpersonal therapy (p. 289):

1. What are some of the side effects of tricyclic antidepressants and MAOIs? How effective are these drugs for treating depression? (pp. 279-280)

2. What are some of the advantages that SSRIs have over other antidepressant medications? (pp. 280-281)

3. What are some of the side effects of SSRIs? (pp. 280-281)

4. What are some of the advantages of bupropion? What are some of the side effects associated with this drug? (p. 281)

5. For whom is ECT prescribed? How effective is ECT and what are some reasons why it remains controversial? (pp. 281-283)

6. How does light therapy for SAD appear to work? (p. 283)

7. How effective is lithium for bipolar disorder? How does it appear to work? What are some side effects and/or difficulties associated with taking it? (p. 284)

8. Other than lithium, what are some drugs used to treat bipolar disorder? (pp. 284-285)

9. Describe some of the techniques used in behavior therapy for depression. (pp. 285-286)

10. Describe some of the techniques used in cognitive-behavioral therapy for depression. (pp. 286-289)

11. Describe how psychodynamic therapy for depression is conducted. (p. 289)

12. Discuss some of the problems addressed by interpersonal therapy for depression. (pp. 289-290)

13. What are the goals of the D/ART program and what are its components? (pp. 290-291)

14. Describe an intervention designed to prevent depression. (pp. 291-292)

15. How do psychotherapies and drug therapies compare in effectiveness? (pp. 292-293)

Bio-Psycho-Social Integration

<u>Guided Review</u>

1. What are some ways in which genes may influence vulnerability to depression in conjunction with the environment? (pp. 294-295)

CASE EXAMPLE
Read the following description and answer the questions below:

Amanda is a successful businesswoman, who apparently has everything going for her. She has plenty of money, a nice car, a good network of friends. Yet she is quite depressed. This depression seems to have been chronic for the past three years. Amanda feels down most of the time, although when good things happen she can feel some pleasure. Amanda says she is chronically tired and drained, like her whole body is weighted down. In part because she stopped exercising when she began feeling depressed, Amanda has gained 30 pounds in the last three years. Despite her success, her self-esteem is low and she frequently makes berating comments about herself and the future. Amanda clearly has continued to function at a rather high level -- at least most of the time. A couple of times in the last three years, however, Amanda has had periods in which her depressive symptoms become much more severe and she cannot function at all. These periods tend to last about a month. Then they pass, but Amanda always returns to her chronic moderately depressed level, rather than ever really feeling good.

1. List all of the specific symptoms of depression that Amanda shows.

2. Which subtype(s) of depression does Amanda have? Specify the symptoms that lead you to this diagnosis.

3. What kinds of information about Amanda would (a) an interpersonal therapist, and (b) a cognitive-behavioral therapist want to know in order to plan a course of treatment for her?

CHAPTER TEST

A. <u>Multiple Choice</u>. Choose the **best answer** to each question below.

1. A person who has experienced (for the past month) a loss of interest in his or her usual activities, in addition to psychomotor agitation, increased appetite, insomnia, and thoughts of committing suicide, would be diagnosed as having:

   A. Double depression.
   B. Biplolar II disorder.
   C. Major depression.
   D. Cyclothymic disorder.

2. Someone who experiences a loss of interest in his or her usual activities, as well as psychomotor retardation, indecisiveness, hypersomnia, and loss of energy for more than two years, would be diagnosed as having:

   A. Dysthymic disorder.
   B. Major depression.
   C. Double depression.
   D. Cyclothymic disorder.

3. With which subtype of depression would the person in the following case example be diagnosed?
   Laura, a 30-year-old graduate student, has always been a "sensitive person." She feels happy at times, but generally feels low. She has been eating more lately and has gained weight. She has also been sleeping a lot lately.

   A. Depression with catatonic features.
   B. Depression with melancholic features.
   C. Depression with psychotic features.
   D. Depression with atypical features.

4. A behavioral disturbance in which one appears to be in a trancelike state, and one's muscles assume a waxy rigidity such that one tends to remain in any position in which one is placed, is known as:

   A. Catalepsy.
   B. Catatonia.
   C. Apraxia.
   D. Psychomotor retardation.

5. Someone who sees, hears, or feels things that are not real would be regarded as having:

    A. Delusions.
    B. Hallucinations.
    C. Depression with psychotic features.
    D. Depression with atypical features.

6. The lowest rates of depression are found among people:

    A. Over 85 years old.
    B. Between 15 and 24 years of age.
    C. Younger than 15 years.
    D. Between 55 and 70 years of age.

7. Depression in children:

    A. Is more common than among adults.
    B. Is underdiagnosed because children manifest depression differently than do adults.
    C. Involves the same cluster of symptoms as adult depression.
    D. Cannot meaningfully be diagnosed before age 14.

8. A person who alternates between episodes of hypomania and moderate depression chronically for at least 2 years would be diagnosed as having:

    A. Bipolar I Disorder.
    B. Bipolar II Disorder.
    C. Rapid cycling bipolar disorder.
    D. Cyclothymic disorder.

9. All of the following suggest that mood disorders have biological underpinnings except:

    A. They represent disruptions in bodily functions.
    B. They tend to be chronic in nature.
    C. They run in families.
    D. They can be induced by certain drugs.

10. Which of the following is <u>false</u> about the role of genetics in mood disorders?

    A. Family history studies have found that the first-degree relatives of people with bipolar disorder are 2-3 times more likely to have either bipolar or unipolar depression.

    B. Family history studies have found that the first-degree relatives of people with unipolar depression are more likely than controls to have either bipolar or unipolar depression.

    C. Twin studies have yielded more equivocal results for unipolar depression than for bipolar depression.

    D. Fewer than 10% of the first-degree relatives of people with bipolar disorder will develop the disorder themselves.

11. All of the following neurotransmitters have been implicated in unipolar depression <u>except</u>:

    A. Glutamate.
    B. Norepinephrine.
    C. Serotonin.
    D. Dopamine.

12. _____ is a neurotransmitter that has numerous receptors in the amygdala. When this neurotransmitter is blocked in people with major depression, they tend to experience significantly reduced depressive symptoms.

    A. Serotonin
    B. Glutamate
    C. Substance P
    D. Dopamine

13. People with depression:

    A. Tend to have increased slow-wave sleep and go into rapid eye movement sleep (REM) earlier in the night than nondepressed people.
    B. Have been found to exhibit decreased metabolic activity in the frontal cortex.
    C. Have less REM sleep per night than nondepressed people.
    D. Have been found to exhibit decreased activation of the nondominant hemisphere.

14. A brain area that appears to be overactive in depressed people is the:

    A. Cerebellum.
    B. Cerebral cortex.
    C. HPA axis.
    D. Dominant hemisphere.

15. All of the following increase a woman's risk of developing postpartum depression except:

   A. Hormonal imbalances.
   B. A past history of depression.
   C. Having a fussy baby.
   D. Lack of social support.

16. The idea that life stress leads to depression by causing a reduction in positive reinforcers is known as:

   A. Learned helplessness theory.
   B. Reformulated learned helplessness theory.
   C. Lewinsohn's behavioral theory.
   D. Depressive realism.

17. The reformulated learned helplessness theory added which of the following notions to learned helplessness theory?

   A. The negative cognitive triad.
   B. Rumination.
   C. Depressive realism.
   D. Causal attributions.

18. Which of the following drugs tends to reduce depressive symptoms the fastest?

   A. MAOIs.
   B. SSRIs.
   C. Tricyclic antidepressants.
   D. The drugs listed above are equally effective.

19. Which of the following statements about ECT is false?

   A. ECT is typically administered bilaterally.
   B. ECT is particularly effective for psychotic depression.
   C. ECT is administered more often in midwestern and eastern states.
   D. About 85% of patients relapse into depression after receiving ECT.

20. Tardive dyskinesia can result from adminstration of which of the following drugs?

   A. Lithium.
   B. Anticonvulsants.
   C. Antipsychotics.
   D. Antidepressants.

B. <u>True-False</u>. Select T (True) or F (False) below.

1. From childhood to adulthood, the specific symptoms of depression that an individual shows tend to change.   T   F

2. The presence of depressed mood is required for a diagnosis of dysthymic disorder, but not for a diagnosis of major depression.   T   F

3. Girls who mature earlier than their peers tend to have lower rates of depression than girls who mature later.   T   F

4. Agitation and irritability are symptoms of both unipolar and bipolar depression.
          T   F

5. Women are more prone than men to both unipolar and bipolar depression.   T   F

C. <u>Short Answer</u>.

1. Contrast cognitive theories of depression with the notion of "depressive realism." Can both theories be accurate? Why or why not?

2. Do women's hormones play a role in their higher rates of depression? Cite evidence from the chapter to support your argument.

3. Describe how ECT is administered. Who is most likely to benefit from it? What are some of the shortcomings of ECT?

4. Describe some of the cognitive-behavioral techniques used to treat depression.

5. What are some of the neurophysiological abnormalities that occur in depression?

ANSWER KEY

<u>Case Example</u>
1. Depressed mood, chronic fatigue, heavy laden feeling in body, weight gain, low self-esteem, hopelessness.
2. Dysthymic disorder with atypical features (chronic depressed mood, low self-esteem, hopelessness, but ability to experience pleasure, weight gain, heavy feelings in body), and double depression (symptoms sometimes become much worse and severely interfere with functioning, but she returns only to dysthymia).
3. A cognitive-behavioral therapist would want to know specifically what "berating comments" Amanda tends to make about herself and the future and what thoughts Amanda has during those times when she feels most down. CB therapist would also want to know how Amanda views her success and her friends and whether she discounts all the good things in her life. An interpersonal therapist would want to know more about Amanda's circle of friends and the quality of those friendships, any recent losses Amanda perceives in her life, whether Amanda is experiencing any role conflicts or role transitions, and the strength of Amanda's interpersonal skills.

<u>Multiple Choice</u>
1. C
2. B
3. D
4. A
5. B
6. D
7. C
8. D
9. B
10. B
11. A
12. C
13. B
14. C
15. A
16. C
17. D
18. B
19. A
20. C

<u>True-False</u>
1. F
2. T
3. F
4. T
5. F

<u>Short Answer</u>
1. See pp. 270-272.
2. See pp. 265-267.
3. See pp. 281-283.
4. See pp. 286-289.
5. See pp. 264-265.

<u>Additional Readings on Chapter 8 Topics</u>
Henriques, J. B., & Davidson, R. J. (1991). Left frontal hypoactivation in depression. <u>Journal of Abnormal Psychology, 100,</u> 535-545.

Jacobson, N. S., Dobson, K. S., Truax, P. A., Addis, M. E., Koerner, K., Gollan, J. K., Gortner, E., & Prince, S. E. (1996). A component analysis of cognitive-behavioral treatment for depression. <u>Journal of Consulting and Clinical Psychology, 64,</u> 295-304.

Nolen-Hoeksema, S., Larson, J., & Grayson, C. (1999). Explaining the gender difference in depressive symptoms. <u>Journal of Personality and Social Psychology, 77,</u> 1061-1072.

Chapter 9: Suicide

LEARNING OBJECTIVES
After reading and studying this chapter, you should be able to:

1. Identify Shneidman's types of people who commit suicide.

2. Discuss suicide rates and how they vary by age, gender, ethnicity, and nationality.

3. Discuss biological, sociocultural, and psychological risk factors for suicide.

4. Identify reasons why it is difficult to study suicide scientifically.

5. Discuss Durkheim's sociological theory of suicide.

6. Discuss suicide contagion and why it might occur.

7. Discuss the mental disorders associated with suicide.

8. Describe the biological, psychological, and sociocultural interventions for suicide.

9. Discuss the relationship between guns and suicide.

ESSENTIAL IDEAS

I. Defining and measuring suicide

   A. Suicide is defined as death from injury, poisoning, or suffocation where there is evidence (either explicit or implicit) that the injury was self-inflicted and that the decedent intended to kill himself/herself.

   B. Death seekers clearly and explicity seek to end their lives. Death initiators also have a clear intention to die, but believe that they are simply hastening an inevitable death. Death ignorers intend to end their lives but do not believe this means the end of their existence. Death darers are ambivalent about dying, and take actions that greatly increase their chances of death, but do not guarantee they will die.

   C. Suicide is the ninth leading cause of death in the United States, and internationally, at least 160,000 people die by suicide and 2 million other people make suicide attempts each year.

   D. Women are more likely than men to attempt suicide, but men are more likely than women to complete suicide.

E. Cross-cultural differences in suicide rates may have to do with religious doctrines, stressors, and cultural norms about suicide.

F. Young people are less likely than adults to commit suicide, but suicide rates have been rising dramatically for young people in recent decades. The elderly, particularly elderly men, are at high risk for suicide.

II. Understanding suicide

A. Suicide notes suggest that mental anguish and escape from pain are behind many suicides.

B. Several negative life events or circumstances increase risk for suicide, including economic hardship, serious illness, loss, and abuse.

C. Durkheim distinguished between egoistic suicide, which is committed by people who feel alienated from others, empty of social contacts, alone in an unsupportive world, anomic suicide which is committed by people who experience severe disorientation because of some large change in their relationships to society, and altruistic suicide which is committed by people who believe that taking their own lives will benefit society in some way.

D. Suicide clusters occur when two or more suicides or attempted suicides are nonrandomly "bunched' in space or time. This phenomenon is sometimes called suicide contagion.

E. Psychodynamic theorists attribute suicide to repressed rage that leads to self-destruction.

F. Several mental disorders increase risk for suicide, including depression, bipolar disorder, substance abuse, schizophrenia, and anxiety disorders.

G. Cognitive-behavioral theorists argue that hopelessness and dichotomous thinking contribute to suicide.

H. Impulsivity is a behavioral characteristic common to people who commit suicide.

I. Family history, twin and adoption studies all suggest there is a genetic vulnerability to suicide.

J. Many studies have found a link between low serotonin levels and suicide.

III. Treatment and Prevention

A. Drug treatments for suicidality most often involve lithium or antidepressant medications to reduce impulsive and violent behavior, and depression and mania. Antipsychotic medications and other medications that treat symptoms of an existing mental disorder may also be used.

B. Psychotherapies for suicide are similar to those used for depression. Dialectical behavior therapy has been specifically designed to address skills deficits and thinking patterns in people who are suicidal.

C. Suicide hot lines and crisis intervention programs provide immediate help to people who are highly suicidal.

D. Community prevention programs aim to educate the public about suicide and encourage suicidal people into treatment.

E. Guns are involved in the majority of suicides and some research suggests restricting access to guns can reduce suicide attempts.

F. Society is debating whether people have a right to choose to commit suicide.

KEY TERMS AND GUIDED REVIEW

Defining and Measuring Suicide

Key Terms

suicide (p. 300):

death seekers (p. 300):

death initiators (p. 301):

death ignorers (p. 301):

death darers (p. 301):

subintentional deaths (p. 301):

Guided Review

1. Explain what this sentence means: "Suicide-like behaviors fall on a continuum." (p. 300)

2. What are the similarities and differences among death seekers, death initiators, death ignorers, and death darers? (pp. 300-301)

3. What are some reasons that it is difficult to obtain accurate suicide rates? (pp. 301-302)

4. How does one's gender affect one's likelihood of attempting or completing suicide? (p. 302)

5. How do suicide rates vary by ethnicity? (pp. 302-304)

6. Discuss the suicide rate among children and adolescents. What are some of the warning signs for suicide in this age group? (pp. 304-305)

7. What contributes to suicide among the elderly? (pp. 305-306)

Understanding Suicide

<u>Key Terms</u>

egoistic suicide (p. 309):

anomic suicide (p. 309):

altruistic suicide (p. 309):

suicide cluster (p. 310):

suicide contagion (p. 310):

hopelessness (p. 313):

dichotomous thinking (p. 314):

<u>Guided Review</u>

1. What are some barriers to research on suicide? (pp. 306-308)

2. What are some sociocultural factors that appear to increase one's risk of suicide? (pp. 308-310)

3. Identify Durkheim's three types of suicide. (p. 309)

4. What is a suicide cluster? What are some contributors to suicide clusters? (pp. 309-310)

5. What is Freud's theory of suicide? (pp. 310-311)

6. What is the evidence that mental disorders are associated with suicide? (pp. 311-313)

7. What are some cognitive and behavioral contributors to suicide? (pp. 313-314)

8. What is the evidence that suicide has a genetic basis? (pp. 314-315)

9. What is the evidence that serotonin is related to suicide? (p. 315)

Treatment and Prevention

Key Terms

crisis intervention (p. 316):

suicide hot lines (p. 316):

lithium (p. 317):

serotonin reuptake inhibitors (p. 317):

dialectical behavior therapy (p. 318):

Guided Review

1. Describe some community-based programs for suicide. (p. 316)

2. What are some medications that may be prescribed to prevent suicide? (pp. 317-318)

3. What psychotherapies may be used to prevent suicide? (p. 318)

4. What are some advantages and disadvantages of sociocultural interventions for suicide? (pp. 318-320)

5. What is the relationship between guns and suicide? (p. 319)

CASE EXAMPLE
Read the following description and answer the questions below:

Brian was fed up and couldn't take it anymore. He had been depressed for quite a while and was living with some people in a house rampant with drug use in a crime-ridden area. Freaks and gangsters would frequently stop by and "hang out." This was not the life Brian had envisioned for himself. In high school, he had been a bright and popular guy, often the object of many women's affections. He was a brilliant artist and musician, and had spent a year at a prestigious art college in Chicago living out his fantasies. However, Brian had been using drugs for several years and had been engaging in risky, impulsive actions at school. He and a friend would ride the subway and spray-paint graffiti on city walls late at night. These excursions would take them into areas ripe with crime. Brian began to develop a feeling of emptiness and he could not explain to himself how he had gotten so far off track. His girlfriend broke up with him and he had lost his job. He wondered if he were gay. His roommates were starting to steal his money and his musical equipment. Some of them were getting involved in gangs. Brian abruptly left one day for Chicago, where for a time he had known peace, but got a speeding ticket on the way. This was too much for him. He taped a suicide note to a highway sign and pulled his car onto a deserted road. With his painting supplies in the back seat, it did not take long for Brian to die once he set his car ablaze while sitting in the front seat.

1. Which one of Shneidman's types of people who commit suicide is Brian?

2. What are some of the warning signs that suggest Brian may be at risk for suicide?

3. Which one of Durkheim's types of suicides is this case?

CHAPTER TEST

A. <u>Multiple Choice</u>. Choose the **best answer** to each question below.

1. Suicide is the _____ leading cause of death in the United States.

      A. second
      B. fifth
      C. ninth
      D. twelfth

2. Which of the following is <u>not</u> part of the CDC's definition of suicide?

      A. There is evidence that the injury was self-inflicted.
      B. There is evidence that the person was depressed or unhappy.
      C. There is evidence that the person intended to kill himself or herself.
      D. Suicide is death from injury, poisoning, or suffocation.

3. Death initiators:

      A. Clearly and explicitly seek to end their lives.
      B. Intend to end their lives but do not believe this means the end of their existence.
      C. Have a clear intention to die, but believe they are simply hastening an inevitable death.
      D. Are ambivalent about dying, and take actions that greatly increase their chances of death, but do not guarantee that they will die.

4. Death ignorers:

      A. Clearly and explicitly seek to end their lives.
      B. Intend to end their lives but do not believe this means the end of their existence.
      C. Have a clear intention to die, but believe they are simply hastening an inevitable death.
      D. Are ambivalent about dying, and take actions that greatly increase their chances of death, but do not guarantee that they will die.

5. According to Shneidman, which of the following terms would apply to someone with skin cancer who continues to frequent tanning booths?

      A. Subintentional death.
      B. Death ignorer.
      C. Death darer.
      D. Death seeker.

6. Women are _____ likely than men to attempt suicide. Men are _____ likely than women to complete suicide.

    A. three times more; two times less
    B. two times more; four times more
    C. three times more; four times more
    D. four times more; three times less

7. Men are more likely than women to do all of the following <u>except</u>:

    A. Take a drug overdose.
    B. Shoot themselves.
    C. Stab themselves.
    D. Drink alcohol when they are distressed.

8. Which ethnic group has the highest suicide rate in the U.S.?

    A. Whites.
    B. African-Americans.
    C. Asians.
    D. Native Americans.

9. Which of the following nations has the highest suicide rate (among the nations listed)?

    A. Mexico.
    B. United States.
    C. Germany.
    D. England.

10. All of the following are warning signs for suicide in adolescents <u>except</u>:

    A. Increased energy.
    B. Decline in school performance.
    C. Loss of appetite.
    D. Increased drug and alcohol use.

11. The single best predictor of future suicide attempts and completions is:

    A. Drug and alcohol abuse.
    B. Ownership of a handgun.
    C. Impulsivity.
    D. A previous history of a suicide attempt.

12. Which of the following statements about barriers to understanding suicide is <u>false</u>?

    A. Suicide is a rare event.
    B. Family members and friends may selectively remember information about the victim.
    C. The majority of people who contemplate suicide never complete it.
    D. The majority of suicide completers leave suicide notes.

13. Suicide committed by people who experience severe disorientation because of a large change in their relationships with society is known as:

    A. Altruistic suicide.
    B. Egoistic suicide.
    C. Anomic suicide.
    D. Confusion suicide.

14. Suicide committed by people who feel alienated from others, empty of social contacts, and alone in an unsupportive world is known as:

    A. Altruistic suicide.
    B. Egoistic suicide.
    C. Anomic suicide.
    D. Confusion suicide.

15. One problem with Freud's theory of suicide is that:

    A. It claims that suicidal people are depressed, but most suicidal people suffer from schizophrenia.
    B. People do not tend to express anger in suicide notes because they cannot express these emotions and are turning the feelings in on themselves.
    C. Suicidal people tend to direct their anger at the part of their ego that represents a lost love object.
    D. It is difficult to test and therefore hard to evaluate.

16. The most common disorder among people who commit suicide is:

    A. Schizophrenia.
    B. Social phobia.
    C. Depression.
    D. Substance abuse.

17. Which of the following is <u>not</u> a common characteristic of suicidal individuals?

      A. Anger and rage.
      B. Guilt and despair.
      C. Hopelessness.
      D. Dichotomous thinking.

18. Which of the following statements is <u>false</u>?

      A. Ten to fifteen percent of people with schizophrenia commit suicide.
      B. Depression increases one's risk of suicide, but mania does not.
      C. Social phobia increases women's risk of suicide.
      D. As many as 10% of people who complete suicide would not have met criteria for a diagnosable mental disorder.

19. All of the following increase one's risk of suicide <u>except</u>:

      A. Impulsivity.
      B. A family history of suicidality.
      C. Dichotomous thinking.
      D. Excessively high serotonin levels.

20. The medication(s) most consistently shown to reduce risk of suicide is/are:

      A. SSRIs.
      B. Antipsychotics.
      C. Lithium.
      D. MAOIs.

B. <u>True-False</u>. Select T (True) or F (False) below.

1. The most common way that women commit suicide is with guns.   T   F

2. More people die from suicide than from homocide.   T   F

3. Suicide is the ninth leading cause of death among 15-24 year-olds.   T   F

4. As many as 20% of college students have attempted suicide at some time in their lives.   T   F

5. The rates of suicide have increased for children and adolescents in recent years, but have declined for the elderly.   T   F

C. <u>Short Answer</u>.

1. Describe some of the risk factors for suicide.

2. What are some interventions that may help reduce or prevent suicide?

3. How do the rates of suicide vary by gender, age, and ethnicity?

4. What are death seekers, initiators, ignorers, and darers?

5. What are some reasons why it is difficult to study suicide?

ANSWER KEY

Case Example
1. A death darer.
2. Male gender, drug use, within the 15-24 age group, social withdrawal, recent loss, impulsivity.
3. Anomic suicide.

Multiple Choice
1. C
2. B
3. C
4. B
5. A
6. C
7. A
8. D
9. C
10. A
11. D
12. D
13. C
14. B
15. D
16. C
17. A
18. B
19. D
20. C

True-False
1. T
2. T
3. F
4. F
5. T

Short Answer
1. See pp. 306-315.
2. See pp. 316-320.
3. See pp. 301-306.
4. See pp. 300-301.
5. See pp. 301-308.

Additional Reading on Chapter 9 Topics

Boergers, J., Spirito, A., & Donaldson, D. (1998). Reasons for adolescent suicide attempts: Associations with psychological functioning. <u>Journal of the American Academy of Child and Adolescent Psychiatry, 37,</u> 1287-1293.

King, C. A. (1998). Suicide across the life span: Pathways to prevention. <u>Suicide and Life-Threatening Behavior, 28,</u> 328-337.

MacLeod, A. K., Williams, J. M., & Linehan, M. M. (1992). New developments in the understanding and treatment of suicidal behaviour. <u>Behavioural Psychotherapy, 20,</u> 193-218.

Chapter 10: Schizophrenia

LEARNING OBJECTIVES
After reading and studying this chapter, you should be able to:

1. Discuss the history of diagnostic criteria for schizophrenia, as well as the current criteria for schizophrenia and disorders that are similar to it.

2. Define and describe delusions and hallucinations, as well as the different types of delusions and hallucinations, and how they vary and do not vary across cultures.

3. Describe the disorganized thought and speech in schizophrenia.

4. Distinguish between Type I and Type II symptoms, as well as between prodromal and residual symptoms.

5. Identify the key features of each of the five subtypes of schizophrenia: paranoid, disorganized, catatonic, undifferentiated, and residual.

6. Discuss the evidence for a genetic transmission of schizophrenia, and which people are most at risk for developing schizophrenia.

7. Discuss the brain areas implicated in schizophrenia, as well as their functions, and be able to discuss how they are different in the brains of people with schizophrenia compared to people without schizophrenia.

8. Discuss the progression of hypotheses that implicate the neurotransmitter dopamine as a key agent in the development and treatment of schizophrenia, and how different drugs can affect dopamine.

9. Discuss the psychosocial factors associated with schizophrenia, the evidence for them, and their limits.

10. Discuss the drug therapies most commonly prescribed for schizophrenia, their side effects, and which symptoms they treat most effectively, and which ones they do not.

11. Discuss the psychological interventions designed for people with schizophrenia.

12. Discuss the prevalence of schizophrenia across cultures, as well as how culture and gender can influence the prognosis for people with schizophrenia.

ESSENTIAL IDEAS

I. Symptoms, diagnosis, and prognosis

A. The positive symptoms of schizophrenia are delusions, hallucinations, disorganized thinking and speech, and disorganized or catatonic behavior. Delusions are beliefs with little grounding in reality. Hallucinations are unreal perceptual experiences, such as hearing voices or having visions of objects that are not really present. The forms of delusions and hallucinations are relatively similar across cultures, but the specific content varies by culture.

B. The negative or Type II symptoms are affective flattening, poverty of speech, and loss of motivation.

C. Other symptoms of schizophrenia include anhedonia, inappropriate affect, and impaired social skills.

D. Prodromal symptoms are more moderate positive and negative symptoms that are present before an individual goes into an acute phase of the illness; residual symptoms are symptoms present after an acute phase.

E. The DSM-IV differentiates between schizophrenia and mood disorders with psychotic features and schizoaffective disorder. Severe mood symptoms are present in both of the latter two disorders. In mood disorders with psychotic features, the mood symptoms occur in the absence of the schizophrenic symptoms at least some of the time, and in schizoaffective disorder, the schizophrenic symptoms occur in the absence of the mood symptoms.

F. The DSM-IV further differentiates between paranoid, disorganized (hebephrenic), catatonic, undifferentiated, and residual schizophrenia.

II. Biological theories of schizophrenia

A. There is strong evidence for a genetic contribution to schizophrenia, although genetics do not fully explain who has the disorder.

B. Many people with schizophrenia, particularly those with predominantly negative symptoms, show significant structural and functional abnormalities in the brain, including low frontal activity and ventricular enlargement.

C. A number of prenatal difficulties and obstetrical problems at birth are implicated in the development of schizophrenia, including prenatal hypoxia and exposure to the influenza virus during the second trimester of gestation.

D. The original dopamine theory of schizophrenia is that the disorder is caused by excessive activity of the dopamine systems in the brain. This theory is probably too simple, but it seems clear that dopamine does play an important role in schizophrenia, especially in the positive symptoms.

E. New research suggests that serotonin and glutamate may also play a role in schizophrenia.

III. Psychological theories of schizophrenia

A. Early psychodynamic theories viewed schizophrenia as the result of harsh and inconsistent parenting that caused an individual to regress to infantile forms of coping.

B. Behavioral theorists view schizophrenic behaviors as the result of operant conditioning.

C. Cognitive theorists see some schizophrenic symptoms as attempts to understand perceptual and attentional disturbances.

IV. Sociocultural perspectives on schizophrenia

A. Early theories suggested that families put schizophrenic members in double-binds or have deviant patterns of communication.

B. Families high in expressed emotion are overinvolved and overprotective, and at the same time critical and resentful. People with schizophrenia who live in families high in expressed emotion may be at increased risk for relapse.

C. People with schizophrenia tend to live in highly stressful circumstances. Most theorists see this as a consequence rather than as a cause of schizophrenia.

V. Treatments for schizophrenia

A. The phenothiazines were the first drugs to have a significant effect on schizophrenia. They are more effective in treating the positive symptoms than the negative symptoms and a significant percentage of people do not respond to them at all. They can induce a number of serious side effects, including tardive dyskinesia.

B. New drugs called the atypical antipsychotics seem more effective in treating schizophrenia than the phenothiazines and have fewer side effects. These include clozapine and risperidone.

C. Psychosocial therapies focus on helping the people with schizophrenia and their families to understand and cope with the consequences of the disorder. They also help the person with schizophrenia gain resources and integrate into the community as possible.

D. Studies show that providing psychosocial therapy along with medication can significantly reduce the rate of relapse in schizophrenia.

E. Community-based comprehensive treatment programs for people with schizophrenia have been underfunded and thus many people with this disorder receive little or no useful treatment.

KEY TERMS AND GUIDED REVIEW

Key Terms

psychosis (p. 326):

schizophrenia (p. 326):

Guided Review

1. Why is schizophrenia a "puzzling" disorder? (p. 326)

2. How common is schizophrenia, and where do many people with schizophrenia reside? (pp. 326-327)

3. How do the rates of schizophrenia vary by gender and ethnicity? (pp. 327-328)

Symptoms, Diagnosis, and Prognosis

Key Terms

positive (Type I) symptoms (p. 330):

negative (Type II) symptoms (p. 330):

delusions (p. 330):

persecutory delusion (p. 331):

delusion of reference (p. 331):

grandiose delusion (p. 331):

delusions of thought control (p. 332):

hallucination (p. 334):

auditory hallucination (p. 334):

visual hallucination (p. 334):

formal thought disorder (p. 335):

word salad (p. 335):

catatonia (p. 335):

catatonic excitement (p. 335):

affective flattening (p. 337):

alogia (p. 338):

avolition (p. 338):

prodromal symptoms (p. 340):

residual symptoms (p. 340):

paranoid schizophrenia (p. 341):

disorganized schizophrenia (p. 341):

catatonic schizophrenia (p. 342):

echolalia (p. 342):

echopraxia (p. 342):

undifferentiated schizophrenia (p. 342):

residual schizophrenia (p. 342):

Guided Review

1. Give some examples of positive and negative symptoms in schizophrenia. (pp. 330-339)

2. How do delusions differ from self-deceptions? (pp. 330-331)

3. Describe some different types of delusions. (pp. 331-332)

4. How do delusions differ across cultures? (p. 333)

5. Describe some different types of hallucinations. (pp. 333-334)

6. How do hallucinations differ across cultures? (pp. 334-335)

7. Describe speech and thought in schizophrenia. (p. 335)

8. What is the evidence that people with schizophrenia have deficits in attention? (pp. 336-337)

9. How might problems in attention be related to the symptoms of schizophrenia? (pp. 336-337)

10. Describe some ways in which affect is exhibited in schizophrenia (pp. 337-339)

11. Why are negative symptoms difficult to diagnose reliably? (p. 338)

12. Summarize how the diagnostic criteria for schizophrenia have changed since the disorder was first conceptualized. (pp. 339-341)

13. What is the difference between prodromal and residual symptoms? (p. 340)

14. What is the difference between Type I and Type II schizophrenia? (p. 340)

15. Describe the five types of schizophrenia. (pp. 341-342)

16. How does schizophrenia vary by age and gender? (pp. 342-344)

17. How do social factors contribute to schizophrenia? (pp. 344-345)

Biological Theories of Schizophrenia

<u>Key Terms</u>

enlarged ventricles (p. 349):

frontal cortex (p. 350):

perinatal hypoxia (p. 351):

dopamine (p. 351):

phenothiazines (neuroleptics) (p. 351):

clozapine (p. 352):

mesolimbic system (p. 352):

<u>Guided Review</u>

1. Summarize the evidence for a genetic contribution to schizophrenia. (pp. 346-349)

2. What are some of the brain areas that exhibit abnormal structure or function in schizophrenia? Which ones appear to contribute to positive symptoms, and which ones appear to contribute to negative symptoms? (pp. 349-350)

3. What appear to be some of the causes of neuroanatomical abnormalities in schizophrenia? (p. 351)

4. What was the original dopamine theory of schizophrenia? Give some examples of evidence that supported it. (pp. 351-352)

5. What are some of the observations that called the original dopamine theory into question? (p. 352)

6. How does dopamine appear to be related to schizophrenia, according to modern views? (pp. 352-353)

Psychological Theories of Schizophrenia

<u>Key Term</u>

schizophrenogenic mothers (p. 353):

<u>Guided Review</u>

1. Describe the early psychodynamic theories of schizophrenia. (pp. 353-354)

2. What cognitive and behavioral factors may play a role in schizophrenia? (p. 354)

Sociocultural Perspectives on Schizophrenia

<u>Key Terms</u>

double bind (p. 355):

communication deviance (p. 355):

expressed emotion (p. 355):

social selection (p. 356):

<u>Guided Review</u>

1. Describe some family interaction patterns that can contribute to or exacerbate schizophrenia. (pp. 355-356)

2. What appears to be the relationship between social selection and schizophrenia? (pp. 356-357)

3. What appears to be the relationship between stress and schizophrenia? (pp. 356-357)

Treatments for Schizophrenia

<u>Key Terms</u>

chlorpromazine (p. 359):

akinesia (p. 360):

akathesis (p. 360):

tardive dyskinesia (p. 360):

atypical antipsychotics (p. 360):

agranulocytosis (p. 361):

risperidone (p. 361):

Guided Review

1. Describe some of the earlier treatments for schizophrenia. (pp. 357-359)

2. What symptoms do phenothiazines help reduce? How do they work? (pp. 359-360)

3. What are some of the side effects of neuroleptics? (pp. 359-360)

4. How does clozapine appear to work? How effective is it? (pp. 360-361)

5. What are some of the side effects of clozapine? (p. 361)

6. Give examples of cognitive, behavioral, and social interventions for schizophrenia. (pp. 361-363)

7. Describe some of the components of family therapy for schizophrenia. (pp. 363-364)

8. Describe some of the community-level interventions for schizophrenia. What is the evidence that they are effective? (pp. 364-366)

9. Identify and describe the models that traditional healers tend to follow in treating schizophrenic symptoms. (p. 366)

CASE EXAMPLE
Read the following description and answer the questions below:

A 29-year-old single Afro-Caribbean woman was admitted to the accident and emergency department with heavy bleeding from a laceration to the right labia majora, self-inflicted with a razor blade. She explained that she wanted to cut off her clitoris as that was the center of her problems. She believed that her genitalia had enlarged due to masturbation and were becoming more masculine, and that this would prevent her from finding a partner and marrying.

She claimed to recall that at the age of 6 two men had put a curse on her because of petty jealousy. She believed that at the age of 17 they started to follow her, and 'made' her 'touch herself'. From age 20 she could hear the voice of a male stranger 'guiding' her, commenting on her actions and the size of her genitals. She felt that articles on female sexuality in women's magazines were specifically directed at her. Occasionally she felt that the direction in which she walked was controlled from outside. Her family reported that from 19 years of age she had become increasingly withdrawn and that in the past six months, she had become even more preoccupied, checking her genital size each time she showered. She found it hard to concentrate at work, felt extremely self-conscious, believing that people could tell that she was abnormal. She became depressed and frequently thought of cutting off her genitalia.

There were seven siblings in the family, of which she was the fourth. She lived with her mother, her parents having divorced, and discipline appeared to be lax. An older brother had been treated for schizophrenia and there was a history of possible schizophrenia in a paternal uncle and aunt.

From her early teens, her schoolwork deteriorated and she ran away frequently. At 14 she was arrested and charged for shoplifting. She left school at 15 with no close friends or qualifications, eventually obtaining work as a catering assistant, a job she held for six years.

At age 17 she started masturbating to heterosexual fantasies. She felt guilty about this, and sometimes experienced the act as being forced from outside. Despite never having seen another woman's external genitalia pictorially or in reality, she believed her own labia were grossly abnormal, and could not be reassured by advice of doctors to the contrary. There was no other psychiatric history or relevant medical history, and no drug or alcohol abuse. Physical examination was normal apart from the wound to her genitalia.

On mental state examination, she was alert and orientated, polite and appropriate in manner but her affect was blunted and rapport was difficult. Her mood was mildly depressed. There was poverty of speech, and some loosening of associations. Her thought content was dominated by her genital size, and she entertained ideas of further mutilation attempts, but not of suicide. She did not think she was ill and only reluctantly accepted hospitalization.

Computerized tomography (CT) showed enlargement of the frontal horn of the left lateral ventricle. (Adapted from Krasucki, Kemp, & David, 1995.)

1. Look carefully at the description of the woman in the case example. What evidence could you cite that would indicate to you whether she is simply self-deceived, or delusional?

2. What types of symptoms does she exhibit that suggest a particular diagnosis? Which of the schizophrenias would you diagnose her with, and why?

3. Given her condition as described in the case study, as well as her family characteristics and personal background, briefly describe what prognosis you would give her as to her condition. What facts about her culture and gender suggest a particular prognosis for her, compared to someone with different characteristics?

CHAPTER TEST

A. <u>Multiple Choice</u>. Choose the **best answer** to each question below.

1. The presence of delusions, hallucinations, and disorganized speech or behavior for at least one day but less than one month would be diagnosed as:

    A. Schizophrenia.
    B. Schizophreniform disorder.
    C. Delusional disorder.
    D. Brief psychotic disorder.

2. Compared to men with schizophrenia, women with schizophrenia:

    A. Tend to develop schizophrenia earlier in life than men, particularly during their late teens or early 20s.
    B. Are more likely to be married.
    C. Are less likely to have had children.
    D. Are less likely to have graduated from high school or college.

3. A man who believes he is Napoleon is suffering from a:

    A. Persecutory delusion.
    B. Delusion of thought control.
    C. Grandiose delusion.
    D. Delusion of reference.

4. The most common type of hallucination is:

    A. Auditory.
    B. Visual.
    C. Somatic.
    D. Tactile.

5. Associations between words that are based on the sounds of the words rather than the content are known as:

   A. Neologisms.
   B. Clangs.
   C. Perseverations.
   D. Word salad.

6. Words that mean something only to the person enunciating them are known as:

   A. Neologisms.
   B. Clangs.
   C. Perseverations.
   D. Word salad.

7. Poverty of speech (reduced speaking) is known as;

   A. Avolition.
   B. Word salad.
   C. Alogia.
   D. Clangs.

8. All of the following are negative symptoms of schizophrenia <u>except</u>:

   A. Avolition.
   B. Alogia.
   C. Affective flattening.
   D. Anhedonia.

9. Emil Kraepelin believed that the disorder he coined _____ resulted from premature deterioration of the brain.

   A. schizophrenia
   B. format thought disorder
   C. dementia praecox
   D. multiple personality disorder

10. A person who exhibits delusions and hallucinations for 2 weeks, but who also experiences a major depressive episode following this 2-week period while continuing to experience delusions and hallucinations, would be diagnosed with:

    A. Mood disorder with psychotic features.
    B. Schizoaffective disorder.
    C. Shared psychotic disorder.
    D. Schizophrenia.

11. Someone who speaks in word salads and does not bathe, dress, or eat if left alone, would most likely be diagnosed with:

    A. Paranoid schizophrenia.
    B. Catatonic schizophrenia.
    C. Undifferentiated schizophrenia.
    D. Disorganized schizophrenia.

12. Repetitive imitation of the movements of another person is known as:

    A. Catalepsy.
    B. Catatonia.
    C. Echolalia.
    D. Echopraxia.

13. Compared to men with schizophrenia, women with the disorder:

    A. Tend to have more severe language impairments.
    B. Tend to develop schizophrenia at an earlier age.
    C. Are hospitalized less often.
    D. More often have enlarged ventricles.

14. A brain area that is important in language, emotional expression, and planning, and which is smaller and shows less activity in people with schizophrenia, is the:

    A. Basal ganglia.
    B. Hippocampus.
    C. Frontal cortex.
    D. Temporal lobe.

15. A newer theory of dopamine and schizophrenia suggests that there is excess dopaminergic activity in the _____, but unusually low dopaminergic activity in the _____.

    A. limbic system; prefrontal area
    B. mesolimbic system; prefrontal area
    C. prefrontal area; limbic system
    D. thalamus; mesolimbic system

16. Julie's son Winston just fell down and hurt himself. She rushes to comfort him and takes him into her arms, saying, "You stupid little boy! Watch where you walk!" This is an example of:

    A. A double bind.
    B. A schizophrenogenic mother.
    C. Communication deviance.
    D. Expressed emotion.

17. Families high in expressed emotion:

    A. Are both overprotective and rejecting of the schizophrenic family member, not letting him or her develop an autonomous sense of self.
    B. Express their thoughts in vague, indefinite ways and communicate misperceptions and misinterpretations.
    C. Are overinvolved with each other, are overprotective of the schizophrenic family member, and are critical and resentful of the schizophrenic family member.
    D. Tend to express their emotions when they should keep them to themselves to avoid hurting the schizophrenic family member's feelings.

18. Chlorpromazine:

    A. Blocks the D3 and D4 receptors for dopamine.
    B. Blocks the D1 and D2 receptors for dopamine.
    C. Can reduce the negative symptoms of schizophrenia.
    D. Is an atypical antipsychotic drug.

19. A common side effect of phenothiazines that consists of agitation which causes patients to pace and be unable to sit still is:

    A. Akathesis.
    B. Agranulocytosis.
    C. Tardive dyskinesia.
    D. Akinesia.

20. A treatment for schizophrenia that binds to the D4 dopamine receptor and influences positive as well as negative symptoms of schizophrenia is known as:

A. Fish oil.
B. Thorazine.
C. Chlorpromazine.
D. Clozapine.

B. <u>True-False</u>. Select T (True) or F (False) below.

1. An individual who exhibits the symptoms of schizophrenia for longer than 1 month, but less than 6 months, would be diagnosed as having schizophreniform disorder.   T   F

2. Delusions and hallucinations are Type II symptoms of schizophrenia.   T   F

3. Compared to other forms of schizophrenia, people with the paranoid subtype show better cognitive and emotional functioning and are more likely to hold down a job.   T   F

4. The earlier the age of onset, the more favorable the course of schizophrenia.   T   F

5. Evidence of lower activity in and/or atrophy of the frontal cortex is found more commonly in people with predominantly positive symptoms of schizophrenia.   T   F

C. <u>Short Answer</u>.

1. What is the relationship between dopamine and schizophrenia? Cite evidence to support your answer.

2. Do psychological factors influence schizophrenia? If so, how? Be specific.

3. Describe the five subtypes of schizophrenia.

4. Describe some ways in which the symptoms of schizophrenia may vary across cultures.

5. Based upon what you read in the chapter, describe the "ideal treatment package" for schizophrenia.

ANSWER KEY

<u>Case Example</u>

1. The woman is delusional, and not simply self-deceived, because she not only occasionally entertains distorted thoughts about her clitoris, but she is preoccupied with them and takes action based upon them.

2. The woman exhibits delusions of reference, hallucinations, poverty of speech, magical thinking, and loosening of associations. Her symptoms suggest a diagnosis of paranoid schizophrenia, because her delusions and hallucinations center around themes of persecution and paranoia. She does not evidence negative symptoms or catatonic symptoms.

3. Though the woman appears to have acute symptoms, her prognosis appears somewhat favorable because paranoid schizophrenia has the best prognosis in general. However, she evidences ventricular enlargement and has a family history of schizophrenia, which suggest strong biological underpinnings and brain atrophy, which make her prognosis less favorable. She shows evidence of being able to hold down a consistent job, which is favorable. Her lack of social support is unfavorable, as is the early onset of her symptoms. However, the course of schizophrenia tends to be more favorable for women. Her residence in a developed country (England) is not favorable for her prognosis.

<u>Multiple Choice</u>

1. D
2. B
3. C
4. A
5. B
6. A
7. C
8. D
9. C
10. B
11. D
12. D
13. C
14. C
15. B
16. A
17. C
18. B
19. A
20. D

<u>True-False</u>
1. T
2. F
3. T
4. F
5. F

<u>Short Answer</u>
1. See pp. 351-353.
2. See pp. 353-357, 361-364.
3. See pp. 341-342.
4. See pp. 333-335, 344-345.
5. A good answer would include biological, psychological, and social components to the treatment package as described in the chapter (e.g., clozapine, individual and family therapy).

<u>Additional Reading on Chapter 10 Topics</u>
Evans, J. D., Heaton, R. K., Paulsen, J. S., McAdams, L. A., Heaton, S. C., Jeste, D. V. (1999). Schizoaffective disorder: A form of schizophrenia or affective disorder? <u>Journal of Clinical Psychiatry, 60,</u> 874-882.

Heinrichs, R. W., & Zakzanis, K. K. (1998). Neurocognitive deficit in schizophrenia: A quantitative review of the evidence. <u>Neuropsychology, 12,</u> 426-445.

Paul, G. L. (1974). Experimental-behavioral approaches to "schizophrenia." In R. Cancro, N. Fox, & L. E. Shapiro (Eds.), <u>Strategic intervention in schizophrenia</u>. New York: Behavioral Publications.

Chapter 11: Dissociative and Somatoform Disorders

LEARNING OBJECTIVES
After reading and studying this chapter, you should be able to:

1. Discuss how early theorists such as Freud viewed dissociation, how Hilgard's experiments provided insight into the "hidden observer" phenomenon, and how these views have shaped our modern understanding of dissociative disorders.

2. Identify the symptoms of dissociative identity disorder (DID) and the different types of alternate personalities that people with DID may exhibit.

3. Identify correlates of DID, including risk factors and comorbid conditions.

4. Summarize the debate and evidence surrounding the possible creation of DID by therapists.

5. Discuss the theories of how DID develops and the different approaches to treating it.

6. Define dissociative fugue, and explain how it is similar to and different from other dissociative disorders.

7. Discuss the conditions that may precede a dissociative fugue.

8. Distinguish among anterograde, retrograde, organic, and psychogenic amnesia, and know the types of information that tend to be lost and retained in each type.

9. Define depersonalization disorder.

10. Distinguish among somatoform disorders, psychosomatic disorders, malingering, and factitious disorders.

11. Define conversion disorder and la belle indifference, and discuss how early physicians and psychodynamic theorists viewed it.

12. Discuss the types of traumas frequently experienced by people with conversion disorder, and the other disorders that often accompany it.

13. Describe the psychodynamic and behavioral treatments for conversion disorder.

14. Distinguish among somatization disorder, pain disorder, conversion disorder, and hypochondriasis.

15. Discuss the cultural and cohort variations in the rates of somatization disorder, as well as the disorders that often accompany it and those that are similar to it, making it difficult to diagnose.

16. Discuss the possible causes of somatization disorder.

17. Summarize how clinicians conduct psychotherapy for people with somatization disorder.

18. Define body dysmorphic disorder, and describe the behaviors that people with this disorder engage in to compensate for their "defective" body part(s).

ESSENTIAL IDEAS

I. Dissociative disorders

    A. The dissociative disorders include dissociative identity disorder, dissociative fugue, dissociative amnesia, and depersonalization disorder.

    B. In all these disorders, people's conscious experiences of themselves become fragmented, they may lack awareness of core aspects of their selves, and they may experience amnesia for important events.

    C. The distinct feature of dissociative identity disorder is the development of multiple separate personalities within the same person. The personalities take turns being in control.

    D. People with dissociative fugue move away from home and assume entirely new identities, with complete amnesia for their previous identities. They do not switch back and forth between different personalities, however.

    E. People with dissociative amnesia lose important memories due to psychological causes.

    F. People with depersonalization disorder have frequent experiences of feeling detached from their mental processes or their bodies.

    G. These disorders are often, although not always, associated with traumatic experiences.

    H. Therapists often treat these disorders by helping people explore past experiences and feelings that they have blocked from consciousness and by supporting them as they develop more integrated experiences of self and more adaptive ways of coping with stress.

II. Somatoform disorders

    A. Somatoform disorders are a group of disorders in which people experience significant physical symptoms for which there is no apparent organic cause.

B. Conversion disorder involves loss of functioning in some part of the body, for no organic reason. Conversion symptoms often occur after trauma or stress, perhaps because the person cannot face memories or emotions associated with the trauma. Treatment for conversion disorder focuses on expression of emotions or memories associated with the symptoms.

C. Somatization disorder involves a long history of multiple physical complaints for which people have sought treatment but for which there is no apparent organic cause. Pain disorder involves only the experience of chronic, unexplainable pain. These disorders appear to be common, particularly among women, young children, and the elderly, and among people of Asian or Hispanic heritage.

D. Hypochondriasis is a condition in which people worry chronically about having a dread disease, despite evidence that they do not. This disorder appears rare.

E. In both somatization and pain disorders, and hypochondriasis, individuals often have a history of anxiety and depression. These disorders may represent acceptable ways of expressing emotional pain. Cognitive theories of the disorders say that they are due to excessive focus on physical symptoms and the tendency to catastrophize symptoms. Treatment for both disorders involves helping people identify feelings and thoughts behind the symptoms and find more adaptive ways of coping.

F. People with body dysmorphic disorder have an obsessional preoccupation with some parts of their bodies and make elaborate attempts to change these body parts. Treatment for body dysmorphic disorder can include psychodynamic therapy to reveal underlying concerns, systematic desensitization therapy to reduce obsessions and compulsions about the body, and serotonin reuptake inhibitors.

KEY TERMS AND GUIDED REVIEW

Key Terms

dissociation (p. 372):

Dissociative Disorders

Key Terms

dissociative identity disorder (DID) (p. 376):

dissociative fugue (p. 382):

dissociative amnesia (p. 384):

organic amnesias (p. 384):

anterograde amnesia (p. 384):

psychogenic amnesia (p. 384):

retrograde amnesia (p. 384):

depersonalization disorder (p. 386):

Guided Review

1. What is the hidden observer phenomenon? What is the evidence that it exists? (pp. 372-373)

2. What are the symptoms of DID? (pp. 376-378)

3. What are some of the gender differences in DID? (pp. 376-377)

4. Describe the common types of alters. (p. 377)

5. Describe some ways in which children tend to manifest DID. (pp. 377-378)

6. What are some reasons why DID has been increasingly diagnosed since 1980? (pp. 378-380)

7. Describe the experiment by Spanos and colleagues. What did it suggest about the diagnosis of DID? (pp. 378-379)

8. What other conditions are often associated with DID? (pp. 379-380)

9. What is an *ataque de nervios*? (p. 380)

10. What are some of the contributors to DID? (p. 381)

11. Describe some techniques used to treat DID. (pp. 381-382)

12. What are some characteristics of people who experience dissociative fugues? (pp. 382-383)

13. What is the difference between organic and psychogenic amnesia? (p. 384)

14. What is the difference between anterograde and retrograde amnesia? (p. 384)

15. What are some of the explanations for psychogenic amnesias? (pp. 384-385)

Somatoform Disorders

<u>Key Terms</u>

somatoform disorders (p. 386):

psychosomatic disorders (p. 386):

malingering (p. 386):

factitious disorders (p. 386):

factitious disorder by proxy (p. 387):

conversion disorder (p. 388):

glove anesthesia (p. 389):

somatization disorder (p. 392):

pain disorder (p. 393):

hypochondriasis (p. 396):

body dysmorphic disorder (p. 397):

<u>Guided Review</u>

1. What is the difference between somatoform disorders and psychosomatic disorders? (p. 386)

2. How do somatoform disorders differ from malingering and factitious disorders? (pp. 386-387)

3. How might somatoform and dissociative disorders be related to one another? (p. 388)

4. Describe the features of conversion disorder and conditions often associated with it. (pp. 388-390)

5. How are medical problems and conversion disorder related? (pp. 390-392)

6. What are some ways to treat conversion disorder? (p. 392)

7. What are the symptoms of somatization disorder? (pp. 392-393)

8. What are some ways in which clinicians attempt to distinguish between somatization and actual symptoms of physical illnesses? (pp. 393-394)

9. How do the rates of somatization disorder vary by age, culture, and gender? (p. 394)

10. What do family history and twin studies suggest about the heritability of somatization and pain disorder? (p. 394)

11. Describe the cognitive theory of somatization and pain disorder. (pp. 394-395)

12. What is the relationship between trauma and somatization and pain disorder? (p. 395)

13. Describe some approaches used to treat somatization disorder. (pp. 395-396)

14. What are some differences between somatization and hypochondriasis? (p. 396)

15. Describe some approaches used to treat body dysmorphic disorder. (pp. 398-399)

CASE EXAMPLE
Read the following description and answer the questions below:

Betty has belonged to the health maintenance organization funded by her health insurance for only three years, but already her medical records fill three large binders. Betty is convinced that she has serious heart disease. She can describe many times when she has had "painful feelings" in her upper chest. When she has these feelings, she stops everything, lays quietly for a long time, and listens to her heart. She reports that her heart "races and pounds" and that there are frequent irregularities in her heart beat. Numerous medical tests, including two occasions when her heart was monitored for a 24-hour period, have revealed no irregularities or abnormalities in her heart beat. Now she is insisting that she should have a cardiac catheterization, an invasive medical procedure that her physicians think is totally unnecessary.

Heart disease is only the latest ailment that Betty is convinced she has. For several years, she has believed she has a kidney disease. She carefully monitors the color of her urine and the frequency of her urination. She has these data charted in a diary she keeps of her health. In her diary, she also lists any pains or twinges she has each day. Betty spends a lot of time researching possible causes of her pains on computer databases. When she goes to her physician, which is at least once a month, she takes along her diary and her notes on the diseases they may indicate. Betty insists on going over each of these entries in her diary, one at a time, with her physician. Over the last three years, in addition to her cardiac tests, she has undergone many X-rays, an MRI scan, multiple ultrasound tests, and almost monthly blood and urine tests (she usually brings in a sample of her urine to her physician when she visits). None of these tests has ever indicated any disease.

1. Which of the somatoform disorders is the most appropriate diagnosis for Betty? How did you, or would you, rule out any of the other somatoform disorders?

2. What family or developmental history might have led Betty to have the concerns she shows?

3. How is Betty likely to respond to a recommendation that she needs to be seeing a psychiatrist instead of a cardiologist?

4. What treatment would you prescribe for Betty?

CHAPTER TEST

A. <u>Multiple Choice</u>. Choose the **best answer** to each question below.

1. A process in which different parts of an individual's identity, memories, or consciousness become split off from one another is known as:

    A. Somatization
    B. Dissociation
    C. Psychogenic amnesia
    D. La belle indifference

2. Which of the following would be most likely to serve as the victim of a trauma?

    A. A child alter
    B. A persecutor personality
    C. The host personality
    D. A helper personality

3. Which of the following statements about children with DID is <u>false</u>?

    A. Children with DID tend to exhibit antisocial behavior.
    B. Children with DID tend to show symptoms of posttraumatic stress disorder.
    C. Children with DID tend to hear voices inside their heads.
    D. Children with DID tend to experience delusions and hallucinations.

4. Research by Spanos and colleagues (1985) demonstrated that:

    A. Symptoms of DID could be induced in normal people through hypnosis.
    B. Clinicians routinely hypnotize patients with DID.
    C. Not all DID patients benefit from hypnosis.
    D. DID is diagnosed more often in the U.S. than in Europe.

5. Which of the following statements about DID is <u>false</u>?

    A. DID is diagnosed more often in the U.S. than in Europe.
    B. In the U.S., DID is rarely diagnosed in Latinos.
    C. The diagnostic criteria for DID first appeared in DSM-III-R, which was published in 1987.
    D. Most people diagnosed with DID are also diagnosed with a personality disorder.

6. Most people with DID do <u>not</u>:

    A. Also meet criteria for major depression.
    B. Have a history of being physically abused.
    C. Tend to be stubborn and resistant to suggestion.
    D. Tend to have significant periods of amnesia.

7. In _____, people cannot remember important facts about their lives and their personal identities, but are aware that there are large gaps in their memories.

    A. dissociative identity disorder
    B. dissociative fugue
    C. depersonalization disorder
    D. dissociative amnesia

8. Psychogenic amnesias:

    A. Rarely involve anterograde amnesia.
    B. Rarely involve retrograde amnesia.
    C. Are caused by brain injury.
    D. Are caused by disease, drugs, accidents, or surgery.

9. The inability to remember new information is known as:

    A. Retrograde amnesia.
    B. Psychogenic amnesia.
    C. Anterograde amnesia.
    D. Dissociative amnesia.

10. All of the following are characterized by the experience of one or more physical symptoms <u>except</u>:

    A. Conversion disorder.
    B. Hypochondriasis.
    C. Body dysmorphic disorder.
    D. Pain disorder.

11. In the somatoform disorders, the physical symptoms:

    A. Are caused by organic factors, but are made worse by the somatoform disorder.
    B. Are consciously produced by the person with the disorder.
    C. Are consistent with possible physiological mechanisms, which makes them hard to distinguish from physical diseases.
    D. Remit when the psychological factors producing them are treated.

12. Someone who fakes a symptom or disorder to avoid some unwanted situation would be regarded as:

   A. Having a factitious disorder by proxy.
   B. Malingering.
   C. Having a psychosomatic disorder.
   D. Having somatization disorder.

13. Someone with a factitious disorder:

   A. Deliberately fakes an illness to avoid an unwanted situation.
   B. Deliberately fakes an illness to gain medical attention.
   C. Experiences psychological stress in the form of physical symptoms.
   D. Has psychological factors that negatively influence an actual physical illness.

14. People who worry chronically that they have a physical disease in the absence of evidence that they do and who frequently seek medical attention would be diagnosed with:

   A. Conversion disorder.
   B. Pain disorder.
   C. Body dysmorphic disorder.
   D. Hypochondriasis.

15. Body dysmorphic disorder involves:

   A. A history of complaints about pain that appears to have no physical cause.
   B. Excessive preoccupation with some part of the body the person believes is defective.
   C. Loss of functioning in some part of the body for psychological rather than physical reasons.
   D. Chronic worry that one has a physical disease in the absence of evidence that one does.

16. Sigmund Freud found that when people tended to recall painful memories or emotions that they had blocked from consciousness, usually under hypnosis:

   A. They experienced relief from glove anesthesia.
   B. They experienced relief from la belle indifference.
   C. They developed symptoms of DID.
   D. They realized that their physical symptoms had psychological causes.

17. People with conversion disorder tend to have high rates of all of the following except:

        A. Antisocial personality disorder.
        B. Depression.
        C. Alcohol abuse.
        D. Schizophrenia.

18. To be diagnosed with somatization disorder, a person must have all of the following except:

        A. Two gastrointestinal symptoms.
        B. Three neurological symptoms.
        C. One sexual symptom.
        D. No organic causes of their physical complaints.

19. People with somatization disorder are more likely to be or have all of the following except:

        A. A history of physical or sexual abuse.
        B. Female.
        C. Caucasian.
        D. Older in age.

20. Body dysmorphic disorder is thought by some researchers to be a form of:

        A. Generalized anxiety disorder.
        B. Hypochondriasis.
        C. Obsessive-compulsive disorder.
        D. Somatization disorder.

B. True-False. Select T (True) or F (False) below.

1. About 90% of patients with DID have a history of suicide attempts.   T   F

2. DID is more commonly diagnosed in the U.S. than in Europe, but body dysmorphic disorder is more often diagnosed in Europe than the U.S.   T   F

3. People with somatoform disorders do not consciously fake their symptoms, but people with psychosomatic disorders do fake their symptoms.   T   F

4. Experiments by Ernest Hilgard showed that researchers could induce the symptoms of DID in normal individuals by using hypnosis.   T   F

5. Body dysmorphic disorder is more common among younger adults, whereas somatization disorder is more common among older adults.   T   F

C. <u>Short Answer</u>.

1. Describe how you would attempt to distinguish between conversion disorder and actual physical maladies.

2. What are the arguments for and against the claim that DID is a spurious diagnosis?

3. How is a dissociative fugue different from dissociative amnesia?

4. What are some of the theories of conversion disorder?

5. How are somatoform disorders different from psychosomatic disorders, malingering, and factitious disorders?

ANSWER KEY

<u>Case Example</u>

1. Hypochondriasis; ruled out somatization disorder because she does not have the variety of complaints necessary for somatization disorder.

2. Having a family member die of heart disease or kidney disease; having a family member who modeled hypochondriasis; having been reinforced by attention from others for her physical complaints.

3. Not well because she truly believes she is ill.

4. Help Betty find more adaptive ways of coping with the stresses in her life and of gaining attention from others; help her confront the irrationality of her medical concerns.

<u>Multiple Choice</u>

1. B
2. A
3. D
4. A
5. C
6. C
7. D
8. A
9. C
10. C
11. D
12. B
13. B
14. D
15. B
16. A
17. D
18. B
19. C
20. C

<u>True-False</u>

1. F
2. T
3. F
4. F
5. T

1. See pp. 390-392.
2. See pp. 378-380.
3. See pp. 382-386.
4. See pp. 388-390.
5. See pp. 386-387.

Additional Readings on Chapter 11 Topics

Eich, E., Macaulay, D., Loewenstein, R. J., & Dihle, P. H. (1997). Memory, amnesia, and dissociative identity disorder. Psychological Science, 8, 417-422.

Phillips, K. A. (2000). Body dysmorphic disorder: Diagnostic controversies and treatment challenges. Bulletin of the Menninger Clinic, 64, 18-35.

Scroppo, J. C., Drob, S. L., Weinberger, J. L., & Eagle, P. (1998). Identifying dissociative identity disorder: A self-report and projective study. Journal of Abnormal Psychology, 107, 272-284.

Chapter 12: Personality Disorders

LEARNING OBJECTIVES
After reading and studying this chapter, you should be able to:

1. Identify the differences between personality disorders and acute disorders.

2. Identify the three clusters of personality disorders, the disorders in each cluster, and the ways in which the disorders in each cluster are related.

3. Discuss the controversies that surround the personality disorders, including claims that they are gender-biased.

4. Identify the similarities and differences between schizophrenia and the odd-eccentric personality disorders.

5. Describe the key symptoms and characteristics of each personality disorder, the theories that attempt to explain it, and the approaches used to treat it.

6. Discuss why some of the personality disorders (such as antisocial personality disorder) are especially difficult to treat.

7. Identify the differences between avoidant personality disorder, social phobia, and schizoid personality disorder.

8. Identify the similarities and differences between obsessive-compulsive disorder and obsessive-compulsive personality disorder.

9. Discuss the criticisms of the DSM's approach to classifying personality disorders.

10. Describe alternative conceptualizations of the personality disorders.

ESSENTIAL IDEAS

I. Defining and diagnosing personality disorders

    A. A personality disorder is a long-standing pattern of behavior, thought, and feeling that is highly maladaptive for the individual or for people around him or her.

    B. A personality disorder must be present continuously from adolescence or early adulthood into adulthood.

    C. Personality disorders are listed on Axis II of the DSM-IV.

D. Some theorists object to the DSM's classification of personality disorders because: (1) it treats these disorders as categories; (2) the diagnostic criteria for these disorders overlap to a large extent; and (3) the diagnostic criteria have low reliability.

E. The DSM-IV construction of personality disorders may be gender biased because some criteria appear to represent extreme stereotypes of masculine or feminine behavior. These criteria may also fail to consider how men and women can exhibit symptoms in different ways.

II. The odd-eccentric personality disorders

A. People with the odd-eccentric personality disorders—paranoid, schizoid, and schizotypal personality disorders—have odd thought processes, emotional reactions, and behaviors similar to those of people with schizophrenia, but they retain their grasp on reality.

B. People with paranoid personality disorder are chronically suspicious of others but maintain their grasp on reality.

C. People with schizoid personality disorder are emotionally cold and distant from others and have great trouble forming interpersonal relationships.

D. People with schizotypal personality disorders have a variety of odd beliefs and perceptual experiences but also maintain their grasp on reality.

E. These personality disorders, especially schizotypal personality disorder, have been linked to familial histories of schizophrenia and some of the biological abnormalities of schizophrenia.

F. People with these disorders tend not to seek treatment, but when they do, therapists pay close attention to their relationships with them and help them learn to reality-test their unusual thinking.

G. Antipsychotics may help schizotypal clients reduce their odd thinking.

III. The dramatic-emotional personality disorders

A. People with the dramatic-emotional personality disorders—antisocial, borderline, histrionic, and narcissistic personality disorders—have histories of unstable relationships and emotional experiences and of behaving in dramatic and erratic ways.

B. People with antisocial personality disorder regularly violate the basic rights of others and often engage in criminal acts.

C. Antisocial personality disorder may have strong biological roots but is also associated with harsh and nonsupportive parenting.

D. People with borderline personality disorder vacillate between "all good" and "all bad" evaluations of themselves and others.

E. People with histrionic and narcissistic personality disorders act in flamboyant manners. People with histrionic personality disorder are overly dependent and solicitious of others, whereas people with narcissistic personality disorder are dismissive of others.

F. None of these personality disorders responds consistently well to current treatments.

IV. The anxious-fearful personality disorders

A. People with the anxious-fearful personality disorders—avoidant, dependent, and obsessive-compulsive personality disorders—are chronically fearful or concerned.

B. People with avoidant personality disorder worry about being criticized.

C. People with dependent personality disorder worry about being abandoned.

D. People with obsessive-compulsive personality disorder are locked into rigid routines of behavior and become anxious when their routines are violated.

E. Some children may be born with temperamental predispositions toward shy and avoidant behaviors, or childhood anxiety may contribute to dependent personalities.

F. These disorders may also arise from lack of nurturing parenting and basic fears about one's ability to function competently.

V. Alternative conceptualizations of personality disorders

A. The DSM-IV scheme for classifying personality disorders has been criticized because it is atheoretical.

B. The five-factor model posits that personality is organized along five broad dimensions: neuroticism, extraversion, openness to experience, agreeableness, and conscientiousness.

C. The interpersonal circumplex model posits that personality can be captured by two primary dimensions: dominance vs. submission, and nurturance vs. cold-heartedness.

KEY TERMS AND GUIDED REVIEW

Key Terms

personality (p. 404):

personality trait (p. 404):

Defining and Diagnosing Personality Disorders

<u>Key Terms</u>

personality disorder (p. 404):

<u>Guided Review</u>

1. Describe some ways in which personality disorders differ from Axis I disorders. (p. 404)

2. What are the three clusters of personality disorders? (p. 404)

3. What are some of the criticisms of the DSM conceptualization of personality disorders? (p. 405)

4. Describe some of the problems with and proposed solutions to the alleged gender bias in DSM criteria for personality disorders. (pp. 405-409)

The Odd-Eccentric Personality Disorders

<u>Key Terms</u>

odd-eccentric personality disorders (p. 409):

paranoid personality disorder (p. 409):

schizoid personality disorder (p. 411):

schizotypal personality disorder (p. 411):

<u>Guided Review</u>

1. What are some characteristics of people with paranoid personality disorder? (pp. 409-410)

2. How do psychoanalytic and cognitive theories attempt to explain paranoid personality disorder? (p. 410)

3. Describe some techniques used to treat paranoid personality disorder. (pp. 410-411)

4. What are some characteristics of people with schizoid personality disorder? (pp. 411-412)

5. How do psychoanalytic and cognitive theories attempt to explain schizoid personality disorder? (p. 412)

6. What are some techniques used to treat schizoid personality disorder? (p. 412)

7. Describe the oddities in cognition found in people with schizotypal personality disorder. (pp. 412-413)

8. What are some biological abnormalities found in people with schizotypal personality disorder? (p. 414)

9. What are some techniques used to treat schizotypal personality disorder? (p. 414)

The Dramatic-Emotional Personality Disorders

Key Terms

dramatic-emotional personality disorders (p. 415):

antisocial personality disorder (p. 415):

serotonin (p. 418):

executive functions (p. 419):

borderline personality disorder (p. 421):

splitting (p. 423):

histrionic personality disorder (p. 426):

narcissistic personality disorder (p. 427):

Guided Review

1. What are some characteristics of people with antisocial personality disorder? (pp. 415-418)

2. What is the evidence that genetics influence antisocial behavior? (p. 418)

3. What kinds of deficits do people with antisocial personality disorder exhibit? (pp. 418-419)

4. How does arousal level appear to relate to antisocial behavior? (p. 419)

5. What are some contributors to domestic violence? (p. 420)

6. Why are people with antisocial personality disorder difficult to treat? (p. 420)

7. What are some characteristics of people with borderline personality disorder? (pp. 421-422)

8. What other conditions tend to be associated with borderline personality disorder? (p. 422)

9. Describe the object relations theory and Linehan's theory of borderline personality disorder. (pp. 422-423)

10. Describe some techniques used to treat borderline personality disorder. (pp. 423-425)

11. What are some characteristics of people with histrionic personality disorder? (p. 426)

12. Summarize the theories of histrionic personality disorder. (pp. 426-427)

13. What are some techniques used to treat histrionic personality disorder? (p. 427)

14. What are some characteristics of people with narcissistic personality disorder? (pp. 427-428)

15. Summarize the theories of and treatments for narcissistic personality disorder. (p. 428)

16. How do the dramatic-emotional personality disorders vary by gender? (pp. 415-428)

The Anxious-Fearful Personality Disorders

Key Terms

anxious-fearful personality disorders (p. 428):

avoidant personality disorder (p. 429):

dependent personality disorder (p. 430):

obsessive-compulsive personality disorder (p. 432):

Guided Review

1. What are some characteristics of people with avoidant personality disorder? (pp. 429-430)

2. Describe the theories of and treatments for avoidant personality disorder. (p. 430)

3. What are some characteristics of people with dependent personality disorder? (pp. 430-431)

4. Describe the theories of and treatments for dependent personality disorder. (pp. 431-432)

5. What are some characteristics of people with obsessive-compulsive personality disorder? (pp. 432-433)

6. Describe the theories of and treatments for obsessive-compulsive personality disorder. (p. 433)

Alternative Conceptualizations of Personality Disorders

Key Terms

five-factor model (p. 434):

interpersonal circumplex model (p. 435):

Guided Review

1. What is the five-factor model and how might it improve the classification of personality disorders? (pp. 434-435)

2. Describe the interpersonal circumplex model. (pp. 435-436)

3. What is the difference between a dimensional and categorical model of personality disorders? What are some advantages and disadvantages of each? (pp. 435-436)

CASE EXAMPLE
Read the following description and answer the questions below:

Horace had lost his job at the post office because he often did not show up for work and when he was at work, he was often unable to complete the tasks he was assigned. He was distressed over his job loss and sought help at a community mental health center.

At the initial interview, Horace was distant and somewhat distrustful of the interviewer. He mentioned that he had few friends. He also did not have a good relationship with his family, and spent long hours thinking angry thoughts about his brother, but then worrying that these thoughts would somehow actually cause harm to his brother.

Horace had a lot on his mind. He told the interviewer he had spent an hour and a half at the pet store debating which dog food to buy, and described in great, irrelevant detail the relative merits of the different brands. He also said he had spent two days studying the washing instructions on a new pair of pants. He wondered whether "wash before wearing" meant that the jeans were to be washed before wearing the first time, or did they need to be washed each time before they were worn. He felt that this question was of great importance, both to him and to the interviewer. Horace also described how he often bought several different brands of the same item, such as different kinds of can openers, and then would keep them in their original bags in his closet, expecting that at some future time he would find them useful. He was usually reluctant to spend money on things that he actually needed, however, even though he had plenty of money. He could recite from memory his most recent monthly bank statement, including the amount of every check and the running balance as each check was written. He knew his balance on any particular day, but sometimes got anxious if he considered whether a certain check or deposit had actually cleared.

He asked the interviewer whether he might be asked to participate in groups if he were to receive counseling. He said that groups made him nervous. He was afraid that he might reveal too much information about himself, which group members would then use to take advantage of him. (Adapted from Spitzer, Gibbon, Skodol, Williams, and First, 1994, pp. 289-290).

1. This person has symptoms that suggest three possible personality disorder diagnoses. What are these symptoms and what are the three possible diagnoses?

2. Which of these three diagnoses do you think best fits this person, and why?

3. Some of this person's thought patterns sound like obsessions. Are they obsessions? Why or why not?

CHAPTER TEST

A. <u>Multiple Choice</u>. Choose the **best answer** to each question below.

1. Personality disorders:

    A. Must be present continuously since childhood.
    B. Are diagnosed in people who meet criteria for more than one of them in the majority of cases.
    C. Are listed on Axis III.
    D. Are more likely to cause people to seek treatment than are acute disorders.

2. All of the following are odd-eccentric personality disorders <u>except</u>:

    A. Avoidant personality disorder.
    B. Schizotypal personality disorder.
    C. Schizoid personality disorder.
    D. Paranoid personality disorder.

3. All of the following are criticisms of the DSM's conceptualization of personality disorders <u>except</u>:

    A. The DSM diagnostic criteria for the personality disorders overlap to a large extent.
    B. The DSM diagnostic criteria for the personality disorders are gender-biased.
    C. The DSM wrongly uses a dimensional classification system for personality disorders.
    D. The DSM's personality disorder criteria have low reliability.

4. Women are more likely than men to be diagnosed with all of the following <u>except</u>:

    A. Histrionic personality disorder.
    B. Borderline personality disorder.
    C. Dependent personality disorder.
    D. Avoidant personality disorder.

5. Psychoanalytic theorists argue that _____ personality disorder results from a person's need to deny his or her true feelings about others and project those feelings onto others.

    A. paranoid
    B. narcissistic
    C. antisocial
    D. avoidant

6. People with _____ personality disorder lack any desire to form interpersonal relationships and are emotionally cold in interactions with others. They view relationships with others as unrewarding, messy, and intrusive.

    A. obsessive-compulsive
    B. avoidant
    C. schizoid
    D. schizotypal

7. All of the following are cognitive oddities in people with schizotypal personality disorder except:

    A. Ideas of reference.
    B. Hallucinations.
    C. Tangential, circumstantial, or vague speech.
    D. Magical thinking.

8. All of the following are abnormalities found in both schizophrenia and schizotypal personality disorder except:

    A. Deficits in sustained attention.
    B. Abnormally high levels of dopamine.
    C. Enlarged ventricles.
    D. Low levels of homovanillic acid.

9. All of the following are dramatic-emotional personality disorders except:

    A. Borderline personality disorder.
    B. Antisocial personality disorder.
    C. Dependent personality disorder.
    D. Narcissistic personality disorder.

10. _____ personality disorder is thought to be characterized by high levels of arousal, whereas _____ personality disorder is thought to be characterized by low levels of arousal.

    A. Dependent; antisocial
    B. Avoidant; schizoid
    C. Borderline; obsessive-compulsive
    D. Avoidant; antisocial

11. People with antisocial personality disorder exhibit all of the following except:

    A. Deficits in the parietal lobes of the brain.
    B. Poor impulse control.
    C. Deficits in executive functions.
    D. Difficulty inhibiting impulsive behaviors.

12. People with _____ personality disorder tend to see themselves and other people as either "all good" or "all bad" -- a process known as splitting.

    A. antisocial
    B. borderline
    C. paranoid
    D. narcissistic

13. The most striking gender difference among the personality disorders appears in _____ personality disorder: men are five times more likely to be diagnosed with it than females.

    A. schizotypal
    B. antisocial
    C. obsessive-compulsive
    D. narcissistic

14. People with _____ are heavy users of mental health services, in contrast to people with other personality disorders.

    A. borderline
    B. antisocial
    C. avoidant
    D. narcissistic

15. Both _____ and _____ personality disorders are correlated with low levels of serotonin.

    A. avoidant; dependent
    B. paranoid; antisocial
    C. antisocial; borderline
    D. obsessive-compulsive; avoidant

16. Psychodynamic theorists view _____ personality disorder as the result of deep dependency needs and repression of emotions, stemming from poor resolution of either the oral or Oedipal stage.

    A. schizoid
    B. narcissistic
    C. histrionic
    D. obsessive-compulsive

17. People with avoidant personality disorder:

    A. Have a pervasive but unwarranted mistrust of others.
    B. Lack any desire to form interpersonal relationships.
    C. Tend to have relatives with schizophrenia.
    D. Are just as likely to be male as female.

18. Men are more likely than women to be diagnosed with all of the following except:

    A. Paranoid personality disorder.
    B. Antisocial personality disorder.
    C. Histrionic personality disorder.
    D. Obsessive-compulsive personality disorder.

19. Individuals low on _____ are cynical, rude, suspicious, uncooperative, and irritable.

    A. Conscientiousness
    B. Agreeableness
    C. Extraversion
    D. Openness to experience

20. The interpersonal circumplex model classifies personality along two dimensions, one of which is:

    A. Introversion - extraversion.
    B. Dominance - submission.
    C. Agreeableness - unagreeableness.
    D. Nurturance - schizoid.

B. <u>True-False</u>. Select T (True) or F (False) below.

1. When clinicians use structured interviews rather than unstructured interviews, they tend to find that women are more often diagnosed with histrionic, borderline, and dependent personality disorders, whereas men are more often diagnosed with antisocial personality disorder.
     T   F

2. People with schizotypal personality disorder view others as deceitful and hostile, and much of their social anxiety emerges from this paranoia.   T   F

3. There is strong, consistent evidence that testosterone plays a role in antisocial behavior.
     T   F

4. Gottman has found that male batterers who are especially violent tend to have lower heart rates during arguments compared to less violent men.   T   F

5. The relatives of people with borderline personality disorder have high rates of mood disorders.
     T   F

C. <u>Short Answer</u>.

1. What are some of the criticisms of the DSM approach to classifying personality disorders? Give an example of an alternative classification system.

2. Describe Linehan's dialectical behavior therapy for borderline personality disorder.

3. Which personality disorders appear to be related to schizophrenia? Explain the ways in which these disorders are similar to and different from schizophrenia.

4. Why do some theorists believe that the DSM personality disorder criteria are gender-biased? What are some ways in which this bias might be reduced?

5. Give examples of how some of the personality disorders described in the chapter may be somewhat adaptive in certain cultures.

ANSWER KEY

<u>Case Example</u>
1. Schizotypal personality disorder: odd beliefs and magical thinking, over-elaborate speaking, paranoia, lack of close friends, social anxiety; schizoid personality disorder: absence of close friends; obsessive-compulsive personality disorder: obsessional thoughts and compulsive behaviors about purchases.
2. Meets all criteria for schizotypal personality disorder, but not for other two.
3. Probably not obsessions because they are ego-syntonic.

<u>Multiple Choice</u>
1. B
2. A
3. C
4. D
5. A
6. C
7. B
8. D
9. C
10. D
11. A
12. B
13. B
14. A
15. C
16. C
17. D
18. C
19. B
20. B

<u>True-False</u>
1. T
2. T
3. F
4. T
5. T

Short Answer
1. See pp. 405, 434-436.
2. See p. 425.
3. See pp. 410-414.
4. See pp. 405-409.
5. See pp. 427-428, 432-433.

Additional Readings on Chapter 12 Topics

Davis, R. D. (1999). Millon: Essentials of his science, theory, classification, assessment, and theory. Journal of Personality Assessment, 72, 330-352.

Huprich, S. K. (1998). Depressive personality disorder: Theoretical issues, clinical findings, and future research questions. Clinical Psychology Review, 18, 477-500.*

Shearin, E. N., & Linehan, M. M. (1994). Dialectical behavior therapy for borderline personality disorder: Theoretical and empirical foundations. Acta Psychiatrica Scandinavica, 89, 61-68.

* Note that depressive personality disorder is not included among the personality disorders in DSM-IV, but is listed instead under "Criteria sets and axes provided for further study."

Chapter 13: Childhood Disorders

LEARNING OBJECTIVES
After reading and studying this chapter, you should be able to:

1. Identify the symptoms of attention-deficit/hyperactivity disorder (ADHD), describe how it affects a child's social and intellectual functioning, and discuss how it affects children as they enter adolescence and adulthood.

2. Discuss the genetic and neurological contributors to ADHD, and the other psychopathological conditions associated with ADHD.

3. Describe the drug and psychosocial therapies for ADHD.

4. Discuss the similarities and differences between conduct disorder, oppositional defiant disorder, and ADHD.

5. Discuss the symptoms and course of conduct disorder and oppositional defiant disorder.

6. Describe the biological and psychosocial contributors to conduct disorder and oppositional defiant disorder.

7. Describe the drug therapies and psychotherapies used to treat conduct and oppositional defiant disorder.

8. Identify the symptoms of separation anxiety disorder and how separation anxiety is related to panic disorder.

9. Discuss the genetic factors and parenting practices that may lead to separation anxiety disorder.

10. Discuss ways to treat separation anxiety disorder.

11. Identify the diagnostic criteria for enuresis and encopresis, the genetic, psychodynamic, and behavioral theories of enuresis, and the most effective treatment for enuresis.

12. Identify the types of developmental disorders that affect only specific skills.

13. Discuss what is required for a diagnosis of mental retardation, the difference between organic and cultural-familial mental retardation, and how the symptoms of the disorder vary in severity from mild to moderate to severe to profound.

14. Discuss and distinguish among the numerous diseases, maternal behaviors, and aspects of pregnancy and birth that can lead to mental retardation.

15. Discuss the sociocultural factors that may contribute to mental retardation.

16. Describe some of the effective interventions for mental retardation.

17. Describe the deficits exhibited by autistic children.

18. Discuss the genetic and biological causes of autism.

19. Discuss the drugs used to treat the symptoms of autism, and the behavioral methods used to treat autistic children.

ESSENTIAL IDEAS

I. Behavior disorders

    A. The behavior disorders include attention deficit/hyperactivity disorder, conduct disorder, and oppositional defiant disorder.

    B. Children with attention deficit/hyperactivity disorder are inattentive, impulsive, and overactive. They often do not do well in school, and their relationships with their peers are extremely impaired.

    C. Many children with attention deficit/hyperactivity disorder grow out of this disorder, but some continue to show the symptoms into adulthood, and they are at high risk for conduct problems and emotional problems throughout their lives.

    D. The two therapies that are effective in treating ADHD are stimulant drugs and behavioral therapies that teach children how to control their behaviors.

    E. Children with conduct disorder engage in behaviors that severely violate societal norms, including chronic lying, stealing, and violence toward others.

    F. Children with oppositional defiant disorder engage in less-severe antisocial behaviors that indicate a negativistic, irritable approach to others.

    G. Some children outgrow oppositional defiant disorder, but a subset develop full conduct disorder.

    H. Children who develop conduct disorder often continue to engage in antisocial behaviors into adulthood and have high rates of criminal activity and drug abuse.

    I. Neurological deficits may be involved in conduct disorder. These deficits may make it more difficult for children with this disorder to learn from reinforcements and punishments and to control their behaviors.

    J. Children with conduct disorder also tend to have parents that are neglectful much of the time and violent when annoyed with them.

K. Children with conduct disorder tend to think about interactions with others in ways that contribute to their aggressive reactions.

II. Separation anxiety disorder

A. Children can suffer from all the emotional disorders, including depression and all the anxiety disorders. Separation anxiety disorder is one disorder specific to children.

B. Children with separation anxiety disorder are excessively fearful about separation from primary caregivers. They may become extremely agitated or ill when they anticipate separation, and curtail usual activities to avoid separation.

C. Separation anxiety disorder may be inherited as part of a larger predisposition to anxiety disorders, particularly panic attacks.

D. Children who are behaviorally inhibited as infants appear at risk for separation anxiety disorder as adults.

E. Parents may enhance a vulnerability to separation anxiety disorder by their reactions to children's distress.

F. Cognitive-behavioral therapies can help children with separation anxiety disorder quiet their anxieties and resume everyday activities.

III. Elimination disorders

A. Enuresis is persistent uncontrolled wetting by children who have previously attained bladder control.

B. Enuresis runs in families and has been attributed to a variety of biological mechanisms. Psychodynamic theories attribute it to emotional distress. Behavioral theories attribute it to poor toilet training.

C. Antidepressants help to reduce enuresis in the short term, but not in the long term, and carry significant side effects.

D. Behavioral methods that help the child learn to awaken and go to the bathroom can help to reduce nighttime enuresis.

E. Encopresis is persistent uncontrolled soiling by children who have previously attained control of defecation.

G. Encopresis typically begins after one or more episodes of constipation, which create distention in the colon and decrease a child's ability to detect needed bowel movements.

H. Medical management and behavioral techniques can help reduce encopresis.

IV. Disorders of cognitive, motor, and social skills

A. Disorders of cognitive, motor, and communication skills include the learning disorders, motor skills disorder, and communication disorders.

B. Learning disorders include reading disorder (inability to read, also known as dyslexia), mathematics disorder (inability to learn math), and disorder of written expression (inability to write).

C. The motor skills disorder is developmental coordination disorder, which involves deficits in fundamental motor skills.

D. Communication disorders include expressive language disorder (inability to express oneself through language), mixed receptive-expressive language disorder (inability to express oneself through language or to understand the language of others), phonological disorder (use of speech sounds inappropriate for the age and dialect), and stuttering (deficits in word fluency).

E. Some of these disorders, particularly reading disorder and stuttering, may have genetic roots. Many other factors have been implicated in these disorders, but they are not well-understood.

F. Treatment usually focuses on building skills in problem areas through specialized training, and now the use of computerized exercises.

V. Mental retardation

A. Mental retardation is defined as subaverage intellectual functioning, indexed by an IQ score of under 70 and deficits in adaptive behavioral functioning.

B. There are four levels of mental retardation, ranging from mild to profound.

C. A number of biological factors are implicated in mental retardation, including metabolic disorders (PKU, Tay-Sachs disease); chromosomal disorders (Down syndrome, Fragile X, Trisomy 13, and Trisomy 18); prenatal exposure to rubella, herpes, syphilis, or illicit drugs (especially alcohol); premature delivery; and head traumas (such as those arising from being violently shaken).

D. There is some evidence that intensive and comprehensive educational interventions, administered very early in an affected child's life, can help to decrease the level of mental retardation.

E. Controversy exists over whether mentally retarded children should be put in special education classes with other mentally retarded children or mainstreamed into normal classrooms.

VI. Autism

A. The pervasive developmental disorders are characterized by severe and lasting impairment in several areas of development, including social interactions, communication with others, everyday behaviors, interests, and activities. They include Asperger's disorder, Rett's disorder, childhood disintegrative disorder, and autism.

B. Autism is characterized by significant interpersonal, communication, and behavioral deficits.

C. Two-thirds of autistic children score in the mentally retarded range on IQ tests.

D. There is wide variation in the outcome of autism, although the majority of autistic children must have continual care as adults. The best predictors of a good outcome in autism are an IQ above 50 and language development before the age of 6.

E. Biological causes of autism may include a genetic predisposition to cognitive impairment, central nervous system damage, prenatal complications, and neurotransmitter imbalances.

F. Drugs reduce some behaviors in autism but do not eliminate the core of the disorder.

G. Behavioral therapy is used to reduce inappropriate and self-injurious behaviors and to encourage prosocial behaviors in autistic children.

KEY TERMS AND GUIDED REVIEW

Guided Review

1. What are some characteristics of children who develop psychological problems, as opposed to those who do not? (pp. 442-443)

Behavior Disorders

Key Terms

attention deficit/hyperactivity disorder (p. 444):

conduct disorder (p. 446):

oppositional defiant disorder (p. 450):

1. What are some problems that children with ADHD tend to have in addition to the ADHD itself? (p. 446)

2. How common is ADHD? How do the rates of ADHD vary by gender and culture? (pp. 446-448)

3. Does ADHD persist into adulthood? What are some problems experienced by adults who had ADHD as children? (p. 448)

4. What are some arguments for and against the claim that ADHD is a "fad diagnosis"? (pp. 446-447)

5. What brain areas are most likely to be involved in ADHD? (p. 448)

6. What conditions tend to run in the families of children who develop ADHD? (p. 448)

7. What pregnancy-related factors are associated with ADHD? (p. 448)

8. Describe the effective treatments for ADHD. (pp. 448-449)

9. What are some characteristics of children with conduct disorder? (pp. 449-451)

10. What are some problems experienced by adults who had conduct disorder as children? (p. 451)

11. How does oppositional defiant disorder differ from conduct disorder? (pp. 450-451)

12. How do the rates and presentation of conduct disorder differ by gender? (p. 451)

13. What are some biological contributors to conduct and oppositional defiant disorder? (pp. 451-452)

14. What are some sociocultural contributors to conduct and oppositional defiant disorder? (pp. 452-453)

15. Describe how children with conduct disorder tend to process information about social interactions. (p. 453)

16. What drug and psychological therapies appear to be effective for children with conduct disorder? (pp. 453-456)

Separation Anxiety Disorder

Key Terms

separation anxiety disorder (p. 457):

Guided Review

1. What are the symptoms of separation anxiety disorder? (p. 457)

2. What is behavioral inhibition, and how does it relate to separation anxiety disorder? (p. 458)

3. What is the evidence that parents and the ability to control one's environment may contribute to separation anxiety disorder? (pp. 458-459)

4. Describe how separation anxiety may be effectively treated. (pp. 459-460)

Elimination Disorders

Key Terms

elimination disorders (p. 462):

enuresis (p. 462):

encopresis (p. 464):

1. What is enuresis? How common is it? (pp. 462-463)

2. What are some biological, psychodynamic, and behavioral contributors to enuresis? (p. 463)

3. What treatments are available for enuresis? (pp. 463-464)

4. What is encopresis? How common is it? (p. 464)

5. Describe how encopresis may be effectively treated. (p. 464)

Disorders of Cognitive, Motor, and Social Skills

Key Terms

learning disorders (p. 465):

reading disorder (p. 465):

mathematics disorder (p. 465):

disorder of written expression (p. 465):

motor skills disorder (p. 465):

developmental coordination disorder (p. 465):

communication disorders (p. 466):

expressive language disorder (p. 466):

mixed receptive-expressive language disorder (p. 466):

phonological disorder (p. 466):

stuttering (p. 466):

Guided Review

1. Under what conditions are learning disorders diagnosed? (p. 465)

2. What are the symptoms of developmental coordination disorder? (pp. 465-466)

3. How are expressive language disorder, mixed receptive-expressive language disorder, phonological disorder, and stuttering similar to and different from one another? (p. 466)

Mental Retardation

Key Terms

mental retardation (p. 467):

phenylketonuria (PKU) (p. 468):

Tay-Sachs disease (p. 468):

Down syndrome (p. 468):

Fragile X syndrome (p. 470):

Trisomy 13 (p. 470):

Trisomy 18 (p. 470):

fetal alcohol syndrome (p. 470):

shaken baby syndrome (p. 471):

Guided Review

1. What are the diagnostic criteria for mental retardation? (pp. 467-468)

2. What are the differences among mild, moderate, severe, and profound mental retardation? (pp. 467-468)

3. Describe some of the genetic conditions that can cause mental retardation. (pp. 468-470)

4. Describe some of the prenatal contributors to mental retardation. (pp. 470-471)

5. What are some consequences of shaking a baby? (p. 471)

6. What are some sociocultural contributors to mental retardation? (pp. 471-472)

7. What behavioral and drug therapies appear to be helpful for mentally retarded children? (p. 472)

8. Describe the Infant Health and Development Program. Was it effective, and if so, why? (p. 473)

9. What are some alternatives to drug or behavior therapy for mentally retarded people? (pp. 473-474)

Autism

Key Terms

pervasive developmental disorders (p. 474):

Asperger's disorder (p. 474):

Rett's disorder (p. 474):

childhood disintegrative disorder (p. 474):

Guided Review

1. What are the symptoms of autism? (pp. 474-477)

2. Describe the course of autism and the factors associated with better outcomes. (p. 477)

3. Describe how parenting and theory of mind relate to autism. (pp. 477-480)

4. What are some biological contributors to autism? (p. 481)

5. Describe some of the treatments that help treat children with autism. (pp. 481-482)

CASE EXAMPLE

Read the following description and answer the questions below:

Karen is a difficult child. At school, she rarely listens to her teacher and often gets up from her chair and wanders around the classroom. When her teacher reprimands her for this, Karen either blatantly ignores the teacher, or says something "smart" to the teacher, such as, "I'm too bored to sit in my seat." Even when she sits in her seat, Karen often disrupts the other children, talking loudly at them when they are trying to concentrate, sometimes insulting them. Karen doesn't finish her own school assignments most of the time. After just a few minutes working on an assignment, Karen declares that it is "stupid" and gets out of her seat to find something more interesting to do. On the playground, few children want to play with Karen because she throws temper tantrums if she doesn't get to do things exactly her way.

At home, Karen frequently disobeys her parents, even though she is punished harshly when she is caught disobeying. Karen is prone to dangerous activities -- one night she crawled out her bedroom window onto the roof of her house, "just because I wanted to." If siblings annoy her, Karen is prone to hitting them, even the brother who is much older and bigger than her. This brother tends to taunt Karen, calling her dumb because she doesn't do well in school. When Karen strikes this brother, he hits her back. He has given her a black eye twice.

1. What two diagnoses may fit Karen's symptoms? Can Karen be given both of these diagnoses?

2. List the symptoms of each of these disorders that Karen shows.

3. What family factors may contribute to Karen's behavior?

CHAPTER TEST

A. <u>Multiple Choice</u>. Choose the **best answer** to each question below.

1. All of the following are classified as pervasive developmental disorders <u>except</u>:

    A. Autism.
    B. Asperger's disorder.
    C. Selective mutism.
    D. Childhood disintegrative disorder.

2. The symptoms of ADHD fall into all of the following categories <u>except</u>:

    A. Inattention.
    B. Defiance.
    C. Impulsivity.
    D. Hyperactivity.

3. Boys are more likely than girls to develop all of the following <u>except</u>:

    A. Separation anxiety disorder.
    B. Encopresis.
    C. ADHD.
    D. Autism.

4. Which of the following brain areas has been implicated in ADHD?

    A. The occipital lobes.
    B. The thalamus.
    C. The frontal lobes.
    D. The hippocampus.

5. Which of the following has not been found to predispose children to ADHD?

    A. Premature delivery.
    B. Consumption of large amounts of sugar.
    C. Maternal nicotine consumption.
    D. Exposure to high concentrations of lead.

6. Which of the following statements about differences between conduct and oppositional defiant disorder is <u>false</u>?

    A. Conduct disorder is more severe than oppositional defiant disorder.
    B. Boys are three times more likely than girls to develop conduct disorder, but the rates of oppositional defiant disorder do not differ by gender.
    C. Twins studies suggest that both conduct and oppositional defiant disorder are influenced by genetics.
    D. Oppositional defiant disorder is diagnosed at an earlier age than conduct disorder.

7. All of the following are associated with conduct and oppositional defiant disorder <u>except</u>:

    A. Lower levels of adrenaline.
    B. ADHD.
    C. Maternal exposure to toxins during pregnancy.
    D. Living in a rural area.

8. Henry has been having problems in school lately. When his gym teacher told him to do 20 push-ups because he called another child a "sissy," Henry blew up and argued with his gym teacher. His teachers say that at times, Henry refuses to pay attention to them. At home, Henry often steals his sister's toys and hides them just to annoy her. He is very jealous of his sister, and pouts whenever she does well at something, calling her "the favorite child." Henry's problems are most consistent with a diagnosis of:

    A. ADHD.
    B. Oppositional defiant disorder.
    C. Conduct disorder.
    D. Separation anxiety disorder.

9. All of the following are symptoms of separation anxiety disorder <u>except</u>:

    A. Persistent and excessive worry about losing, or harm coming to, caregivers.
    B. Excessively fearful about being alone.
    C. Repeated nightmares involving themes of separation.
    D. Excessive sleeping when caregivers are not present.

10. Which of the following is <u>not</u> associated with separation anxiety disorder?

    A. A family history of panic attacks.
    B. Behavioral disinhibition.
    C. Having a family that is close-knit and does not encourage independence.
    D. Exposure to traumatic events.

11. Encopresis:

    A. Must occur at least twice a week for 3 months to be diagnosed.
    B. May be effectively treated with the bell and pad method.
    C. Is less common than enuresis.
    D. Tends to run in families.

12. Dyslexia is a term often used to refer to:

    A. Reading disorder.
    B. Receptive language disorder.
    C. Phonological disorder.
    D. Disorder of reading comprehension.

13. Which of the following disorders is least common?

    A. Reading disorder.
    B. Developmental coordination disorder.
    C. Expressive language disorder.
    D. Mathematics disorder.

14. Children with _____ mental retardation have very limited vocabularies, speak in two-to-three-word sentences, and have IQ scores between 20 and 35.

    A. mild
    B. moderate
    C. severe
    D. profound

15. Which of the following childhood diseases resembles Alzheimer's disease in that both consist of tangles and plaques on neurons in the brain as well as memory loss and an inability to care for oneself?

    A. Trisomy 21.
    B. Fragile X syndrome.
    C. Phenylketonuria.
    D. Fetal alcohol syndrome.

16. A disorder marked by deficits in social interactions and in activities and interests, but not in language or basic cognitive skills, is known as:

    A. Autism.
    B. Rett's disorder.
    C. Asperger's disorder.
    D. Childhood disintegrative disorder.

17. All of the following characterize organic mental retardation, but not cultural-familial mental retardation, except:

    A. It is typically diagnosed in infancy.
    B. It occurs in lower socioeconomic groups.
    C. Physical health is poorer than in the general population.
    D. Impairments are generalized across situations.

18. Which of the following childhood diseases is the most common cause of mental retardation?

    A. Trisomy 21.
    B. Fragile X syndrome.
    C. Trisomy 18.
    D. Phenylketonuria.

19. All of the following are groups of deficits in autism except:

    A. Activities and Interests.
    B. Communication.
    C. Social Interactions.
    D. Inattention.

20. The best predictors of outcome in autism are:

    A. The child's IQ and language development before age 6.
    B. The child's capacity to reach developmental milestones on time.
    C. The child's capacity for nonverbal communication.
    D. The quality of parenting the child receives.

B. True-False. Select T (True) or F (False) below.

1. Most children with ADHD have a history of brain injury.   T   F

2. All of the childhood disorders described in this chapter are more common in boys than in girls.
    T   F

3. When a child obtains an IQ score less than 70, he or she meets criteria for mental retardation.
    T   F

4. In Down syndrome, chromosome 21 is present in triplicate rather than in duplicate.
    T   F

5. The majority of children with autism go on to develop schizophrenia as adults.   T   F

C. <u>Short Answer</u>.

1. Describe how cognitive-behavioral techniques may be used to treat conduct disorder.

2. What are some ways in which ADHD and conduct disorder are related?

3. Describe some of the methods used to treat mental retardation.

4. What are some of the biological contributors to conduct disorder?

5. Present arguments for and against the claim that ADHD is a "fad diagnosis."

ANSWER KEY

Case Example

1. Attention deficit disorder and oppositional defiant disorder. Yes, Karen can be given both of these diagnoses.

2. ADHD: not listening to the teacher, getting up and walking around class, difficulty being quiet in class, disrupting the other children, temper tantrums, dangerous impulsive behaviors like going out on the roof and striking a larger brother. Oppositional defiant disorder: chronically defies teacher and parents, deliberately annoys other children and siblings, easily annoyed, often loses temper, argues with adults.

3. Use of harsh punishment by parents, modeling of aggressive behaviors by brother.

Multiple Choice

1. C
2. B
3. A
4. C
5. B
6. B
7. D
8. B
9. D
10. B
11. C
12. A
13. D
14. C
15. A
16. C
17. B
18. A
19. D
20. A

True-False

1. F
2. F
3. F (Importantly, this is not the only criterion for mental retardation)
4. T
5. F

Short Answer
1. See pp. 455-456.
2. See pp. 444-457.
3. See pp. 472-474.
4. See pp. 451-452.
5. See pp. 446-448.

Additional Readings on Chapter 13 Topics

Gaub, M., & Carlson, C. L. (1997). Gender differences in ADHD: A meta-analysis and critical review. Journal of the American Academy of Child and Adolescent Psychiatry, 36, 1036-1045.

McEachin, J. J., Smith, T., & Lovaas, O. I. (1993). Long-term outcome for children with autism who received early intensive behavioral treatment. American Journal on Mental Retardation, 97, 359-372.

Moffitt, T. E. (1993). The neuropsychology of conduct disorder. Development and Psychopathology, 5, 135-151.

Chapter 14: Eating Disorders

LEARNING OBJECTIVES

After reading and studying this chapter, you should be able to:

1. Discuss the societal pressures on people (especially women) to maintain a slim appearance, and the behaviors people engage in to meet these expectations.

2. Discuss the key symptoms of anorexia nervosa, and distinguish between the restricting and binge-purge type.

3. Discuss the prevalence of anorexia and its associated health risks.

4. Discuss the contributions of Sir William Gull and Charles Lasegue to our understanding of anorexia.

5. Discuss the key symptoms of bulimia nervosa, and distinguish between the purging and nonpurging type.

6. Discuss the prevalence of bulimia and its associated health risks.

7. Identify the similarities and differences between anorexia and bulimia.

8. Discuss binge-eating disorder and how it differs from anorexia and bulimia.

9. Discuss the physiological and emotional effects of dieting, and how dieting may lead to both anorexia and bulimia.

10. Discuss the gender similarities and differences in the eating disorders.

11. Discuss the cross-cultural differences in the eating disorders.

12. Summarize the theories of Hilda Bruch and Salvador Minuchin.

13. Discuss the proposed explanations for why girls are at an increased risk for eating disorders compared to boys.

14. Discuss the argument that eating disorders result from sexual abuse, and summarize what the evidence suggests about this idea.

15. Discuss the evidence that genetic factors contribute to the development of eating disorders.

16. Discuss the link between eating disorders and mood disorders.

17. Discuss the biological abnormalities in anorexia and bulimia.

18. Discuss the difficulties faced by therapists who treat anorexic clients, and the ingredients of effective therapy for anorexia.

19. Discuss interpersonal, supportive-expressive, cognitive-behavioral, and behavioral therapies for bulimia, and their respective efficacy.

20. Describe how efficacious or inefficacious tricyclic antidepressants, MAO inhibitors, and selective serotonin reuptake inhibitors are for treating anorexia and bulimia.

ESSENTIAL IDEAS

I. Anorexia nervosa

    A. Anorexia nervosa is characterized by self-starvation, a distorted body image, intense fears of becoming fat, and amenorrhea.

    B. People with the restricting type refuse to eat in order to prevent weight gain.

    C. People with the binge/purge type periodically engage in binging and then purge to prevent weight gain.

    D. The lifetime prevalence of anorexia is about 1%, with 90 to 95% of cases being female.

    E. Anorexia usually begins in adolescence, and the course is variable from one person to another.

    F. It is a very dangerous disorder, and the death rate among anorexics is 15%.

    G. There may be cultural differences in the manifestation of anorexia nervosa.

II. Bulimia nervosa

    A. Bulimia nervosa is characterized by uncontrolled binging followed by behaviors designed to prevent weight gain from the binges.

    B. People with the purging type use self-induced vomiting, diuretics, or laxatives to prevent weight gain.

    C. People with the nonpurging type use fasting and exercise to prevent weight gain.

    D. The definition of a binge has been controversial, but the DSM-IV specifies that it must involve the consumption of an unusually large amount of food in a short time, and a sense of lack of control.

E. Binge-eating disorder is a provisional category in the DSM-IV. People with this disorder regularly binge eat but do not engage in behaviors to compensate for the binges.

F. Although overconcern with weight and occasional binging is common among college students, the prevalence of the full syndrome of bulimia nervosa is only about 1.0% in women and 0.2% in men.

G. The onset of bulimia nervosa is most often in adolescence, and its course, if left untreated, is unclear.

H. Although people with bulimia nervosa do not tend to be severely underweight, there are a variety of possible medical complications of the disorder.

III. Understanding eating disorders

A. Cultural and societal norms regarding beauty may play a role in the eating disorders. Eating disorders are more common in groups that consider extreme thinness attractive than in groups that consider a heavier weight attractive.

B. Eating disorders develop as a means of gaining some control or coping with negative emotions. In addition, people with eating disorders tend to show rigid, dichotomous thinking.

C. People who develop eating disorders come from families that are overcontrolling and perfectionistic but discourage the expression of negative emotions.

D. People who are so unaware of their own bodily sensations that they can starve themselves may develop anorexia nervosa. People who remain aware of their bodily sensations and cannot starve themselves but who are prone to anxiety and impulsivity may develop binge-eating disorder or bulimia nervosa.

E. Girls may be more likely than boys to develop eating disorders in adolescence because girls are not given as much freedom as boys to develop independence and their own identities.

F. People with eating disorders are more likely than people without eating disorders to have a history of sexual abuse, but a history of sexual abuse is also common among people with several other disorders.

G. There is evidence that both anorexia nervosa and bulimia nervosa are heritable.

H. Depression also runs in the families of people with eating disorders. Many theorists believe that the eating disorders should not be considered just a variant of depression, however.

I. Eating disorders may be tied to dysfunction in the hypothalamus, a part of the brain that helps to regulate eating behavior.

J. Some studies show abnormalities in levels of the neurotransmitters serotonin and norepinephrine in people with eating disorders.

IV. Treatments for eating disorders

A. People with anorexia nervosa often must be hospitalized because they are so emaciated and malnourished that they are in a medical crisis.

B. Behavior therapy for anorexia nervosa involves making rewards contingent upon the client eating. Clients may be taught relaxation techniques to handle their anxiety about eating.

C. Family therapy focuses on understanding the role of anorexic behaviors in the family unit. Therapists challenge parents' attitudes toward their anorexic children's behaviors and try to help the family find more adaptive ways of interacting with each other.

D. Individual therapy for anorexia may focus on helping clients identify and accept their feelings and to confront their distorted cognitions about their bodies.

E. Psychotherapy can be helpful for anorexia but is usually a long process and the risk for relapse is high.

F. Several studies show that cognitive-behavioral therapy, which focuses on the bulimic's distorted cognitions about eating, is effective in the treatment of bulimia.

G. Tricyclic antidepressants and serotonin reuptake inhibitors have been shown to be helpful in the treatment of bulimia. The MAO inhibitors can also be helpful, but are not usually prescribed because they require dietary restrictions to avoid side effects.

H. Antidepressants have not proven as useful in the treatment of anorexia nervosa, but some small studies suggest the serotonin reuptake inhibitors may be helpful.

I. Prevention programs can help to make students more aware of eating disorders and available treatments, but may backfire if the prevention message is not carefully tailored for audiences with different needs.

KEY TERMS AND GUIDED REVIEW

Anorexia Nervosa

<u>Key Terms</u>

anorexia nervosa (p. 492):

amenorrhea (p. 493):

restricting type (p. 493):

binge/purge type (p. 494):

Guided Review

1. What are the symptoms of anorexia nervosa? (pp. 492-493)

2. What are some differences between the restricting and binge/purge types of anorexia nervosa? (pp. 493-495)

3. Describe the prevalence of anorexia nervosa. (p. 495)

4. How does the presentation of anorexia nervosa differ by culture? (pp. 495-496)

5. What are some medical consequences of anorexia nervosa? (p. 495)

Bulimia Nervosa

Key Terms

bulimia nervosa (p. 497):

bingeing (p. 497):

purging type (p. 498):

nonpurging type (p. 498):

binge-eating disorder (p. 499):

Guided Review

1. Describe some of the similarities and differences between anorexia and bulimia nervosa. (p. 497)

2. What are some of the differences between the purging and nonpurging types of bulimia nervosa? (p. 498)

3. What are the symptoms of binge-eating disorder? (pp. 499-500)

4. How common is bulimia nervosa? (pp. 500-501)

5. What are some medical consequences of bulimia? (pp. 501-502)

Understanding Eating Disorders

<u>Key Terms</u>

enmeshed families (p. 510):

hypothalamus (p. 512):

serotonin (p. 513):

norepinephrine (p. 513):

<u>Guided Review</u>

1. What are some of the societal pressures that may contribute to eating disorders? (pp. 502-505)

2. How do the eating disorders differ by socioeconomic status and ethnicity? (p. 505)

3. What psychopathological features characterize people with eating disorders? (pp. 505-510)

4. According to Hilde Bruch, how do family dynamics contribute to eating disorders? (pp. 510-511)

5. According to psychodynamic theorists, why do eating disorders develop during adolescence, and why are they more common among women? (p. 511)

6. What is the relationship between sexual abuse and eating disorders? (pp. 511-512)

7. What is the evidence that eating disorders are influenced by genetics? (p. 512)

8. How are eating disorders related to depression? (p. 512)

9. What are some biological contributors to eating disorders? (pp. 512-513)

Treatments for Eating Disorders

Key Terms

behavior therapy (p. 514):

cognitive-behavioral therapy (p. 516):

interpersonal therapy (p. 516):

supportive-expressive psychodynamic therapy (p. 516):

tricyclic antidepressants (p. 517):

serotonin reuptake inhibitors (p. 517):

Guided Review

1. Why are people with anorexia nervosa often difficult to treat? (pp. 513-514)

2. Describe some of the methods used to treat anorexic clients in individual therapy. (pp. 514-515)

3. Describe how family therapy for anorexia nervosa is conducted. (p. 515)

4. What is the evidence that psychotherapy is effective for anorexia nervosa? What are some of the shortcomings of psychotherapy for this disorder? (p. 515)

5. Describe some cognitive-behavioral techniques used to treat bulimia nervosa. (pp. 515-516)

6. Describe some alternative types of therapy for bulimia nervosa. (pp. 516-517)

7. Which medications appear to be helpful for anorexia and bulimia nervosa? (p. 517)

8. What are some important features of programs designed to prevent eating disorders? (pp. 517-518)

CASE EXAMPLE
Read the following description and answer the questions below:

Tammy's family is just too perfect. Her parents are both very successful lawyers. Her older brother went to West Point and graduated at the top of his class. Her sister is a junior at an Ivy League college, carrying nearly a perfect grade point average, and has a great boyfriend. Tammy, on the other hand, is barely making it through high school, at least in her parents' eyes. She just can't seem to get her grades up to the standards set by her brother and sister. Her parents are constantly annoyed at her for not doing as well as they think she should. They have hired numerous tutors for Tammy, have transfered her to a private school (which she hates), and are constantly asking her about her exams and grades. They forbid her to date or even go out with friends much because they want her to spend all her time working on her grades and on "activities" that will help her get into a prestigious college. Tammy's parents don't have a lot of time for her, however. They both work about 80 hours a week and see Tammy mostly right before she goes to bed and for short periods on the weekend. Tammy seldom complains to her parents, however. She is grateful for any little time she can get with them and doesn't want to spoil that time with conflict.

1. What characteristics of Tammy's family would Hilde Bruch and Salvador Minuchin say put Tammy at risk for an eating disorder?

2. If Tammy does develop an eating disorder, what characteristics of Tammy might determine whether she develops anorexia or bulimia?

CHAPTER TEST

A. <u>Multiple Choice</u>. Choose the **best answer** to each question below.

1. Men who develop eating disorders:

    A. Display different symptoms of eating disorders than women.
    B. Have high rates of comorbid substance abuse (like women), but do not have high rates of comorbid depression.
    C. Are more likely than women to have a history of being overweight.
    D. Are more likely than women to be athletes.

2. All of the following are diagnostic criteria for anorexia nervosa <u>except</u>:

    A. Intense fear of gaining weight or becoming fat.
    B. Absence of at least three menstrual cycles (in women who have reached menarche).
    C. Refusal to maintain body weight at or above a minimally normal weight for one's age and height.
    D. Recurrent inappropriate behaviors to prevent weight gain.

3. Which of the following characterizes the binge/purge type of anorexia nervosa, but not the restricting type?

    A. Sense of lack of control over eating.
    B. Amenorrhea in females.
    C. Severely disturbed body image.
    D. Body weight at least 15% underweight.

4. Which of the following characterizes the binge/purge type of anorexia, but not bulimia nervosa?

    A. Binges, purges, or other compensatory behaviors.
    B. Body weight at least 15% underweight.
    C. Absence of amenorrhea in females.
    D. Sense of lack of control over eating.

5. People with the restricting type of anorexia are more likely than those with the binge/purge type of anorexia:

    A. To have problems with unstable moods.
    B. To have problems controlling their impulses.
    C. To have problems with self-mutilation.
    D. To have a deep mistrust of others and deny they have a problem.

6. The death rate among anoxexics is _____ %.

    A. 5
    B. 15
    C. 25
    D. 30

7. Which of the following is a known difference in the presentation of anorexia nervosa in Asian cultures, compared to American and European cultures?

    A. Asians with anorexia nervosa are more preoccupied with being fat than Americans or Europeans with anorexia.
    B. Asians with anorexia nervosa are more commonly restricted types, whereas more Americans and Europeans are binge/purge types.
    C. Asians with anorexia nervosa do not have the distorted body images that are characteristic of American and European anorexia patients, and will often admit that they are thin.
    D. More men than women have anorexia nervosa in Asian cultures.

8. Who coined the term "anorexia nervosa" and first noted its prevalence among females and tendency to begin in adolescence?

    A. Sir William Gull
    B. Charles Lasegue
    C. Hilde Bruch
    D. Richard Morton

9. People with the binge/purge type of anorexia differ from people with bulimia nervosa in that:

    A. Their body weight need not be 15% below normal.
    B. They do not tend to experience amenorrhea.
    C. They engage in binging and purging.
    D. They have a grossly distorted body image.

10. For several months, Lisa has been very concerned about her weight, even thought it is actually 5 pounds below normal for her age and height. She believes she looks fat and often exercises for 2 to 3 hours after eating a meal. At other times, though, she will exercise for as long as 4 hours after eating a large meal, during which she feels she cannot stop eating. She has become concerned because she recently stopped menstruating. Which of the following diagnoses would Lisa likely receive?

    A. Anorexia nervosa, binge/purge type
    B. Binge-eating disorder
    C. Bulimia nervosa, purging type
    D. Bulimia nervosa, nonpurging type

11. Which of the following is <u>not</u> included in the DSM-IV definition of a binge?

    A. A binge includes a feeling of a lack of control over one's eating.
    B. A binge must include a minimum of 1,500 calories.
    C. A binge includes eating an amount of food that is definitely larger than most people would eat under similar circumstances.
    D. A binge occurs in a discrete period of time.

12. All of the following are medical complications of anorexia nervosa <u>except</u>:

    A. Irregular heart rate.
    B. Tooth decay.
    C. Dehydration.
    D. Electroencephalogram abnormalities.

13. Epidemiological studies cited in the chapter found that _____ % of college students met the criteria for bulimia nervosa.

    A. 0-1.
    B. 5-10.
    C. 15-20.
    D. 25.

14. People with which of the following eating disorders do <u>not</u> engage in binge eating?

    A. Purging type of bulimia
    B. Nonpurging type of bulimia
    C. Binge-purge type of anorexia
    D. Restricting type of anorexia

15. Eating disorders are more common among:

    A. Hispanics.
    B. Caucasians.
    C. People of lower socioeconomic status.
    D. African Americans.

16. What appears to be crucial to the development of anorexia nervosa is:

    A. A history of sexual abuse.
    B. Themes of control and perfectionism in the family.
    C. A girl's lack of awareness of her own bodily sensations.
    D. Discouraged expression of negative emotions.

17. A brain area thought to be dysregulated in eating disorders is/are the:

    A. Hippocampus.
    B. Thalamus.
    C. Hypothalamus.
    D. Parietal lobes.

18. A disorder that runs in the families of people with eating disorders, and for which 75% of people with eating disorders meet criteria, is:

    A. Generalized anxiety disorder.
    B. Major depression.
    C. Obsessive-compulsive disorder.
    D. Histrionic personality disorder.

19. Studies of bulimic people have found that they have abnormally low levels of:

    A. Norepinephrine.
    B. Epinephrine.
    C. Acteylcholine.
    D. Dopamine.

20. Behavior therapies for anorexia:

    A. Have a low relapse rate.
    B. Benefit the majority of anorexic patients, who gain weight to within 15% of normal body weight.
    C. Are not an effective treatment for this disorder.
    D. Should involve the entire family.

B. <u>True-False</u>. Select T (True) or F (False) below.

1. Binge/purge anorexics are more likely than restricting type anorexics to have a more chronic course of the disorder.   T   F

2. People are more likely to die from bulimia than anorexia.   T   F

3. Tricyclic antidepressants and MAO inhibitors have not proven effective in the treatment of anorexia in controlled clinical trials.   T   F

4. People with eating disorders are more likely to have a history of sexual abuse than people with other psychological problems.   T   F

5. The families of girls with eating disorders are more likely than the families of children with depression to have high levels of conflict, and to discourage the expression of negative emotions.
    T   F

C. <u>Short Answer</u>.

1. Describe the two types of anorexia and the two types of bulimia. How are these four disorders similar to and different from one another?

2. Describe Hilde Bruch's theory of anorexia nervosa.

3. What are some of the societal pressures that may contribute to eating disorders?

4. What treatments are effective for anorexia and bulimia nervosa?

5. Describe some biological contributors to the eating disorders.

ANSWER KEY

<u>Case Example</u>
1. "Perfectionism in family"; parents overcontrolling but uninvolved emotionally; chronic tension between Tammy and her parents, which is not openly expressed.
2. If Tammy is able to ignore or is unable to read her body's signals about hunger, she is more likely to develop restricting anorexia. If she finds that binge-eating helps to relieve her negative emotions, she is more likely to develop bulimia.

<u>Multiple Choice</u>
1. C
2. D
3. A
4. B
5. D
6. B
7. C
8. A
9. D
10. D
11. B
12. D
13. A
14. D
15. B
16. C
17. C
18. B
19. A
20. B

<u>True-False</u>
1. T
2. F
3. T
4. F
5. F

<u>Short Answer</u>
1. See pp. 493-498.
2. See pp. 510-511.
3. See pp. 502-505.
4. See pp. 513-517.
5. See pp. 512-513.

Additional Readings on Chapter 14 Topics

Fairburn, C. G., Shafran, R., & Cooper, Z. (1999). A cognitive behavioural theory of anorexia nervosa. Behaviour Research and Therapy, 37, 1-13.

Kaye, W. H., Gendall, K., & Strober, M. (1998). Serotonin neuronal function and selective serotonin reuptake inhibitor treatment in anorexia and bulimia nervosa. Biological Psychiatry, 44, 825-838.

Wilson, G. T. (1999). Cognitive behavior therapy for eating disorders: Progress and problems. Behaviour Research and Therapy, 37 (Suppl 1), S79-S95.

Chapter 15: Sexual Disorders and Gender Identity Disorder

LEARNING OBJECTIVES
After reading and studying this chapter, you should be able to:

1. Describe the five stages of the sexual response cycle, and the gender differences evident in it.

2. Distinguish between hypoactive sexual desire and sexual aversion disorder.

3. Describe female sexual arousal disorder and male erectile disorder.

4. Describe female orgasmic disorder (anorgasmia), male orgasmic disorder, and premature ejaculation.

5. Describe dyspareunia and vaginismus.

6. Discuss the biological causes of sexual dysfunctions, including specific medical conditions and drugs, and how biologically-caused dysfunctions differ from those caused by psychological factors.

7. Discuss the relationship problems, traumas, and attitudes that can cause sexual dysfunctions.

8. Discuss some cultural differences in sexual dysfunctions.

9. Discuss the drugs and biological procedures used to treat sexual dysfunctions.

10. Discuss the components of sex therapy with particular respect to sensate focus therapy, the stop-start technique, and the squeeze technique.

11. Describe how couples therapy and individual psychotherapy can be useful to treat sexual dysfunctions.

12. Discuss how clinicians should confront clients whose values about sex differ from their own.

13. Discuss the differences between paraphilias and normal sexual fantasies.

14. Describe fetishism, sexual sadism, sexual masochism, voyeurism, exhibitionism, and frotteurism.

15. Discuss the causes, characteristics, and available treatments for pedophilia.

16. Distinguish among gender identity, gender role, and sexual orientation.

17. Discuss the characteristics of and treatments for gender identity disorder.

18. Distinguish between transsexualism and transvestitism.

ESSENTIAL IDEAS

I. Sexual dysfunctions

A. The sexual response cycle includes five phases: desire, excitement or arousal, plateau, orgasm, and resolution.

B. People with disorders of sexual desire have little or no desire to engage in sex. These disorders include hypoactive sexual desire disorder and sexual aversion disorder.

C. People with sexual arousal disorders do not experience the physiological changes that make up the excitement or arousal phase of the sexual response cycle. These disorders include female sexual arousal disorder and male erectile disorder.

D. Women with female orgasmic disorder do not experience orgasm or have greatly delayed orgasm after reaching the excitement phase. Men with premature ejaculation reach ejaculation before they wish. Men with male orgasmic disorder have a recurrent delay in or absence of orgasm following sexual excitement.

E. The two sexual pain disorders are dyspareunia, genital pain associated with intercourse, and vaginismus, involuntary contraction of the vaginal muscles in women.

F. Biological causes of sexual dysfunctions include undiagnosed diabetes or other medical conditions, prescription or recreational drug use, and hormonal or vascular abnormalities.

G. Psychological causes include other psychological disorders and maladaptive attitudes and cognitions (especially performance concerns).

H. Sociocultural causes include problems in intimate relationships, traumatic experiences, and an upbringing or cultural milieu that devalues or degrades sex.

I. When the cause of a sexual dysfunction is biological, treatments that eradicate the cause can cure the sexual dysfunction. Alternately, drug therapies or prostheses can be used.

J. Sex therapy corrects the inadequate sexual practices of a client and his or her partner. The techniques of sex therapy include sensate focus therapy, teaching masturbation, the stop-start and squeeze techniques, and deconditioning of vaginal contractions.

K. Couples therapy focuses on decreasing conflicts between couples over their sexual practices or over other areas of their relationship.

L. Individual psychotherapy helps people recognize conflicts or negative attitudes behind their sexual dysfunctions and resolve these.

II. Paraphilias

A. The paraphilias are a group of disorders in which people's sexual activity is focused on (1) nonhuman objects, (2) nonconsenting adults, (3) suffering or humiliation of oneself or one's partner, or (4) children.

B. Fetishism involves the use of inanimate objects (such as panties or shoes) as the preferred or exclusive source of sexual arousal or gratification. One elaborate fetish is transvestism, in which a man dresses in the clothes of a woman to sexually arouse himself.

C. Voyeurism involves observing another person nude or engaging in sexual acts, without that person's knowledge or consent, in order to become sexually aroused.

D. Exhibitionism involves exposing oneself to another without his or her consent, in order to become sexually aroused.

E. Frotteurism involves rubbing up against another without his or her consent, in order to become sexually aroused.

F. Sadism and masochism involve physically harming another or allowing oneself to be harmed for sexual arousal.

G. Pedophilia involves engaging in sexual acts with a child.

H. Most paraphilics are men. Their behavior may represent the acting out of hostile or aggressive impulses.

I. Behavioral theories suggest that paraphilics' sexual preferences are the results of chance classical conditioning.

J. Treatment of the paraphilias can include biological interventions to reduce sexual drive, behavioral interventions to decondition arousal to paraphillic objects, and training in interpersonal and social skills.

III. Gender identity disorder

A. Gender identity disorder is diagnosed when individuals believe they were born with the wrong sex's genitals and are fundamentally persons of the opposite sex. This disorder in adults is also called transsexualism.

B. Biological theories suggest that unusual exposure to prenatal hormones affects the development of the hypothalamus and other brain structures involved in sexuality, leading to gender identity disorder.

C. Socialization theories suggest that parents of children (primarily boys) with gender identity disorder did not socialize "gender appropriate" behaviors. Other theories suggest that parents of children who develop this disorder have high rates of psychopathology.

D. Some people with this disorder undergo gender reassignment treatment to change their genitalia, and live as a member of the sex they believe they are.

KEY TERMS AND GUIDED REVIEW

Sexual Dysfunctions

<u>Key Terms</u>

sexual dysfunctions (p. 524):

sexual desire (p. 524):

arousal phase (p. 524):

vasocongestion (p. 524):

myotonia (p. 525):

plateau phase (p. 525):

orgasm (p. 525):

resolution (p. 526):

hypoactive sexual desire disorder (p. 530):

sexual aversion disorder (p. 531):

sexual arousal disorders (p. 531):

female sexual arousal disorder (p. 531):

male erectile disorder (p. 531):

female orgasmic disorder (p. 532):

premature ejaculation (p. 532):

male orgasmic disorder (p. 533):

dyspareunia (p. 533):

vaginismus (p. 533):

substance-induced sexual dysfunction (p. 536):

performance anxiety (p. 537):

sensate focus therapy (p. 542):

stop-start technique (p. 542):

squeeze technique (p. 543):

<u>Guided Review</u>

1. Define each of the five stages of the sexual response cycle. (pp. 524-526)

2. Describe some of the differences between male and female sexual responses. (p. 526)

3. Why are more people seeking sex therapy? (p. 529)

4. What is the difference between a generalized and situational sexual desire disorder? (pp. 530-531)

5. How does hypoactive sexual desire differ by gender? (p. 531)

6. What is the difference between the primary and secondary forms of male erectile disorder? (p. 531)

7. What are the criteria for female orgasmic disorder? (p. 532)

8. How do premature ejaculation and male orgasmic disorder differ? (pp. 532-533)

9. Describe how dyspareunia is manifested in both men and women. (p. 533)

10. What are some areas that a clinician should assess when he or she suspects a sexual dysfunction? (p. 534)

11. What are some common medical causes of sexual dysfunction? (pp. 534-535)

12. What is the relationship between hormones and sexual functioning in men and women? (p. 535)

13. Give some examples of drugs that can affect sexual functioning. (p. 535)

14. What are some differences between biologically and psychologically caused sexual dysfunctions? (p. 536)

15. Give some examples of psychological disorders and attitudes or cognitions that can interfere with sexual functioning. (pp. 536-537)

16. How does performance anxiety disrupt sexual activity? (p. 537)

17. What are some ways in which men gain ejaculatory control? (p. 537)

18. Give some examples of how problems in relationships (e.g., communication difficulties) can lead to sexual dysfunctions. (pp. 537-539)

19. What are some ways in which trauma can lead to sexual dysfunctions? (p. 539)

20. Give some examples of cross-cultural differences in sexual behavior or sexual dysfunctions. (p. 539)

21. Describe some of the biological treatments available for sexual dysfunctions. (pp. 540-541)

22. What are the elements of sensate focus therapy? (p. 542)

23. Give an example of how (1) premature ejaculation and (2) vaginismus may be treated. (pp. 542-543)

24. What are some issues addressed in couple or individual psychotherapy for sexual dysfunctions? (pp. 543-544)

25. Give some examples of folk remedies for sexual dysfunctions. (pp. 547-548)

Paraphilias

Key Terms

paraphilias (p. 549):

fetishes (p. 550):

transvestism (p. 550):

sexual sadism (p. 551):

sexual masochism (p. 551):

sadomasochism (p. 551):

voyeurism (p. 552):

exhibitionism (p. 552):

frotteurism (p. 553):

pedophilia (p. 553):

sadomasochism:

aversion therapy (p. 556):

desensitization (p. 556):

Guided Review

1. What are some characteristics of people with paraphilias? (p. 549)

2. Give some examples of fetishes. (p. 550)

3. Why do some clinicians question if fetishism should qualify as a psychiatric diagnosis? (p. 551)

4. What is the source of sexual excitement in sadomasochism, voyeurism, exhibitionism, and frotteurism? (pp. 551-553)

5. What must be present for someone to be diagnosed with pedophilia? (p. 553)

6. What are some effects of child sexual abuse? (pp. 553-554)

7. What are the psychodynamic, behavioral, social learning, and cognitive theories of paraphilias? (pp. 554-555)

8. Describe some of the effective treatments for paraphilias. (pp. 555-556)

Gender Identity Disorder

<u>Key Terms</u>

gender identity (p. 557):

gender role (p. 557):

sexual orientation (p. 557):

gender identity disorder (p. 557):

transsexualism (p. 558):

<u>Guided Review</u>

1. How do the terms gender identity, gender role, and sexual orientation differ from one another? (p. 557)

2. What are the criteria for gender identity disorder? (pp. 557-559)

3. How does transsexualism differ from transvestism? (p. 558)

4. What are some biological contributors to gender identity disorder? (pp. 560-561)

5. How might parents contribute to the development of gender identity disorder in their children? (pp. 560-561)

6. Describe gender reassignment and its advantages and disadvantages. (pp. 561-562)

CASE EXAMPLE
Read the following description and answer the questions below:

Alan and Kim have requested couples therapy because their "sex life has all but ended." For the past several months, whenever they have tried to have sex together, Alan has not been able to sustain an erection and Kim has not had an orgasm. They now report that neither of them has much interest in having sex with the other. Their problems began after Alan started a new job that he finds highly stressful and tiring. He works 6 days a week every week, and often 7 days a week. He comes home each night at 8 or 9 P.M., exhausted. When Kim tries to talk with him about the events of the day, he recounts all the disagreements he had with people on the job, and how frustrated he is. He doesn't listen when Kim tries to tell him about her own day. Kim's response to this has been to withdraw, to do dishes while Alan watches television and falls asleep. Kim has also begun to have "dates" with a man she works with. These dates started as casual lunches during the work day. But now when Alan is on a business trip, Kim has dinner with this man, and once she kissed this man passionately at the end of one of these dates. Kim feels badly about "cheating" on Alan, and wants to maintain her marriage. Alan knows his marriage is in trouble, and he also wants to save it.

1. What diagnoses, if any, do Alan's and Kim's behaviors and feelings warrant?

2. What might be an effective course of therapy for Alan and Kim?

CHAPTER TEST

A. <u>Multiple Choice</u>. Choose the **best answer** to each question below.

1. Which of the following is <u>not</u> one of Masters and Johnson's five phases of the sexual response cycle?

    A. resolution
    B. arousal
    C. orgasm
    D. refractory period

2. Enlargement of the clitoris, swelling of the labia, and moistening of the vagina is caused by:

    A. myotonia
    B. engorgement
    C. orgasm
    D. the refractory period

3. During the _____ phase, vasocongestion and myotonia occur.

    A. desire
    B. orgasm
    C. arousal
    D. plateau

4. Recurrent inability to attain or maintain the swelling-lubrication response of sexual excitement is known as:

    A. sexual aversion disorder.
    B. female orgasmic disorder.
    C. female sexual arousal disorder.
    D. vaginismus.

5. The most common complaint of people seeking sex therapy is:

    A. lack of sexual desire.
    B. inability to experience orgasm.
    C. pain or discomfort during sex.
    D. difficulty staying sexually aroused.

6. Genital pain associated with sexual intercourse is known as:

    A. hypoactive sexual desire disorder.
    B. dyspareunia.
    C. vaginismus.
    D. sexual aversion disorder.

7. Hypoactive sexual desire disorder is:

    A. diagnosed only in individuals who have never enjoyed sex.
    B. diagnosed when low sexual desire results from pain during intercourse.
    C. more common in younger women and older men.
    D. more often connected to anxiety or depression in men than in women.

8. The most common orgasmic disorder in men is:

    A. premature ejaculation.
    B. male orgasmic disorder.
    C. male erectile disorder.
    D. dyspareunia.

9. Which of the following statements about the causes of sexual dysfunction is <u>true</u>?

    A. In men, low levels of prolactin and estrogen can cause sexual dysfunctions.
    B. In women, hormones have a consistent, direct effect on sexual desire.
    C. Psychologically caused sexual dysfunctions tend to be global and consistent.
    D. Biologically caused sexual dysfunctions tend to appear gradually.

10. "Spectatoring" involves:

    A. voyeurs watching people engaged in sex without the people's consent or awareness.
    B. exhibitionists revealing themselves to large groups of people at the same time.
    C. individuals closely monitoring their own behaviors and feelings while engaging in sexual relations with another person.
    D. parents allowing their children to watch them engage in sexual intercourse.

11. Men gain ejaculatory control through all of the following processes <u>except</u>:

    A. a regular rhythm of being sexual.
    B. adherence to the same intercourse position.
    C. increased comfort with practice.
    D. a more give-and-take pleasuring process.

12. Men seeking treatment for hypoactive sexual desire disorder are more likely than women:

      A. to report problems in their marriage.
      B. to be experiencing other types of sexual dysfunction.
      C. to report other stressful events in their lives.
      D. to have higher levels of psychological distress.

13. The traditional Chinese medical system teaches that:

      A. loss of semen is detrimental to a man's health.
      B. if a man does not have an erection, then he does not want sex.
      C. pregnancy is more likely when women's vaginas are dry and tight for sexual intercourse.
      D. masturbation has very positive effects on one's health.

14. The stop-start technique is used primarily:

      A. to help a paraphilic stop engaging in paraphilic behavior and start engaging in normal sexual behavior.
      B. to help men who have premature ejaculations learn to control their ejaculations.
      C. to help women with vaginismus gain some control over their vaginal contractions.
      D. to help women with dyspareunia learn they can stop sexual interactions when they feel pain and start them again when the pain passes.

15. Psychodynamic theorists believe that women with _____ are overidentified with their mothers and unconsciously equate having sex as a rejection of their mothers.

      A. anorgasmia.
      B. sexual aversion disorder.
      C. female sexual arousal disorder.
      D. vaginismus.

16. All of the following medical and surgical treatments for male erectile disorder are effective except:

      A. vacuum pumps.
      B. vasomax.
      C. topical creams.
      D. inflatable prosthesis.

17. Someone who obtains sexual arousal by compulsively and secretly watching another person being naked or engaging in sex would most likely be diagnosed with:

    A. exhibitionism.
    B. frotteurism.
    C. voyeurism.
    D. fetishism.

18. Someone who obtains sexual gratification from stealing women's underwear and masturbating into them would most likely be diagnosed with:

    A. fetishism.
    B. transsexualism.
    C. transvestism.
    D. exhibitionism.

19. All of the following are true of pedophiles except:

    A. pedophiles have typically been abused as children.
    B. pedophiles are typically homosexual.
    C. the typical victims of pedophiles are relatives or close acquaintances.
    D. pedophiles must be, by definition, at least 5 years older than their victim(s).

20. All of the following are criteria for gender identity disorder except:

    A. intense desire to participate in the stereotypical games and pastimes of the other sex.
    B. strong preference for playmates of the other sex.
    C. repeatedly stated desire to be, or insistence that he or she is, the other sex.
    D. evidence of prenatal hormonal abnormalities is present.

B. True-False. Select T (True) or F (False) below.

1. In most cases of hypoactive sexual desire, the individual has never had much interest in sex.
    T   F

2. Most pedophiles are homosexual men abusing young boys.   T   F

3. In transsexualism, people dress as a member of the opposite gender in order to gain sexual satisfaction.   T   F

4. Serotonin reuptake inhibitors often produce sexual side effects, but also may be used to treat certain sexual dysfunctions.   T   F

5. Lesbian women are more likely than heterosexual women to have aversions to oral sex.
    T   F

C. <u>Short Answer</u>.

1. How does Bem's exotic-becomes-erotic theory attempt to explain sexual orientation?

2. Identify and describe the five phases of the sexual response cycle as it occurs in both men and women.

3. Describe how a clinician would treat: (1) premature ejaculation, and (2) female anorgasmia, using psychological interventions.

4. Describe the behavioral and social-learning theories of paraphilias.

5. What are some of the proposed explanations for gender identity disorder?

ANSWER KEY

<u>Case Example</u>
1. Male erectile disorder for Alan and female orgasmic disorder for Kim. Hypoactive sexual desire would not be diagnosed for either of them because it is secondary to the primary disorders.
2. Couples therapy focusing on couple's "seduction rituals" and on the communication patterns between Alan and Kim. If Kim reveals her dating of another man, therapy will need to deal with Alan's reactions to this and whether the couple is committed enough to the relationship to learn to ask for what they need from each other and to give what each other needs.

<u>Multiple Choice</u>
1. D
2. B
3. C
4. C
5. A
6. B
7. C
8. A
9. D
10. C
11. B
12. B
13. A
14. B
15. D
16. C
17. C
18. A
19. B
20. D

<u>True-False</u>
1. F
2. F
3. F
4. T
5. T

<u>Short Answer</u>
1. See pp. 546-547.
2. See pp. 524-526.
3. See pp. 541-543.
4. See pp. 554-555.
5. See pp. 560-561.

Additional Readings on Chapter 15 Topics

Bradley, S. J., & Zucker, K. J. (1997). Gender identity disorder: A review of the past 10 years. Journal of the American Academy of Child and Adolescent Psychiatry, 36, 872-880.

Maletzky, B. M. (1993). Factors associated with success and failure in the behavioral and cognitive treatment of sexual offenders. Annals of Sex Research, 6, 241-258.

Scholinski, D. (1998). The last time I wore a dress. New York: Riverhead Books. *This is a very interesting story about gender identity disorder.*

Chapter 16: Substance-Related Disorders

LEARNING OBJECTIVES
After reading and studying this chapter, you should be able to:

1. Discuss the prevalence, patterns, and trends of substance use over the past several decades, and how the rates of substance use vary by culture, gender, and age.

2. Distinguish among and define substance intoxication, withdrawal, abuse, and dependence, and the factors associated with different manifestations of intoxication, withdrawal, and dependence.

3. Describe the intoxication and withdrawal effects (when such effects exist) of alcohol, benzodiazepines, barbiturates, inhalants, cocaine, amphetamines, opioids, hallucinogens, PCP, cannabis, and nicotine.

4. Discuss the negative effects of the substances described in this chapter on physical and mental health.

5. Describe the stages of alcohol withdrawal.

6. Discuss the typical patterns of alcohol, benzodiazepine, barbiturate, and cocaine use that lead to dependence on these substances.

7. Define and describe Wernicke's encephalopathy, Korsakoff's psychosis, alcohol-induced dementia, and fetal alcohol syndrome.

8. Discuss the effects of a pregnant woman's use of alcohol, cocaine, and nicotine on her developing fetus and newborn child.

9. Distinguish between the disease model of alcoholism and controlled drinking perspective.

10. Summarize the contributions of the mesolimbic dopamine system and opponent processes to substance use behavior.

11. Discuss the role of genetics in alcoholism and describe what might be inherited in the children of alcoholics.

12. Summarize the arguments and evidence for and against the idea that alcoholism is a form of depression.

13. Discuss the appropriate uses of methadone, naltrexone, naloxone, disulfiram, and antidepressants to treat people with particular substance-related disorders.

14. Describe Alcoholics Anonymous and its treatment philosophy.

15. Discuss the behavioral treatments for alcoholism: aversive classical conditioning, covert sensitization therapy, and cue exposure and response prevention.

16. Describe the elements of behavioral and cognitive therapies for alcoholism, and the elements of relapse prevention programs.

17. Discuss why different treatment approaches may be indicated for men and women.

ESSENTIAL IDEAS

I. Society and substance use

    A. Cultures differ in their predominant attitudes and legal policies regarding substances. Many Muslim countries strictly prohibit alcohol. The British consider substance addiction to be a medical disease, and refer most users for treatment rather than punishment. The Dutch distinguish "hard" drugs (such as heroin) from "soft" drugs (such as cannabis) and only aggressively prosecute the use and sale of "hard" drugs in an attempt to avoid driving users of "soft" drugs underground where they might begin using more potent substances.

    B. Many substances, including stimulants, opioids, and hallucinogens, have been used by various cultures throughout history for medicinal or religious purposes. People who deliberately use substances to alter their moods, thoughts, and behaviors as ends in themselves and who experience significant distress and/or impairment in their daily functioning are said to have a substance-related disorder.

II. Defining substance-related disorders

    A. Substance intoxication is a set of behavioral and psychological changes that result directly from the physiological effects of a substance on the central nervous system.

    B. Substance withdrawal is a set of physiological and behavioral symptoms that result from a reduction or cessation of substance use following a prolonged period of heavy use. Withdrawal symptoms are typically the opposite of symptoms experienced during intoxication and tend to begin and end more quickly for substances that quickly exit the body, and more slowly for substances that slowly exit the body.

    C. Substance abuse is diagnosed when an individual experiences recurrent problems in at least one of the following four areas over a 12-month period: (1) failure to fulfill important obligations at work, school, or home; (2) use of substances in physically hazardous situations; (3) legal problems as a result of substance use; and (4) recurrent substance use despite significant social or legal problems that result from the substance use.

    D. Substance dependence is diagnosed when a person compulsively uses a substance despite significant social, occupational, psychological, or medical problems as a result of the use. Substances vary in their potential to lead to dependence: those that are rapidly and efficiently absorbed (e.g., by injection), that act more rapidly on the central nervous system, that cause intoxication quickly, and whose effects wear off quickly, are most likely to lead to dependence.

III. Depressants

A. At low doses, alcohol produces relaxation and a mild euphoria. At higher doses, it produces the classic signs of depression and cognitive and motor impairment.

B. A large proportion of deaths due to accidents, murders, and suicides are alcohol-related.

C. Alcohol withdrawal symptoms can be mild or so severe as to be life threatening.

D. Alcohol abusers and dependents experience a wide range of social and interpersonal problems and are at risk for many serious health problems.

E. Persons of Asian descent typically are less prone to alcohol-related problems, although exceptions to this include Native Americans and Koreans. Women drink less alcohol than do men in most cultures and are less likely to have alcohol-related disorders than are men.

F. Benzodiazepines and barbiturates are sold legally by prescription for the treatment of anxiety and insomnia. Inhalants are solvents such as gasoline or paint thinner.

G. These substances can cause an initial rush plus a loss of inhibitions. These pleasurable sensations are then followed by depressed mood, lethargy, and physical signs of central nervous system depression. Benzodiazepines and barbiturates are dangerous in overdose and when mixed with other substances.

H. Inhalants can cause permanent organ and brain damage and accidental deaths due to suffocation or dangerous delusional behavior.

IV. Stimulants

A. Cocaine and amphetamines produce a rush of euphoria, followed by increases in self-esteem, alertness, and energy. With chronic use, however, they can lead to grandiosity, impulsiveness, hypersexuality, agitation, and paranoia.

B. Withdrawal from cocaine and amphetamines causes symptoms of depression, exhaustion, and an intense craving for more of the substances.

C. Cocaine seems particularly prone to lead to dependence, because it has extraordinarily rapid and strong effects on the brain and its effects wear off quickly.

D. The intense activation of the central nervous system caused by cocaine and amphetamines can lead to a number of cardiac, respiratory, and neurological problems, and these substances are responsible for a large percentage of substance-related medical emergencies and deaths.

E. Nicotine is an alkaloid found in tobacco, and affects the release of several neurochemicals in the body. Nicotine subjectively reduces stress but causes physiological arousal similar to that seen in the fight-or-flight response.

F. Smoking is associated with higher rate of heart disease, lung cancer, emphysema, and chronic bronchitis, and substantially increases mortality rates.

G. The majority of people who smoke wish they could quit, but have trouble doing so, in part because tolerance to nicotine develops and withdrawal symptoms are difficult to tolerate.

H. Caffeine is the most commonly used stimulant drug. Caffeine intoxication can cause agitation, tremors, heart irregularities, and insomnia. People can develop tolerance and withdrawal from caffeine.

V. Opioids

A. The opioids include heroin, morphine, codeine, and methadone.

B. They cause an initial rush or euphoria followed by a drowsy, dream-like state. Severe intoxication can cause respiratory and cardiovascular failure.

C. Withdrawal symptoms can include dysphoria, anxiety, and agitation; an achy feeling in the back and legs; increased sensitivity to pain; and craving for more opioids.

D. Opioid users who inject drugs can contract HIV and a number of other disorders by sharing needles.

VI. Hallucinogens and PCP

A. The hallucinogens create perceptual illusions and distortions, sometimes fantastic, sometimes frightening. Some people feel more sensitive to art, music, and other sensations. They also create mood swings and paranoia. Some people experience frightening flashbacks to experiences under the hallucinogens.

B. PCP causes euphoria or affective dulling, abnormal involuntary movements, and weakness at low doses. At intermediate doses, it leads to disorganized thinking, depersonalization, feelings, and aggression. At higher doses, it produces amnesia and coma, analgesia sufficient to allow surgery, seizures, severe respiratory problems, hypothermia, and hyperthermia.

VII. Cannabis

A. Cannabis creates a high feeling, cognitive and motor impairments, and in some people hallucinogenic effects.

B. Cannabis use is high and significant numbers of people, especially teenagers, have impaired performance at school or on the job, and in relationships as a result of chronic use. Marijuana use can also lead to a number of physical problems, especially respiratory problems.

VIII. Theories of Substance Use, Abuse, and Dependence

A. Psychoactive substances have powerful effects on the parts of the brain that register reward and pleasure, including the mesolimbic dopamine system. Repeated use of a substance may sensitize this system, causing craving for more of the substance.

B. Some types of alcoholism, particularly among males, may be genetically transmitted. Men genetically predisposed to alcoholism are less sensitive to the effects of low doses of alcohol. One reason women may be less prone to alcoholism is that their bodies are more reactive to low doses of alcohol.

C. Some theorists view alcoholism as a form of depression, although the prevailing evidence suggests that alcoholism and depression are distinct disorders.

D. Behavioral theories of alcoholism note that people are reinforced or punished by other people for their alcohol-related behaviors.

E. Cognitive theories argue that people who develop alcohol-related problems have strong expectations that alcohol will help them feel better and cope better when they face stressful times.

F. Sociocultural theorists note that alcohol and drug use increases among people under severe stress. In addition, the gender differences in substance-related disorders may be tied to different reinforcements and punishments for men and women for using substances.

IX. Treatments for substance-related disorders

A. Detoxification is the first step in treating substance-related disorders.

B. Antianxiety and antidepressant drugs can help ease the withdrawal symptoms from other substances. Antagonist drugs can block the effects of substances, reducing desire for the drug, or making the ingestion of the drug aversive.

C. Methadone maintenance programs substitute methadone for heroin in the treatment of heroin addicts. These programs are controversial, but may be the only way some heroin addicts will get off the streets.

D. Behavioral therapies based on aversive classical conditioning are sometimes used to treat alcoholism.

E. Treatments based on social learning and cognitive theories focus on training the alcoholic in more adaptive coping skills and challenging his or her positive expectations about the effects of alcohol.

F. The most common treatment for alcoholism is Alcoholics Anonymous, a self-help group that encourages alcoholics to admit their weaknesses and call on a higher power and other group members to help them remain completely abstinent from alcohol. A related group called Narcotics Anonymous is available for people dependent on other substances.

G. Prevention programs for college students aim to teach them responsible use of alcohol.

H. Different treatments may be needed for men and women that take into account the different contexts for their substance use.

KEY TERMS AND GUIDED REVIEW

Key Terms

substance (p. 568):

drug addicts (p. 568):

Society and Substance Use

Key Terms

substance-related disorder (p. 570):

Guided Review

1. Give some examples of how different societies view substance use. (pp. 569-570)

2. What are some reasons that societies may want to regulate substance use? (p. 570)

Defining Substance-Related Disorders

<u>Key Terms</u>

substance intoxication (p. 570):

substance withdrawal (p. 573):

substance abuse (p. 573):

substance dependence (p. 573):

tolerance (p. 573):

<u>Guided Review</u>

1. What is substance intoxication? Under what circumstances is it diagnosed? (pp. 571-572)

2. The symptoms of intoxication depend on which factors? (p. 572)

3. What is substance withdrawal? When it is diagnosed? (p. 573)

4. What is substance abuse? What must be present for it to be diagnosed? (p. 573)

5. What is substance dependence? (p. 573)

6. What is physiological dependence? (p. 574)

7. Why is the route of administration used to ingest a substance important? (p. 575)

Depressants

<u>Key Terms</u>

blackout (p. 576):

alcohol abuse (p. 577):

alcohol dependence (p. 577):

alcohol withdrawal (p. 577):

delirium tremens (DTs) (p. 581):

alcohol-induced persisting amnestic disorder (p. 581):

Wernicke's encephalopathy (p. 581):

Korsakoff's psychosis (p. 581):

alcohol-induced dementia (p. 581):

fetal alcohol syndrome (p. 582):

benzodiazepines (p. 584):

barbiturates (p. 584):

inhalants (p. 585):

Guided Review

1. What are some of the intoxication and withdrawal effects of depressants? (pp. 575-576)

2. How are alcohol abuse and dependence different from one another? (pp. 577-578)

3. Describe the patterns of alcohol use by alcohol abusers and dependents. (p. 578)

4. How do alcoholics with antisocial personalities differ from alcoholics without antisocial personalities? (p. 580)

5. What is negative affect alcoholism? (p. 580)

6. Describe the stages of alcohol withdrawal. (pp. 580-581)

7. What are some of the long-term health effects of alcohol abuse? (p. 581)

8. Identify and describe some of the neurological disorders that can result from alcohol abuse. (p. 581)

9. Describe some cross-cultural differences in alcohol abuse and dependence. (pp. 582-583)

10. How do the rates of alcohol problems vary by age and gender? (pp. 583-584)

11. What are the common patterns in the development of benzodiazepine or barbiturate abuse and dependence? (p. 585)

12. What are some negative effects of inhalant abuse? (p. 585)

Stimulants

Key Terms

cocaine (p. 586):

amphetamines (p. 589):

nicotine (p. 590):

caffeine (p. 592):

Guided Review

1. What are some of the intoxication and withdrawal effects of stimulants? (pp. 586-587)

2. Why is cocaine more likely than other substances to result in patterns of substance abuse and dependence? (pp. 586-588)

3. What are some of the negative consequences of amphetamine abuse? (p. 589)

4. What is the evidence that nicotine is an addictive drug? (pp. 591-592)

5. What are some arguments for and against declaring nicotine a drug? (p. 592)

6. What are the symptoms of caffeine intoxication? (p. 592)

Opioids

Key Term

opioids (p. 593):

Guided Review

1. What are some of the intoxication and withdrawal effects of opioids? (pp. 593-594)

2. What are the pathways to opioid abuse or dependence? (p. 594)

Hallucinogens and PCP

Key Terms

hallucinogens (p. 596):

flashbacks (p. 597):

phenylcyclidine (PCP):

Guided Review

1. Describe the intoxication effects of hallucinogens and PCP. (pp. 596-597)

Cannabis

Key Term

cannabis (p. 597):

Guided Review

1. Describe the intoxication effects of cannabis. (p. 598)

Theories of Substance Use, Abuse, and Dependence

<u>Key Terms</u>

mesolimbic dopamine system (p. 599):

disease model (p. 600):

<u>Guided Review</u>

1. How might the mesolimbic dopamine system be involved in substance use? (p. 599)

2. What is the evidence that genetics contribute to alcohol and substance dependence? (p. 600)

3. What is alcohol reactivity, and how might it contribute to drinking behavior? (pp. 601-602)

4. How and why do men and women differ in terms of their sensitivity to alcohol? (p. 602)

5. Give some reasons why alcoholism should be viewed as a form of depression, and some reasons why it should not. (p. 602)

6. Explain how modeling may contribute to patterns of alcohol use in families. (p. 602)

7. Explain how alcohol expectancies may contribute to drinking behavior. (p. 603)

8. Give some reasons why the rates of alcohol use differ between men and women. (p. 604)

Treatment for Substance-Related Disorders

<u>Key Terms</u>

detoxification (p. 605):

antidepressants (p. 605):

antagonist drugs (p. 605):

naltrexone (p. 605):

naloxone (p. 605):

disulfiram (p. 606):

methadone (p. 606):

methadone maintenance programs (p. 606):

aversive classical conditioning (p. 606):

covert sensitization therapy (p. 606):

cue exposure and response prevention (p. 607):

abstinence violation effect (p. 608):

relapse prevention programs (p. 608):

Guided Review

1. How do the disease model and harm-reduction approach differ? (p. 605)

2. Discuss the appropriate use(s) of the following biological treatments: (1) antidepressants; (2) naltrexone; (3) naloxone; (4) disulfiram; and (5) methadone. (pp. 605-606)

3. Describe how aversive classical conditioning, covert sensitization therapy, and cue exposure and response prevention may be used to treat alcoholism. (p. 606)

4. Describe how cognitive techniques may be used to treat alcoholics. (pp. 607-608)

5. What is the controlled drinking controversy? (p. 608)

6. What contributes to the abstinence violation effect? (p. 608)

7. Describe how relapse prevention programs may assist people to stop drinking. (pp. 608-609)

8. What is Alcoholics Anonymous and how does it work? (p. 609-610)

9. Describe the Alcohol Skills Training Program (ASTP) and how it works. (pp. 610-611)

10. Why might it be important to treat male and female substance abusers in different ways? (pp. 611-612)

CASE EXAMPLE

Read the following description and answer the questions below:

Ben had a long history of violent and impulsive behavior, beginning when he was a preschooler, and continuing now that he is in his mid-twenties. He got into trouble constantly in school, and was eventually kicked out of high school for drinking on school property repeatedly. Ben has held a number of jobs for a short period of time. He has gotten fired from every one of these jobs because he came to work drunk or missed many days of work due to hangovers.

When he is drunk, Ben can get mean. He frequently picks fights with other men over trivial issues. He has hit his wife a number of times. Ben also will race off in his car when he is drunk, driving fast and erratically down the rural roads near where he lives. He has had a few accidents and lost his driver's license when he was caught driving drunk. He continues to drive without a license, however.

1. What substance related disorder does Ben likely have? What symptoms of this disorder does he show?

2. What other Axis II disorder might Ben's symptoms indicate?

3. How would a cognitive-behavioral therapist treat Ben?

CHAPTER TEST

A. <u>Multiple Choice</u>. Choose the **best answer** to each question below.

1. Which of the following people would be diagnosed with other substance-related disorder?

    A. Someone who abuses alcohol but is not dependent on it.
    B. Someone who inhales antifreeze and experiences significant anxiety and hallucinations as a result.
    C. Someone who smokes rat poison and experiences mild, transient effects from it.
    D. Someone who uses opioids, but who does not exhibit significant tolerance or withdrawal symptoms.

2. Substance dependence is:

    A. a diagnosis given when recurrent substance use leads to significant harmful consequences.
    B. the experience of clinically significant distress in social, occupational, or other areas of functioning due to the cessation or reduction of substance use.
    C. the experience of significant maladaptive behavioral and psychological symptoms due to the effect of a substance on the central nervous system.
    D. a diagnosis given when substance use leads to tolerance and withdrawal symptoms or significant impairment or distress.

3. A DSM-IV diagnosis can be given for withdrawal symptoms from all of the following substances <u>except</u>:

    A. barbiturates.
    B. amphetamines.
    C. cannabis.
    D. nicotine.

4. Which of the following is <u>not</u> included in the diagnostic criteria for substance abuse?

    A. There is a persistent desire or unsuccessful efforts to cut down or control substance use.
    B. Failure to meet important obligations at work, school, or home.
    C. Use of the substance in situations in which it is physically hazardous to do so.
    D. Legal problems as a result of substance use.

5. Which of the following is <u>not</u> a criterion for substance dependence?

    A. The substance is often taken in larger amounts or over a longer period than was intended.
    B. Repeated legal problems as a result of substance use.
    C. A great deal of time is spent in activities necessary to obtain the substance, use the substance, or recover from its effects.
    D. Important social, occupational, or recreational activities are given up or reduced because of substance use.

6. All of the following are present among alcoholics with antisocial personalities more so than in alcoholics without such personalities <u>except</u>:

    A. more severe symptoms of alcoholism.
    B. heavier drug involvement.
    C. experience of depressive and anxiety symptoms as children.
    D. increased likelihood of coming from alcoholic families.

7. A loss of memory for recent events, problems in recalling distant events, and confabulation are features of:

    A. Wernicke's Encephalopathy.
    B. alcohol-induced dementia.
    C. substance intoxication.
    D. Korsakoff's psychosis.

8. The ethnic group at highest risk for alcohol abuse and dependence is:

    A. Caucasians.
    B. African Americans.
    C. Native Americans.
    D. Hispanics.

9. Which of the following is a <u>true</u> explanation for why rates of alcohol problems are higher among older people?

    A. The rates of alcohol problems are actually lower, not higher, among older people.
    B. Older people have more free time and financial security than younger people, which makes it possible for them to tolerate hangovers and negative effects of alcohol.
    C. Older people have grown up under fewer prohibitions against alcohol use and abuse, since alcohol problems were much less common during their younger years.
    D. Older people metabolize alcohol at a slower rate than younger people, which leads them to become intoxicated more quickly.

10. Which of the following is a biological cause of cravings for a substance?

    A. neural sensitization in the mesolimbic dopamine system
    B. neural desensitization in the mesolimbic dopamine system
    C. opponent processes
    D. increased levels of serotonin

11. The sons of alcoholics have been found to exhibit all of the following characteristics <u>except</u>:

    A. lower reactivity to moderate doses of alcohol.
    B. low physiological tolerance to alcohol, which leads them to achieve intoxication easily.
    C. less intoxication in their cognitive and motor performance.
    D. significantly greater likelihood of becoming an alcoholic.

12. Which of the following statements about alcoholism and depression is <u>true</u>?

    A. Depression among alcoholics typically remains even after the alcoholism is treated.
    B. Alcohol-related disorders and depression run together in families.
    C. The odds of alcoholism preceding depression are lower than the odds of depression preceding alcoholism.
    D. Depressed adolescents are more likely to become alcoholics than those who are not depressed.

13. Alcohol cravings can be reduced with:

    A. naloxone.
    B. methadone.
    C. disulfiram.
    D. naltrexone.

14. A drug that makes the user feel sick and dizzy when he or she ingests alcohol while taking the drug is:

    A. naloxone.
    B. methadone.
    C. disulfiram.
    D. naltrexone.

15. In which of the following treatments are alcoholics caused to experience their favorite types of alcohol, encouraged to hold glasses to their lips, and smell the alcohol, but are not allowed to drink any of the alcohol?

    A. cue exposure and response prevention
    B. aversive classical conditioning
    C. covert sensitization therapy
    D. controlled drinking treatment

16. The most widely-used illicit substance(s) in the world is/are:

    A. inhalants
    B. cannabis
    C. cocaine
    D. opioids

17. Abuse of all of the following may be diagnosed in DSM-IV except:

    A. alcohol.
    B. nicotine.
    C. amphetamines.
    D. opioids.

18. All of the following are intoxication symptoms of depressants except _____, which is a withdrawal symptom.

    A. slurred speech
    B. stupor or coma
    C. psychomotor agitation
    D. attention and memory problems

19. Delirium tremens can occur after withdrawal from:

    A. alcohol.
    B. cocaine.
    C. opioids.
    D. hallucinogens.

20. The lowest rates of alcoholism are found in which of the following cultures?

    A. United States
    B. New Zealand
    C. Puerto Rico
    D. China

B. <u>True-False</u>. Select T (True) or F (False) below.

1. The symptoms of intoxication remit once the amount of substance in people's blood and/or tissues declines, and the substance is no longer detectable in the body.   T   F

2. For a person to be diagnosed with substance dependence, he or she must exhibit tolerance and withdrawal to the substance.   T   F

3. Binge drinking is no more common among members of fraternities and sororities than it is among the general college population.   T   F

4. Alcohol-induced dementia is the second most common cause of adult dementia.
     T   F

5. The use of cocaine has declined since the mid-1980s.   T   F

C. <u>Short Answer</u>.

1. When someone uses a substance, the specific symptoms that he or she will exhibit depend upon several factors. Identify five of these factors.

2. How do the rates of alcohol disorders vary by culture, gender, and age? What are some of the proposed reasons for these differences?

3. Explain how the mesolimbic dopamine system is related to substance use.

4. Describe two of the cognitive-behavioral treatments and two biological treatments for alcoholism described in the chapter.

5. Contrast the disease model of alcoholism with the controlled drinking perspective. Do you think that some alcoholics can learn to control their drinking? Why or why not?

ANSWER KEY

Case Example

1. Alcohol dependence. He shows withdrawal symptoms (hangovers), continued use of alcohol despite several negative consequences (losing jobs, losing his license, being kicked out of school, getting into fights).
2. Antisocial personality disorder. He has a life-long history of violent and impulsive behavior that violates the fundamental rights of others (fights, hitting his wife, driving drunk and without a license).
3. First detoxification, perhaps using naltroxone to block the effects of the alcohol. Second, help him identify thoughts or situations that trigger impulsive behaviors and drinking. Third, help him develop alternative coping strategies for these situations and to challenge the thoughts that contribute to drinking.

Multiple Choice
1. B
2. D
3. C
4. A
5. B
6. C
7. D
8. C
9. A
10. A
11. B
12. B
13. D
14. C
15. A
16. B
17. B
18. C
19. A
20. D

True-False
1. F
2. F
3. F
4. T
5. T

Short Answer
1. See pp. 572, 574-575.
2. See pp. 582-584.
3. See pp. 599-600.
4. See pp. 605-608.
5. See p. 608.

Additional Readings on Chapter 16 Topics

Kopelman, M. D. (1995). The Korsakoff syndrome. British Journal of Psychiatry, 166, 154-173.

Nesse, R. M., & Berridge, K. C. (1997). Psychoactive drug use in evolutionary perspective. Science, 278, 63-66.

Robinson, T. E., & Berridge, K. C. (1993). The neural basis of drug craving: An incentive-sensitization theory of addiction. Brain Research: Brain Research Reviews, 18, 247-291.

Chapter 17: Psychology and Physical Health

LEARNING OBJECTIVES
After reading and studying this chapter, you should be able to:

1. Discuss the three predominant models for how psychological factors affect physical disease.

2. Describe the fight-or-flight response and the phases of the general adaptation syndrome.

3. Discuss the characteristics of events that lead people to perceive them as stressful.

4. Describe some of the earlier notions in health psychology, such as the "ulcer-prone personality," and why they were discredited.

5. Discuss the relationship between psychological factors and coronary heart disease, as well as hypertension.

6. Discuss how psychological factors can influence immunocompetence and the evidence that psychological factors influence the development and course of physical illness.

7. Discuss the negative physiological and psychological effects of sleep deprivation.

8. Distinguish among the various sleep disorders, including primary sleep disorders, dyssomnias, and parasomnias.

9. Discuss some of the treatments available for sleep disorders.

10. Explain how dispositional pessimism may contribute to physical illness, and the specific evidence that supports this view.

11. Distinguish between Type A and Type B personalities, and the evidence that Type A personality is associated with early mortality and coronary heart disease.

12. Identify the specific aspects of Type A personality that are most detrimental to health.

13. Discuss why men are more likely than women to develop Type A personalities.

14. Define repressive coping style, and summarize the evidence for its negative effect on physical health.

15. Define John Henryism, and explain how it might partly explain higher rates of hypertension in African American men.

16. Describe the elements of guided mastery techniques, cognitive therapy, biofeedback, and time management training.

17. Summarize the evidence for the idea that seeking social support, including support groups and religion, positively impacts upon physical health.

ESSENTIAL IDEAS

I. Stress and health

A. Three characteristics of stressful events are that they are uncontrollable, unpredictable, and they challenge our capabilities and self-concept.

B. Health psychologists formerly thought that ulcers, asthma, and chronic headaches were due to specific personality characteristics. Research support for these views have been inconsistent, but stress and distress can worsen these diseases in people who already have them.

C. There is substantial evidence that stress, particularly uncontrollable stress, increases risks for coronary heart disease and hypertension, probably through chronic hyperarousal of the body's fight-or-flight response.

D. There is mounting evidence from animal and human studies that stress may also impair the functioning of the immune system, possibly leading to higher rates of infectious diseases.

II. Sleep and health

A. The sleep disorders are divided into sleep disorders due to other mental disorders, medical conditions, or substances, and primary sleep disorders.

B. The primary sleep disorders are further divided into dyssomnias and parasomnias.

C. The most common dyssomnia is insomnia. Hypersomnia, narcolepsy, and breathing-related sleep disorder are also dyssomnias.

D. The parasomnias include nightmare disorder, sleep terror disorder, and sleepwalking disorder. Many people experience symptoms of these disorders occasionally, but only a small percentage of the population ever develops one of these sleep disorders.

E. Sleep disorders, particularly insomnia, can be treated with a variety of drugs, or through behavioral and cognitive-behavioral therapies that change sleep-related behavior and thinking patterns.

III. Personality and health

A. People who are chronically pessimistic may show poorer physical health because they appraise more events as uncontrollable or because they engage in poorer health-related behaviors.

B. People with the Type A behavior pattern are highly competitive, time urgent, and hostile. The Type A behavior pattern significantly increases risk for coronary heart disease. The most potent component of this pattern is hostility, which alone significantly predicts heart disease.

C. People with repressive coping styles deny their negative emotions and may be at increased risk for poor health.

D. John Henryism is a coping style in which people work diligently against tremendous obstacles but apparently put their physical health at risk in doing so.

IV. Interventions to improve health

A. Guided mastery techniques help people learn positive health-related behaviors, by teaching them the most effective ways of engaging in these behaviors and giving them opportunity to practice the behaviors in increasingly challenging situations.

B. Cognitive-behavioral techniques can be used to challenge catastrophizing cognitions people may have about illnesses that maintain high states of physiological arousal.

C. Biofeedback is used to help people learn to control their own negative physiological responses.

D. Time management techniques can help people reduce the overall levels of stress in their lives, thereby improving their health.

E. A variety of cognitive-behavioral techniques have been combined into an effective treatment package to reduce Type A behavior pattern and the risk of further coronary disease in men.

F. Seeking social support is one coping strategy associated with better health, as long as other provide positive social support rather than social conflict.

G. Support groups are one source of social support for some people. Some research suggests that they can improve both psychological and physical well-being.

H. Religious people tend to be healthier than nonreligious people. It is not clear whether this is due to religious people having better social support or to other factors.

KEY TERMS AND GUIDED REVIEW

Key Terms

health psychology (p. 618):

mind-body question (p. 618):

Guided Review

1. Describe the direct effects, interactive, and indirect effects models. (pp. 618-619)

Stress and Health

Key Terms

fight-or-flight response (p. 619):

general adaptation syndrome (p. 619):

stress (p. 620):

safety signal hypothesis (p. 621):

ulcers (p. 622):

asthma (p. 622):

migraines (p. 623):

muscle contraction headaches (p. 623):

coronary heart disease (p. 623):

hypertension (p. 624):

immune system (p. 624):

immunocompetence (p. 625):

lymphocytes (p. 625):

Guided Review

1. What are the phases of the general adaptation syndrome described by Selye? (p. 619)

2. What is the evidence that uncontrollable events are more stressful than controllable events? (pp. 620-621)

3. Why do unpredictable events appear to be more stressful than predictable events? (p. 621)

4. For ulcers and asthma, describe what health psychologists used to think about these problems, and what the current evidence suggests. (pp. 622-623)

5. What psychological factors are related to migraine headaches? (p. 623)

6. What are some contributors to coronary heart disease (CHD)? (pp. 623-624)

7. What is the evidence that stress is related to hypertension? (p. 624)

8. What is the evidence that: (1) stress; and (2) controllability are related to reduced immunocompetence? (pp. 624-626)

Sleep and Health

Key Terms

sleep disorders related to another mental disorder (p. 628):

sleep disorders due to a general medical condition (p. 628):

substance-induced sleep disorders (p. 628):

primary sleep disorders (p. 628):

dyssomnias (p. 628):

parasomnias (p. 628):

insomnia (p. 628):

stimulus control therapy (p. 630):

sleep restriction therapy (p. 630):

hypersomnia (p. 630):

narcolepsy (p. 630):

cataplexy (p. 630):

breathing-related sleep disorder (p. 630):

Guided Review

1. Identify several of the negative health and safety effects of sleep deprivation. (pp. 626-627)

2. What are some psychological effects of sleep deprivation? (p. 627)

3. What are some ways in which people can reduce sleepiness and sleep deprivation? (pp. 627-628)

4. What are some of the medical conditions that can disturb sleep? (p. 628)

5. What must be present for someone to be diagnosed with insomnia? (pp. 628-630)

6. Describe how: (1) stimulus control therapy; and (2) sleep restriction therapy may be used to treat insomnia. (p. 630)

7. What must be present for someone to be diagnosed with hypersomnia? (p. 630)

8. What are the symptoms of narcolepsy? (p. 630)

Personality and Health

Key Terms

Type A behavior pattern (p. 633):

repressive coping style (p. 636):

John Henryism (p. 638):

Guided Review

1. What is the evidence that pessimism is related to health? (pp. 631-632)

2. What are some mechanisms through which pessimism is related to health? (pp. 631-632)

3. Describe the Type A behavior pattern. (pp. 633-634)

4. What is the evidence that the Type A behavior pattern is related to coronary heart disease (CHD)? (pp. 634-635)

5. Which aspect(s) of Type A behavior appear to be most strongly related to negative health outcomes? What evidence led researchers to this conclusion? (p. 635)

6. What are some mechanisms through which Type A behavior(s) may lead to CHD? (p. 635)

7. How is gender related to Type A behavior and CHD? (pp. 635-636)

8. What is the evidence that repressive coping is related to negative health outcomes? (pp. 636-637)

9. Describe Pennebaker's research and what it demonstrated. (p. 637)

10. What is John Henryism and how is it related to health? (p. 638)

Interventions to Improve Health

<u>Key Terms</u>

guided mastery techniques (p. 639):

biofeedback (p. 641):

<u>Guided Review</u>

1. How do guided mastery techniques appear to work? (p. 639)

2. Give some examples of catastrophizing cognitions. What are some techniques used to combat them? (pp. 640-641)

3. What is biofeedback and what are some of its uses? (pp. 641-642)

4. What are some limitations of biofeedback? (p. 642)

5. In time management, what is the difference between important and urgent activities? (p. 642)

6. What are four principles in time management? (pp. 642-644)

7. What techniques appear to be helpful for reducing Type A behavior? (pp. 645-646)

8. What is the evidence that social support is beneficial for physical health? (pp. 646-648)

CASE EXAMPLE
Read the following description and answer the questions below:

Tonya is a very successful young businesswoman. Her previous accomplishments are, she feels, only the beginning. She intends to be a millionaire by age thirty. Her father and older brother both made their fortunes early and she intends to better both of them. In her office, it is commonly said that it is easier to move a mountain than to disagree with Tonya. She is notorious for demanding things on time and keeps herself and her staff going at a whirlwind pace all the time. When anything goes wrong, however, Tonya often blows up at others. When confronted about her behavior, Tonya points out that the victory belongs to the strong and that you have to play hard ball to get ahead.

1. What personality type does Tonya's behavior fit? What characteristics of this personality type does Tonya show?

2. For what disease is Tonya at increased risk due to her behavior? Which of her symptoms seems, according to recent studies, most related to her increased risk of disease?

3. Describe a therapy that might help reduce her risk of illness.

CHAPTER TEST

A. <u>Multiple Choice</u>. Choose the **best answer** to each question below.

1. The interactive model suggests that:

    A. psychological factors can only cause or exacerbate physical illness in people who already have a biological vulnerability to an illness, or a mild form of the illness.
    B. psychological factors influence the development and progress of physical illness by affecting people's health-related behaviors.
    C. physiological factors interact with cognitive and emotional functioning.
    D. psychological factors influence the development and progress of physical illness by causing physiological changes that lead to or exacerbate disease.

2. All of the following are highly active during the fight-or-flight response <u>except</u> the:

    A. hypothalamus.
    B. parasympathetic nervous system.
    C. sympathetic nervous system.
    D. adrenal-cortical system.

3. The general adaptation syndrome consists of which phases?

    A. resistance → alarm → resilience → exhaustion
    B. alarm → resistance → resilience → exhaustion
    C. resistance → resilience → alarm
    D. alarm → resistance → exhaustion

4. The safety signal hypothesis asserts that:

    A. knowing when a negative event will occur makes it less stressful because it is more predictable and we can prepare for it better.
    B. uncontrollable events are more stressful than controllable events.
    C. negative events are more likely than positive events to be stressful and negatively affect physical and mental health.
    D. even positive life events can be stressful and negatively affect physical and mental health.

5. All of the following have been found to predict the experience of headaches <u>except</u>:

    A. serotonin deficiencies.
    B. a passive personality.
    C. dopamine deficiencies.
    D. chronic feelings of helplessness.

6. Coronary heart disease (CHD) is not:

    A. more common among men than women.
    B. the leading cause of death for women.
    C. an acute condition.
    D. a condition that runs in families.

7. Hypertension is not:

    A. traceable to genetic causes in 90% of cases.
    B. typically due to unknown causes.
    C. more common among African-Americans.
    D. associated with a heightened response to stress among offspring of people who have it.

8. T-cells:

    A. are types of natural killer cells, which are types of lymphocytes.
    B. multiplied just as well in rats who could control their exposure to shock as those rats who were not shocked.
    C. are more prevalent among animals who have been exposed to loud noise, electric shock, or separation from their mothers.
    D. are types of lymphocytes that seek out and destroy viruses.

9. The DSM-IV recognizes all of the following categories of sleep disorders except:

    A. sleep disorder due to a general medical condition.
    B. substance-induced sleep disorder.
    C. sleep disorder due to another mental disorder.
    D. sleep disorder due to stress.

10. All of the following are dyssomnias except:

    A. narcolepsy.
    B. nightmare disorder.
    C. primary hypersomnia.
    D. primary insomnia.

11. All of the following are parasomnias except:

    A. sleep terror disorder.
    B. sleepwalking disorder.
    C. narcolepsy.
    D. nightmare disorder.

12. Someone who experiences cataplexy would be likely be diagnosed with:

    A. narcolepsy.
    B. nightmare disorder.
    C. breathing-related sleep disorder.
    D. circadian rhythm sleep disorder.

13. Someone who experiences repeated awakenings with detailed recall of extended and extremely frightening dreams, usually involving threats to survival, security, or self-esteem, would be most likely diagnosed with:

    A. sleepwalking disorder.
    B. sleep terror disorder.
    C. primary hypersomnia.
    D. nightmare disorder.

14. Research suggests that pessimistic people:

    A. are less likely to make medical visits.
    B. are more likely to die after being diagnosed with cancer than optimists.
    C. are more likely to engage in healthy behaviors.
    D. have lower blood pressure than optimists.

15. According to Friedman and Rosenman, all of the following are components of the Type A pattern except:

    A. impatience.
    B. easily aroused hostility.
    C. competitive achievement strivings.
    D. a sense of time urgency.

16. Which of the following is the best predictor of coronary heart disease?

    A. time urgency
    B. competitiveness
    C. classification as Type A vs. Type B behavior pattern
    D. hostility

17. Which of the following has been most consistently related to hypertension?

    A. hostility
    B. repressive coping
    C. John Henryism
    D. Type A personality

18. Which of the following has been found to be effective at reducing symptoms of irritable bowel syndrome?

    A. time management
    B. guided mastery techniques
    C. cognitive therapy
    D. biofeedback

19. Biofeedback has been found to be effective for treating all of the following <u>except</u>:

    A. migraine headaches.
    B. Type A personality.
    C. chronic pain.
    D. hypertension.

20. Which of the following is <u>not</u> an element of effective time management as described in this chapter?

    A. scheduling specific times to accomplish urgent activities
    B. breaking large tasks into smaller tasks
    C. distinguishing between distal goals and proximal goals
    D. rewarding yourself

B. <u>True-False</u>. Select T (True) or F (False) below.

1. The effects of sleep deprivation are cumulative; for example, if one gets 2 hours of sleep less than one needs for three nights, then one has a 6-hour "sleep debt." T   F

2. Repressive coping is an important predictor of ulcers.   T   F

3. Lymphocytes are types of natural killer cells that attack viruses.   T   F

4. Women who sleep fewer than 6 hours per night have a higher mortality rate than women who get 8 hours of sleep per night, but this difference is not present in men.   T   F

5. Sleep apnea is a breathing-related sleep disorder.   T   F

C. <u>Short Answer</u>.

1. What are three characteristics of events that contribute to their being perceived as stressful? Describe each of these characteristics and give some examples.

2. A client presents to your clinic seeking therapy for "stress." After a thorough assessment, you conclude that he has a Type A behavior pattern. Describe why it is important to treat this personality style, what the most important aspect(s) of it to treat would be, and how you would approach treating this client.

3. Describe the steps involved in effective time management.

4. What is biofeedback, what is it used for, and how does it appear to work?

5. What is social support? Describe some of the evidence which suggests that it improves health. What kinds of social support may be detrimental?

ANSWER KEY

Case Example

1. Type A behavior pattern. She is hard-driving, over-working, competitive, stubborn, hostile, and easily blows up.
2. Coronary heart disease. Hostility.
3. Cognitive-behavioral therapy, in which Tonya learns to reduce stress in her life, to challenge assumptions that she must be very successful and hard-driving, to be more patient and able to wait for others, and to reduce her hostile feelings and behaviors.

Multiple Choice

1. A
2. B
3. D
4. A
5. C
6. C
7. A
8. B
9. D
10. B
11. C
12. A
13. D
14. B
15. A
16. D
17. C
18. C
19. B
20. A

True-False

1. T
2. F
3. F
4. F
5. T

Short Answer

1. See pp. 620-622.
2. See pp. 633-636 and 644-646.
3. See pp. 642-644.
4. See pp. 641-642.
5. See p. 646.

Additional Readings on Chapter 17 Topics

Baum, A., & Posluszny, D. M. (1999). Health psychology: Mapping biobehavioral contributions to health and illness. Annual Review of Psychology, 50, 137-163.

Taylor, S. E., Kemeny, M. E., Reed, G. M., Bower, J. E., & Gruenewald, T. L. (2000). Psychological resources, positive illusions, and health. American Psychologist, 55, 99-109.

Taylor, S. E., Repetti, R. L., & Seeman, T. (1997). Health psychology: What is an unhealthy environment and how does it get under the skin? Annual Review of Psychology, 48, 411-447.

Chapter 18: The Cognitive Disorders: Dementia, Delirium, and Amnesia

LEARNING OBJECTIVES
After reading and studying this chapter, you should be able to:

1. Explain why the cognitive disorders are no longer known as "organic brain disorders."

2. Identify when a set of symptoms should be diagnosed as a cognitive disorder, and when it should not be.

3. Identify the types of cognitive impairment in dementia.

4. Describe the symptoms of Alzheimer's disease,

5. Identify and describe the brain changes that occur in Alzheimer's disease and the conditions thought to cause them.

6. Discuss the evidence for a genetic contribution to Alzheimer's disease.

7. Describe vascular dementia and identify its causes.

8. Distinguish between penetrating injuries and closed head injuries.

9. Describe the symptoms of Parkinson's disease, HIV-associated dementia, and Huntington's disease.

10. Discuss the available treatments for dementia.

11. Discuss how culture and gender may affect dementia.

12. Identify the symptoms of delirium, their typical progression, and the conditions that make a diagnosis likely.

13. Discuss the ways in which delirium can be treated.

14. Distinguish between anterograde and retrograde amnesia.

15. Identify how amnesic disorders may be treated.

ESSENTIAL IDEAS

I. Dementia

    A. Dementia is typically a permanent deterioration in cognitive functioning, often accompanied by emotional changes.

B. The five types of cognitive impairments in dementia are memory impairment, aphasia, apraxia, agnosia, and loss of executive functioning.

C. The most common type of dementia is due to Alzheimer's disease.

D. The brains of Alzheimer's patients show neurofibrillary tangles, plaques made up of amyloid protein, and cortical atrophy.

E. Recent theories of Alzheimer's disease focus on three different genes that might contribute to the buildup of amyloid in the brains of Alzheimer's disease patients.

F. Dementia can also be caused by cerebrovascular disorders, head injury, and progressive disorders such as Parkinson's disease, HIV disease, Huntington's disease, Pick's disease, Creutzfeldt-Jakob disease, and a number of other medical conditions. Finally, chronic drug abuse and the nutritional deficiencies that often accompany it can lead to dementia.

G. There is no effective treatment for dementia, although drugs help to reduce the cognitive symptoms and accompanying depression, anxiety, and psychotic symptoms in some patients.

H. Gender, culture, and education all play roles in vulnerability to dementia.

II. Delirium

A. Delirium is characterized by disorientation, recent memory loss, and clouding of consciousness.

B. The onset of delirium can be either sudden or slow.
C. The many causes of delirium include medical diseases, the trauma of surgery, illicit drugs, medications, high fever, and infections.

D. Delirium must be treated immediately by treating its underlying causes, to prevent brain damage and to prevent people from hurting themselves.

III. Amnesia

A. The amnesic disorders are characterized only by memory loss.

B. Retrograde amnesia is loss of memory for past events, and anterograde amnesia is the inability to remember new information.

C. Amnesia can be caused by brain damage due to strokes, head injuries, chronic nutritional deficiencies, exposure to toxins (such as through carbon monoxide poisoning), and chronic substance abuse.

D. Treatment of amnesia can involve removal of the agents contributing to the amnesia and helping the person develop memory aids.

KEY TERMS AND GUIDED REVIEW

<u>Guided Review</u>

1. Why was the term "organic brain disorders" discontinued in DSM-IV? (p. 654)

Dementia

<u>Key Terms</u>

dementia (p. 655):

aphasia (p. 656):

echolalia (p. 656):

palialia (p. 656):

apraxia (p. 656):

agnosia (p. 656):

Alzheimer's disease (p. 658):

neurofibrillary tangles (p. 661):

amyloid (p. 661):

vascular dementia (p. 663):

cerebrovascular disease (p. 663):

stroke (p. 663):

<u>Guided Review</u>

1. How prevalent is Alzheimer's disease (AD)? (p. 655)

2. Describe each of the five types of cognitive deficits in dementia: memory impairment, aphasia, apraxia, agnosia, and deficits in executive functioning. (pp. 656-657)

3. Describe some of the symptoms of AD. (p. 658)

4. What is the "sandwich generation of women"? (p. 658)

5. Describe the brain abnormalities in AD. Where in the brain are these abnormalities concentrated? (pp. 660-662)

6. What are some of the proposed causes of AD? (p. 662)

7. What is ApoE4? How is it related to AD? (pp. 662-663)

8. How are AD and Down's syndrome related? (p. 663)

9. Abnormalities on which chromosomes have been associated with increased risk of AD? (pp. 662-663)

10. Describe the neurotransmitter abnormalities in AD. (p. 663)

11. What must be present for someone to be diagnosed with vascular dementia? (p. 663)

12. Among stroke patients, what factors are associated with increased risk of developing dementia? (pp. 663-664)

13. What are some common causes of brain damage? (p. 666)

14. What is dementia pugilistica? (p. 666)

15. What is Parkinson's disease? (p. 667)

16. Describe the cognitive side effects that can result from HIV. (p. 667)

17. What is the difference between mild neurocognitive disorder and HIV-associated dementia? (p. 667)

18. What is Huntington's disease? (p. 667)

19. Describe the treatments that are available for dementia. (pp. 667-668)

20. How does dementia vary by gender and ethnicity? (pp. 668-670)

21. Describe Snowdon's study of nuns. (pp. 670-671)

Delirium

Key Terms

delirium (p. 672):

Guided Review

1. Describe the symptoms of delirium. (p. 672)

2. Describe the onset of delirium. (pp. 672-673)

3. What are some causes of delirium? (p. 673)

4. What are some risk factors for delirium? (p. 674)

5. Why is it important to treat delirium quickly? How can it be treated? (pp. 673-674)

Amnesia

Key Terms

amnesic disorders (p. 674):

amnesia (p. 674):

anterograde amnesia (p. 674):

retrograde amnesia (p. 675):

<u>Guided Review</u>

1. What is the difference between anterograde and retrograde amnesia? (pp. 674-675)

2. What are some causes of amnesia? (p. 675)

3. What is Korsakoff's psychosis? (p. 675)

4. What are some ways to treat amnesic disorders? (p. 675)

CASE EXAMPLE
Read the following description and answer the questions below:

A 70-year-old college professor named Marshall has shown progressive deterioration in many areas of functioning over the last year. When he is alone in a store or in the woods near his home, he often gets lost and can't find his way out. He is easily distracted, and frequently forgets where he puts things. When this happens, Marshall often becomes angry and accuses others of taking his things. Marshall's wife has discovered a number of grave errors in his accounting in the family finances, such as major mathematical errors in the checkbook. When she has confronted him about these errors, Marshall has denied that there is anything wrong, and has stomped off in a rage.

Marshall's interest in his usual activities has diminished. He no longer wants to garden or read, when he formerly engaged in these activities almost daily. He is content to sit for long periods of time, or to shuffle and reshuffle the old letters and newspapers he has been collecting in his home office for the last couple of years.

Conversations with Marshall can be difficult because he often uses odd words to refer to objects, such as calling a cup a vase, or goes on long tirades that are irrelevant to the subject being discussed. He does not seem to know anything that is going on in the world, although he sits in front of the television news programs every night. He recently asserted that John Kennedy was still president.

Marshall has undergone extensive physical examinations in the past year, and no serious medical disease has been found. He has been only a light drinker of alcohol most of his life.

1. What cognitive disorder is Marshall most likely suffering from? What symptoms of this disorder does he show?

2. If Marshall's body undergoes an autopsy upon his death, what is likely to be found in his brain?

3. What treatments are available for Marshall's condition?

CHAPTER TEST

A. <u>Multiple Choice</u>. Choose the **best answer** to each question below.

1. By definition, a cognitive disorder cannot be caused by:

    A. medical diseases.
    B. substance intoxication or withdrawal.
    C. psychiatric disorders.
    D. infections.

2. Dementia is:

    A. typically reversible with appropriate treatments.
    B. caused by biological factors, whereas other disorders are not.
    C. acute and usually transitory disorientation and memory loss.
    D. gradual and usually permanent.

3. Dementia occurs:

    A. only in people over 60 years of age.
    B. in 2-5% of people over age 65.
    C. more often in men than in women.
    D. in 80% of people over age 85.

4. Which of the following is a term that refers to an impaired ability to execute common actions, such as waving goodbye?

    A. apraxia.
    B. alogia.
    C. agnosia.
    D. aphasia.

5. Which of the following would <u>not</u> be considered to reflect a deficit in executive functioning?

    A. interpreting the proverb, "People who live in glass houses shouldn't throw stones" to mean, "People don't want their windows broken"
    B. failing to recognize objects or people
    C. difficulty planning how to carry out a sequence of actions
    D. trouble stopping oneself from engaging in a behavior

6. Repeating sounds or words over and over is known as:

    A. palialia.
    B. aphasia.
    C. echolalia.
    D. apraxia.

7. The most common cause of dementia is ____, the least common cause is _____, and _____ falls in between these two causes.

    A. stroke; brain injury; Parkinson's disease
    B. Alzheimer's disease; Parkinson's disease; brain injury
    C. brain injury; Alzheimer's disease; stroke
    D. Alzheimer's disease; brain injury; stroke

8. Plaques are most likely to be found in the:

    A. precentral gyri.
    B. occipital lobe.
    C. hippocampus.
    D. superior temporal lobe.

9. All of the following are pathological brain changes that occur in AD <u>except</u>:

    A. neurofibrillary tangles.
    B. loss of dendrites.
    C. shrunken ventricles.
    D. extensive cell death.

10. Genetic abnormalities on which of the following chromosomes are associated with an increased risk of late-onset Alzheimer's disease?

    A. 4
    B. 14
    C. 19
    D. 21

11. AD has been attributed to all of the following except:

    A. viral infections.
    B. excessive folate.
    C. immune system dysfunction.
    D. excessive aluminum.

12. Genetic abnormalities on which of the following chromosomes is responsible for a protein on the membrane of cells known as S182, and may be responsible for up to 80% of early-onset Alzheimer's disease?

    A. 4
    B. 14
    C. 19
    D. 21

13. Deficits in which of the following neurotransmitters are associated with declines in memory function in AD?

    A. acetylcholine
    B. norepinephrine
    C. serotonin
    D. peptide Y

14. All of the following are symptoms of frontal lobe injuries except:

    A. apathy.
    B. uncharacteristic lewdness.
    C. lability of affect.
    D. visual-perceptual disturbances.

15. The most common causes of closed head injuries are:

    A. gunshot wounds.
    B. falls.
    C. motor vehicle accidents.
    D. blows to the head during violent assaults.

16. Someone who experiences tremors, muscle rigidity, dementia, and inability to initiate movement would be most likely diagnosed with:

    A. dementia pugilistica.
    B. Huntington's disease.
    C. HIV-associated dementia.
    D. Parkinson's disease.

17. Which of the following disorders is transmitted by a single dominant gene?

    A. Huntington's disease
    B. Parkinson's disease
    C. Alzheimer's disease
    D. Pick's disease

18. The nun study by Snowdon et al. (1996) showed that:

    A. religious people are more likely to become demented.
    B. people who had greater linguistic skills earlier in life were less likely to develop Alzheimer's disease in late life.
    C. better-educated people were more likely to become demented because they had more abilities to lose once dementia took hold.
    D. people with low levels of education are less likely to be diagnosed with Alzheimer's disease than people with higher levels of education.

19. The diagnostic criteria for delirium include all of the following except:

    A. not caused by the direct physiological consequences of a medical condition.
    B. perceptual disturbance that is not accounted for by a dementia.
    C. reduced ability to focus, sustain, or shift attention.
    D. disturbance develops over a short time and tends to fluctuate.

20. Korsakoff's syndrome is an amnestic disorder caused by damage to the _____.

    A. cerebral cortex
    B. amygdala
    C. hippocampus
    D. thalamus

B. True-False. Select T (True) or F (False) below.

1. Dementia, delirium, and amnesia cannot be diagnosed if they appear to be the results of a psychiatric disorder, such as schizophrenia.   T   F

2. Alzheimer's disease cannot be definitively diagnosed in living humans.   T   F

3. The degree of cognitive decline seen in AD is significantly correlated with the degree of deficits in acetylcholine.   T   F

4. The majority of stroke patients develop vascular dementia.   T   F

5. Parkinson's disease results from the death of cells that produce acetylcholine.   T   F

C. <u>Short Answer</u>.

1. Describe the cognitive and biological deficits in AD.

2. Not all people who have strokes develop dementia. Which stroke patients are at the greatest risk of developing dementia?

3. What genetic factors are associated with increased risk of AD?

4. Describe some ways in which dementia can be treated.

5. What is delirium? How is it similar to and different from dementia? How can it be treated?

ANSWER KEY

<u>Case Example</u>
1. Dementia of the Alzheimer's type. Memory impairment, impairment in abstract thinking, aphasia. This dementia is probably due to Alzheimer's because other illnesses that can cause dementia (e.g., Parkinson's disease, cerebrovascular disease, Huntington's disease, chronic alcoholism) have been ruled out.
2. Neurofibrillary plaques and tangles, cell death and dendritic shrinkage, enlarged ventricles, and neurotransmitter deficits.
3. Medications such as tacrine and donepezil, as well as antioxidants, ginkgo biloba, and anti-inflammatories. Behavior therapy may also be useful. None of these treatments will cure the disorder, but they may slow its progression or lead to slight improvement in symptoms.

<u>Multiple Choice</u>
1. C
2. D
3. B
4. A
5. B
6. A
7. D
8. C
9. C
10. C
11. B
12. B
13. A
14. D
15. C
16. D
17. A
18. B
19. A
20. D

<u>True-False</u>
1. T
2. T
3. T
4. F
5. F

Short Answer
1. See pp. 658-662.
2. See pp. 663-664.
3. See pp. 662-663.
4. See pp. 667-668.
5. See pp. 672-674.

Additional Readings on Chapter 18 Topics

      Bondi, M. W., Salmon, D. P., Galasko, D., Thomas, R. G., & Thal, L. J. (1999). Neuropsychological function and apolipoprotein E genotype in the preclinical detection of Alzheimer's disease. Psychology and Aging, 14, 295-303.

      Massman, P. J., Delis, D. C., Butters, N., & Levin, B. E. (1990). Arc all subcortical dementias alike? Verbal learning and memory in Parkinson's and Huntington's disease patients. Journal of Clinical and Experimental Neuropsychology, 12, 729-744.

      McKhann, G., Drachman, D., Folstein, M., Katzman, R., Price, D., & Stadlan, E.M. (1984). Clinical diagnosis of Alzheimer's disease: Report of the NINCDS-ADRDA Work Group under the auspices of Department of Health and Human Services Task Force on Alzheimer's Disease. Neurology, 34, 939-944.

Chapter 19: Mental Health, Social Policy, and the Law

LEARNING OBJECTIVES
After reading and studying this chapter, you should be able to:

1. Discuss the limitations of psychological research to inform legal decisions.

2. Discuss how competency to stand trial is determined.

3. Discuss the characteristics of people most likely to be referred for competency evaluations, and the characteristics of people most likely to be found incompetent to stand trial.

4. Discuss the frequency with which the insanity defense is used, and the typical judgments that result when it is used.

5. Summarize how insanity pleas are evaluated according to the M'Naghten Rule, irresistible impulse rule, Durham Rule, ALI Rule, and the American Psychiatric Association's definition of insanity.

6. Discuss the pros and cons of each rule above and describe how each rule either broadened or constricted the legal definition of insanity.

7. Discuss the significance of *Barrett vs. United States* (1977).

8. Discuss the use of the verdict guilty but mentally ill (GBMI).

9. Discuss the need for treatment as a justification for civil commitment.

10. Discuss the modern criteria used to enable civil commitment, and the variations in how states treat the legal issue of civil commitment.

11. Discuss the significance of *Donaldson vs. O'Connor* (1975).

12. Discuss the problems with predictions of dangerousness to others, and the factors that predict violence over the short term.

13. Describe the prevalence of violence among mentally ill people.

14. Discuss the rights of patients to treatment and to refuse treatment.

15. Discuss the circumstances in which patients' rights can be violated.

16. Summarize the goals of the deinstitutionalization movement as well as its accomplishments and failures.

17. Identify and describe the clinician's duties to the client and society.

18. Discuss when confidentiality may be broken, and when it may not be broken.

19. Summarize the recent trends in family law and child custody law.

20. Identify the guidelines that clinicians should follow when conducting independent assessments in child custody disputes.

21. Discuss the roles that psychologists assume in child maltreatment cases, and the pros and cons of having psychologists involved in these matters.

22. Identify and describe the controversy in the repressed/recovered/false memory debate, the viewpoints held, and the evidence that supports or weakens each viewpoint.

ESSENTIAL IDEAS

I. Judgments about people accused of crimes

A. One judgment mental health professionals are asked to make is about an accused person's competency to stand trial.

B. Another judgment is whether the accused person was "sane" at the time he or she committed a crime.

C. The insanity defense has undergone many changes over recent history, often in response to its use in high profile crimes.

D. Five different rules have been used to evaluate the acceptability of a plea of not guilty by reason of insanity: the M'Naghten Rule, the irresistible impulse rule, the Durham Rule, the ALI Rule, and the American Psychiatric Association definition.

E. All of these rules require that the defendant be diagnosed with a "mental disease" but do not clearly define *mental disease*.

F. Most of these rules also require that the defendant have been unable to understand the criminality of his or her actions or conform his or her actions to the law in order to be judged not guilty by reason of insanity.

G. Many states have introduced the alternative verdict of "guilty but mentally ill."

II. Involuntary commitment and civil rights

A. People can be held in mental health facilities involuntarily if they are judged to have grave disabilities that make it difficult for them to meet their own basic needs or that pose imminent danger to themselves or to others. Each of the criteria used to make such judgments has its flaws, however, creating concerns about the appropriateness of civil commitment.

B. Short-term commitments can occur without court hearings on the certification of mental health professionals that individuals are in emergency situations. Such commitments are most likely to happen for individuals who are actively suicidal.

C. Longer-term commitments require court hearings. Patients have the rights to have attorneys and to appeal rulings.

D. Other basic rights of patients are the right to be treated while being hospitalized and the right to refuse treatment (at least in some states).

E. The deinstitutionalization movement was intended to stop the warehousing of mental patients and to reintegrate them into society through community-based mental health centers. Thousands of patients were subsequently released from long-term mental institutions, but unfortunately, not enough community mental health centers were built and funded to serve all these people's needs.

F. The National Alliance for the Mentally Ill is a patients' advocacy group that works to educate the public on mental disorders and increase resources for patients and their families.

III. Clinicians' duties to clients and society

A. First and foremost, clinicians have a duty to provide competent care to their clients.

B. Clinicians must also avoid multiple relationships with their clients, particularly sexual relationships.

C. They must protect their clients' confidentiality, except under special circumstances. One of these occurs when therapists believe clients need to be committed involuntarily.

D. Two other duties therapists have to society require them to break clients' confidentiality: the duty to protect people clients are threatening to harm and the duty to report suspected child or elder abuse.

E. Recently, clinicians' have been charged to provide ethnical service to diverse populations.

IV. Family law and mental health professionals

A. Psychologists and other mental health professionals can provide a number of services in family law courts hearing cases of custody disputes, charges of child maltreatment, or charges by adults that they were sexually abused as children.

B. Mental health professionals can help to investigate cases, employing proper interviewing techniques with great caution to obtain information that is as objective as possible without further traumatizing the parties involved.

C. They can act as expert witnesses, providing the court with information about research relevant to a case.

D. They can assist in getting family members into appropriate treatment if necessary after a case is decided.

E. In each of these areas of involvement, however, there are pitfalls to avoid. In interviewing people for a case, the mental health professional must be careful not to be overly suggestive, leading a person to fabricate a story that is not true or to misremember events.

F. In giving expert testimony, the mental health professional must not overstate the research evidence pertinent to a case or make inappropriate generalizations from the research to a specific case being tried.

G. In assisting parties in getting treatment, the mental health professional must follow all the ethical guidelines of clinicians, including that of not being involved in multiple relationships with the parties.

H. Child custody, child maltreatment, and repressed memory cases create highly charged atmospheres with great potential for further harm of the children and adults involved. Mental health professionals must act with the greatest objectivity and skill to help reduce this harm rather than add to it.

KEY TERMS AND GUIDED REVIEW

Key Term

mentally ill (p. 680):

Guided Review

1. What are some limitations on the ability of mental health professionals to assist the law and society? (p. 680)

Judgments About People Accused of Crimes

Key Terms

incompetent to stand trial (p. 681):

insanity (p. 681):

insanity defense (p. 682):

M'Naghten Rule (p. 683):

irresistible impulse rule (p. 684):

Durham Rule (p. 684):

ALI Rule (p. 684):

Insanity Defense Reform Act (p. 685):

American Psychiatric Association definition of insanity (p. 685):

guilt but mentally ill (GBMI) (p. 686):

Guided Review

1. Give some examples of impairments that might lead an individual to be regarded as incompetent to stand trial. (p. 681)

2. What are some characteristics of people that increase their likelihood of being considered incompetent to stand trial? (p. 681)

3. What is the fundamental premise underlying the insanity defense? (pp. 681-682)

4. How often do people plead not guilty by reason of insanity? (p. 682)

5. What is the M'Naghten Rule? What are two major problems with it? (pp. 682-683)

6. How did the irresistible impulse rule broaden the legal definition of insanity over the M'Naghten rule? (p. 684)

7. What was the Durham Rule? What was its major flaw? (p. 684)

8. What it the ALI Rule? Explain how it is broader than the M'Naghten Rule but not as broad as the Durham Rule. (pp. 684-685)

9. What was the significance of *Barrett vs. United States* (1977)? (p. 685)

10. What is the American Psychiatric Association definition of insanity? (p. 685)

11. What are arguments for and against the GBMI verdict? (p. 686)

Involuntary Commitment and Civil Rights

Key Terms

need for treatment (p. 687):

civil commitment (p. 687):

grave disability (p. 687):

dangerousness to self (p. 688):

dangerousness to others (p. 688):

right to treatment (p. 691):

right to refuse treatment (p. 692):

informed consent (p. 693):

Guided Review

1. Describe some of the problems with the "need for treatment" criterion for civil commitment? (p. 687)

2. What are the current criteria used to determine if someone should be committed involuntarily? (pp. 687-688)

3. What is the significance of *Donaldson vs. O'Connor* (1975)? (p. 688)

4. What are the three best predictors of violence over the short term? (p. 688)

5. Which patients are most likely to engage in violence after being discharged, and who are their most common targets? (pp. 688-690)

6. How common are involuntary admissions to psychiatric hospitals? (p. 690)

7. What is the significance of *Wyatt vs. Stickney* (1972)? (p. 691)

8. What are some limitations of treatment provided to prison inmates? (pp. 691-692)

9. What are some limitations of the right to refuse treatment? (p. 692)

10. What were the goals of the patients' rights movement? (pp. 692-693)

11. Describe NAMI and its objectives. (p. 694)

Clinicians' Duties to Clients and Society

Guided Review

1. Why do clinicians have a duty not to become involved in multiple relationships with clients? (p. 695)

2. How often do clinicians have sexual relationships with their clients? (p. 695)

3. What is the significance of *Tarasoff vs. Regents of the University of California* (1974)? (pp. 696-697)

4. What are the conditions under which a clinician may appropriately violate a client's confidentiality? (pp. 695-697)

Family Law and Mental Health Professionals

Key Term

repressed memory debate (p. 701):

1. What is the role of mental health professionals in child custody disputes? (p. 700)

2. How do psychologists assess allegations of child maltreatment? (pp. 700-701)

3. What are some limitations of psychologists' expert testimony in child maltreatment cases? (p. 701)

4. What are the two major viewpoints in the repressed memory debate? (pp. 701-704)

CHAPTER TEST

A. Multiple Choice. Choose the **best answer** to each question below.

1. All of the following increase one's likelihood of being judged incompetent to stand trial except:

   A. being female.
   B. being Caucasian.
   C. being poorly educated.
   D. being accused of a violent crime.

2. The insanity defense:

   A. will only be successful if it can be proven that the defendant has been chronically insane.
   B. is usually successful when it is used as one's plea.
   C. is most often used to acquit schizophrenic individuals.
   D. is used in only about 5% of felony cases.

3. The idea that someone cannot be held responsible for a crime if he or she did not know the nature or quality of the act being performed, or if he or she knew but did not know that his or her actions were wrong, is known as the:

   A. M'Naghten rule.
   B. Durham rule.
   C. ALI rule.
   D. irresistible impulse rule.

4. The condition most commonly recognized as a "disease of the mind" is:

    A. severe depression.
    B. psychosis.
    C. alcoholism.
    D. antisocial personality disorder.

5. A person can still be found not guilty by reason of insanity even if he or she knows the act being performed is wrong (i.e., criminal) under which of the following legal principles?

    A. ALI Rule
    B. M'Naghten Rule
    C. American Psychiatric Association definition of insanity
    D. Durham Rule

6. The case which established that the term "mental disease or defect" did not include an abnormality manifested only by repeated criminal or otherwise antisocial conduct was:

    A. *Durham vs. United States (1954)*.
    B. *Donaldson vs. O' Connor (1975)*.
    C. *Wyatt vs. Stickney (1972)*.
    D. *Barrett vs. United States (1977)*.

7. The Insanity Defense Reform Act adopted which of the following legal definitions of insanity?

    A. ALI Rule
    B. M'Naghten Rule
    C. American Psychiatric Association definition of insanity
    D. irresistible impulse rule

8. If an individual is not held responsible for a crime because, at the time of the crime, as a result of mental disease or defect, the person lacked substantial capacity either to appreciate the criminality (wrongfulness) of the act or to conform his or her behavior to the law, we are using which of the following criteria?

A. ALI Rule
B. M'Naghten Rule
C. American Psychiatric Association definition of insanity
D. Durham rule

9. As a result of _____, most states began requiring the defense to prove that the defendant was insane at the time of the crime, as opposed to requiring the prosecution to prove that the defendant was sane.

    A. the Lorena Bobbitt verdict
    B. the "twinkie defense" of Dan White
    C. *Donaldson vs. O' Connor (1975)*
    D. the John Hinckley verdict

10. Which of the following is not a criterion used to commit someone to a psychiatric facility?

    A. imminent danger to self
    B. imminent danger to others
    C. diagnosis of a mental disorder
    D. need for treatment

11. *Donaldson vs. O'Connor* (1975) established:

    A. the right to treatment.
    B. the unconstitutionality of confining a nondangerous individual.
    C. the clinician's duty to protect others from harm.
    D. the need to refine to irresistible impulse rule.

12. Which of the following is one of the best predictors of violence over a short term?

    A. having a diagnosis of schizophrenia
    B. being male
    C. having a diagnosis of substance abuse
    D. being African American

13. Violence among people who have been discharged from a psychiatric hospital:

    A. most often targets strangers.
    B. occurs more frequently among mentally ill men.
    C. occurs more frequently among mentally ill African Americans.
    D. does not occur among the majority of people.

14. *Wyatt vs. Stickney* (1972) established:

    A. the right to treatment.
    B. the unconstitutionality of confining a nondangerous individual.
    C. the right to treatment among prison inmates.
    D. the right to refuse treatment.

15. Studies of female prison inmates have shown that the most common mental disorder in that population is:

    A. antisocial personality disorder.
    B. substance abuse or dependence.
    C. major depression.
    D. borderline personality disorder.

16. Which of the following cases established the clinician's duty to protect people who might be in danger because of his or her client?

    A. *Durham vs. United States (1954)*
    B. *Tarasoff vs. Regents of The University of California (1974)*
    C. *Donaldson vs. O' Connor (1975)*
    D. *Wyatt vs. Stickney (1972)*

17. Which of the following is not a guideline for ethical service to culturally diverse populations?

    A. Psychologists avoid racist practices and do not consider ethnicity or culture as significant parameters in understanding psychological processes; rather, they emphasize the individual client.
    B. Psychologists are cognizant of relevant research and practice issues as related to the population being served.
    C. Psychologists interact in the language requested by the client and, if this is not feasible, make an appropriate referral.
    D. Psychologists attend to, as well as work to eliminate, biases, prejudices, and discriminatory practices.

18. Which of the following is not a part of the American Psychological Association's guidelines for psychologists acting as expert evaluators in child custody proceedings?

    A. The psychologist strives to acknowledge any limitations in the methods or data used.
    B. The psychologist acknowledges and confronts his or her own biases.
    C. The psychologist strives to present his or her client's best possible case.
    D. The psychologist strives to emphasize the child's best interests.

19. Clinicians may not violate a client's confidentiality:

    A. to report suspected child abuse.
    B. to report suspected abuse of elderly persons.
    C. to consult with the client's physician about his or her symptoms.
    D. to protect persons who might be in danger because of their clients.

20. Which of the following statements about the evidence related to the repressed memory debate is <u>true</u>?

    A. One study found that people could be made to believe that events happened to them that actually did not.

    B. One study found that 49 of 129 women with documented histories of abuse could not remember any abuse incidents at all from their childhood.

    C. One study found that a large number of people who identified themselves as abuse victims could not remember their abuse at some point before their eighteenth birthday, specifically due to repression.

    D. One study found that three-fourths of a group of women with repressed memories of sexual abuse found confirming evidence of their abuse.

B. <u>True-False</u>. Select T (True) or F (False) below.

1. Insanity is a medical term, not a psychological term.   T   F

2. Women are more likely to be acquitted by reason of insanity than are men.   T   F

3. Mentally ill men are more likely to be violent than are mentally ill women.   T   F

4. The right to refuse treatment is not recognized in all states.   T   F

5. The majority of homeless people are mentally ill.   T   F

C. <u>Short Answer</u>.

1. Which types of people are most likely to be acquitted by reason of insanity? How common are such acquittals? What happens to people who are found not guilt by reason of insanity?

2. What is the American Psychiatric Association's definition of insanity? How is it similar to and different from the M'Naghten rule and ALI rule?

3. What are the criteria used to commit someone to a psychiatric facility involuntarily? Explain each of these criteria.

4. Why do clinicians have a duty to protect clients' confidentiality? Under what circumstances might a clinician justifiably violate a client's confidentiality? Give two examples of when a clinician should <u>not</u> violate a client's confidentiality.

5. Describe the appropriate role of a clinician in a child custody hearing.

ANSWER KEY

<u>Multiple Choice</u>
1. B
2. C
3. A
4. B
5. D
6. D
7. C
8. A
9. D
10. D
11. B
12. C
13. D
14. A
15. B
16. B
17. A
18. C
19. C
20. A

<u>True-False</u>
1. F; it is a legal term.
2. F
3. F
4. T
5. F

<u>Short Answer</u>
1. See pp. 681-683.
2. See pp. 683-685.
3. See pp. 687-688.
4. See pp. 695-697.
5. See pp. 699-700.

<u>Additional Readings on Chapter 19 Topics</u>

Alper, J. S. (1998). Genes, free will and criminal responsibility. <u>Social Science and Medicine, 46,</u> 1599-1611.

Berman, M. F., & Coccaro, E. F. (1998). Neurobiologic correlates of violence: Relevance to criminal responsibility. <u>Behavioral Sciences and the Law, 16,</u> 303-318.

Nestor, P. G., Daggett, D., Haycock, J., & Price, M. (1999). Competence to stand trial: A neuropsychological inquiry. <u>Law and Human Behavior, 23,</u> 397-412.